2004

THE BIGGEST JOB WE'LL EVER HAVE

The Hyde School Program
for Character-Based Education and Parenting

LAURA AND MALCOLM GAULD

Foreword by Marc Brown, best-selling author of the *Arthur* series

SCRIBNER
New York   London   Toronto   Sydney   Singapore

SCRIBNER
1230 Avenue of the Americas
New York, NY 10020

SCRIBNER and design are trademarks of Macmillan Library Reference USA, Inc., used under license by Simon & Schuster, the publisher of this work.

For information about special discounts for bulk purchases, please contact Simon & Schuster Special Sales: 1-800-456-6798 or business@simonandschuster.com

DESIGNED BY ERICH HOBBING

Text set in Berthold Garamond

Manufactured in the United States of America

10 9 8 7 6 5 4 3 2 1

Library of Congress Cataloging-in-Publication Data
Gauld, Laura.
The biggest job we'll ever have: the Hyde School program for character-based education and parenting / Laura and Malcolm Gauld; foreword by Marc Brown.
p. cm.
Includes index.
1. Hyde School (Bath, Me.) 2. Character—Study and teaching—United States—Case studies. 3. Moral education—United States—Case studies. 4. Parenting—Moral and ethical aspects—Case studies. I. Gauld, Malcolm. II. Title.

LC311.G38 2002
370.11'4'0973—dc21
              2001049660

ISBN 0-7432-1058-1

To Mahalia, Scout, Harrison,
and their grandparents

Foreword

Dear Fellow Parents,

Being a parent is a lot like being a trapeze artist. You need courage, trust in large quantities, but most important, you've got to know when to let go.

"Letting go" is a concept I continue to struggle with, and I know I am not alone. But before our family was fortunate enough to find ourselves at the Hyde School, I had no clue just what "letting go" really meant or that it was an issue that was interfering with my parenting.

When I summon up our years at the Hyde School, I now view them as most difficult and most wonderful. My son, Tolon, led us there when we thought we had found a school to "fix" *his* problems. I will never forget his first interview (our family's interview, actually), which we all failed. And later his brother Tucker's interview, when the interviewer said politely, "Don't take this personally, but you have the worst attitude I've ever seen."

I thought we were doing everything right. But then, what was wrong? I soon found out. That's when the work began. I was sure the old adage "No pain, no gain" had originated at Hyde School.

It was horrifying to learn that I was part of the problem, painful to find out why, and hard work to change patterns of behavior.

None of us are really prepared for the most *important* job of parenting. We bring to it our experiences—both good and bad. Our parents are our teachers and if your parents were not perfect teachers, as mine weren't, we need some help. And helping families is what the Hyde School does better than anyone.

Laura and Malcolm have worked successfully with thousands of families, and in this book they distill the powerful process of Hyde School into one accessible and very helpful book. Please read these pages with humility and an open mind. It is a gift.

Marc Brown

Contents

Contents

To the Reader

Exceptional Parenting
It is hard.
It is doable.
It is never too late.

We are the parents of three school-aged children. We began our professional careers as teachers over twenty years ago and have spent the years since working with hundreds of teenagers and their families. The experiences we have had and the lessons we have learned in both roles, as parents and as teachers, form the heart of this book.

The bottom-line point we make in these pages is simple. We believe that parents are the primary teachers and the home is the primary classroom. The job of parenting asks us to accept and honor a commitment to develop the best in our children, the best in our families, and the *best in ourselves.* No job is more important than parenting, and while most people we talk with profess to agree, we have observed that many parents do not organize and prioritize their lives in accordance with this notion. It is our hope that this book and its 10 Priorities can help parents focus their efforts by presenting a program that has provided meaningful experiences and valuable lessons to hundreds of parents.

Many of these experiences and lessons have occurred at the Hyde Schools, a group of schools and programs dedicated to character development and family growth. Both of us graduated from Hyde's original campus in Bath, Maine, in the 1970s. Our time there as students was life-changing. Our teachers challenged us to test our character and we were rewarded with a sense of purpose that has guided us as individuals, as educators, and as parents ever since. Today we serve as leaders of the Hyde organization: Malcolm as president and Laura as director of the Biggest Job workshops, a national parenting program. In these roles we strive to offer the same challenges and rewards to students, parents, and teachers in a variety of settings. Whether at a boarding school in rural New England or an urban public K–12 school in Washington, D.C., it has been deeply gratifying to see the promise of genuine character development unfold for American kids and families from all walks of life.

Although this book has been written with parents foremost in our minds, it is actually for anyone committed to the personal growth and character development of children. In attempting to identify those families that will find it especially meaningful, we are reminded of a one-page piece written by Hyde students in 1970. Entitled "Statement to the Prospective Student," it has since been offered to hundreds of students and families considering a Hyde education. It is intended to help families answer the simple question: Is Hyde right for me? The statement begins:

> If you have the desire to take an honest look at yourself and are willing to commit yourself to the pursuit of excellence, then Hyde may be for you.

Later the statement notes:

> If you are happy and content with yourself, then Hyde may not be for you. You must want to change and grow.

Near the conclusion, the central point of the piece is made:

> As a Hyde student, you should accept the following premise as your basic responsibility: that you make and keep a total commitment to pursue excellence.

Such a commitment is not easy to make, and, once made, it requires effort to keep. We feel that we have made such a commitment. That is why we are at Hyde School and why we have experienced growth.

This book is offered in the spirit of this statement and is designed to be especially helpful to those committed to the pursuit of personal and family excellence. In accordance with the statement, those parents who are happy and content with themselves probably will not find it as useful as those motivated by a deep desire to change and grow. The book calls upon families to make and keep a total commitment to pursue excellence while at the same time it recognizes that each family's goals and objectives will vary. It comes with the fair warning that this commitment is difficult to make and maintain. As parents and teachers, we have made such a commitment and we strive to keep it on a daily basis. This commitment and the accompanying growth we have experienced in the form of various ups and downs have fueled our motivation to write this book.

Our personal and professional experiences have taught us three things about this commitment:

1. It is *hard.*
2. It is *doable.*
3. It is *never too late.*

To add a fourth: It is *never too early.*

This book and its 10 Priorities outline and support our belief that, at any age, a person's character is more important than his or her innate abilities. Who we are is more important than what we can do. If asked, most people would agree that the right attitude and a commitment to principles are keys to a fulfilling life rich with achievement, strong personal relationships, and a sense of purpose. Unfortunately, in today's results-driven culture, the element of character is overlooked more than those same people would care to admit. How else can we explain the dramatic rise in cheating in schools across our country? How else can we explain the students who, often on the advice of adult role models, might choose to avoid taking a particularly challenging advanced high school course because the low grade they might receive would hurt their chances for admission to an elite college? The logic of this choice is understandable, but it most certainly is not aimed at developing the student's character.

The "results" culture that prevails in most schools is damaging to students in a number of ways. Those who try hard but don't have the aptitude of the class stars come to feel as if they're fighting a losing battle and begin to ask "Why bother?" Meanwhile, the top performers gain a false sense of accomplishment when they are not challenged to explore their full potential. Across the board, these teenagers sense the hypocrisy at work and become alienated and apathetic. Creativity, curiosity, and enthusiasm flag, and restless energy looks for less constructive outlets.

Similar troubles emerge in the home when the principles that most parents believe they value—honesty, responsibility, accountability—don't actually govern family life. In fact, it's often difficult to determine which ideas *do* lie at the heart of a family, since many of us are so focused on avoiding the mistakes our parents made that we unwittingly neglect to devise a positive parenting plan of our own. In a sense, we're steering without a rudder, and each time the desire to "get along," to placate a volatile family member, or to quickly repair a problem that someone else has created overrides our purported principles, parents and children veer farther off course. Cynicism and hostility creep in along with secretiveness, making each new challenge that much more difficult to face.

In visualizing a guide for parents, we imagined the metaphor of a map and compass. When hiking in the woods, a map and compass, working hand in hand, are essential tools. A map without a compass is of limited value because we are then forced to guess our direction. A compass without a map not only leaves the destination in doubt, it leaves us unable to identify and connect with critical landmarks along the way. We not only need both, we need both simultaneously. Thus, our book is intended to offer a philosophical framework, the "compass," accompanied by a set of ten parenting Priorities, the "map."

This book parallels the program followed in the Biggest Job workshops, a program we created and have presented to thousands of parents across the country. We call these workshops the Biggest Job for two reasons. First, we want to clearly establish our belief that parenting is a very difficult undertaking. In fact, we sometimes tell parents: "Even when you do it *right*, you will feel like a sucked lemon!" Thus, we offer fair warning that this book will not appeal to the parent seeking a "quick fix." Parenting is hard work. However, we have observed that anyone with a genuine commitment can be pretty good at it.

The second reason for the title Biggest Job derives from a regular theme of the many interviews and conferences we have conducted with students and their parents over the years. In these sessions we have repeatedly observed a phenomenon we initially regarded as a fascinating irony but have come to expect as a common occurrence. Sitting before us are men and women who, on the one hand, are confident, highly competent, and very successful professionals, yet, on the other hand, are uncertain, perhaps even frightened, parents. We often say to them, "What works at the office may not work at home. No matter how successful you have become in your professional lives, remember that this is the *big leagues*. This is the *biggest job* you will ever have."

Laura and Malcolm Gauld
Bath, Maine
April 2001

PART ONE

CHARACTER:
SOME FUNDAMENTALS

"Character Is Inspired; It Is Not Imparted"

When we became teachers in the seventies, we looked forward to teaching subjects like math and history to the teenagers in our classrooms. Our motivation, however, was deeper than the development of academic skills and the transfer of intellectual knowledge. We saw ourselves as trying to develop the whole person. We wanted to teach character. Therefore, we spent a good deal of time just talking with kids, getting to know them outside of our classrooms. We coached sports—soccer, basketball, and lacrosse—three seasons a year. We were engaged in extracurricular activities like performing arts and community service. Some of these activities were as foreign to us as they were to the students who were required to experience them. We simply wanted to be where the action was in as many ways as possible.

Fresh out of college, we were flush with the confidence that we possessed enough charisma, commitment, and capability to make a difference in the life of any teenage boy or girl. We quickly discovered that often we also needed to make a difference in their parents' lives if we were going to have any lasting, effective influence. This was harder than it sounded, as we, like all teachers, had been trained to work with kids. In our early attempts to bring parents into the learning equation, it seemed that they fell into four categories:

1. School and home are in "sync" in regard to what is important regarding the values and priorities of proper education. We could really "hum" with these families.

2. School and home are basically in agreement, but both parties need to sometimes engage in some good old heart-to-heart discussions in order to either get on or stay on the same page. Sometimes these discussions led to inspiring understanding and personal growth.

3. School and home hold sharper disagreements. Although we might never quite be on the same page, we might at least be in the same chapter. For example, perhaps a student was late for school and lied about the reason. We might focus on the lie while the parent focused on the tardiness rule. In more troubling cases, the parent might even regard the lie as insignificant. In such cases, the family would move into category four.

4. School and home are not even reading the same book. In these cases, there might be obvious family dysfunction at work—parental denial over substance abuse issues, fallout over an ugly divorce, or perhaps psychological problems in the home.

In a number of these instances, particularly those in category four, it often seemed that *our* best teaching would consistently lose out to *their* worst parenting. We learned that good teaching cannot overcompensate for bad parenting, regardless of how either is defined. We were sure that we had the correct perspective as teachers and we were fairly confident that we saw what the parents needed to do. Then something happened: *We became parents ourselves* (our first child was born in 1990). Once in the dual role of teacher *and* parent, we struggled to find the point where one role ended and the other began. We were sure that we needed to separate the two roles, but we were not sure how. Eventually we realized that the trick lies in finding the critical connections between them.

TWO THINGS WE HAVE LEARNED ABOUT CHARACTER

All parents hope to raise children who will grow up to be adults of character. As teachers, we have dedicated our professional careers to this same hope. When pressed to describe what we have learned about character development, we offer a two-sentence response: (1) Character is inspired; it is not imparted. (2) Character development cannot be limited to a *site;* it must include a *context.*

CHARACTER IS INSPIRED

We won't teach much character if we simply post a list of ideals (e.g., respect, tolerance, honesty) and beg the kids to pay heed. In his book *Dumbing Us Down,* John Gatto presents a comparison of the painter and the sculptor as a metaphor for great teaching. Gatto observes that a painter begins with a blank canvas and transforms it by *adding* patterns of color to create a new design. A sculptor begins with a mass of stone and transforms it by *subtracting* matter to reveal a shape that was always there waiting to be exposed to the world. Gatto maintains that the great teachers are sculptors rather than painters. We agree. We don't pour character into our students; we summon it forth with value-forming challenges and experiences. With this view, character is a miracle that must be developed. Once developed, it must be maintained: "Use it or lose it!"

Over the years, we have been approached at graduation ceremonies by appreciative parents who have made comments like, "Thank you so much! You and this school truly *gave* my kid character." We would be less than honest if we didn't acknowledge that such compliments are gratifying. But they are inaccurate. We don't *give* our students anything. We help them *uncover* something that was always there. It may be buried under a lack of confidence or under a heap of family dysfunction, but great teachers remove the barriers and

21

ignite a dormant confidence that can help a kid "take off." Parents play a similar role.

SITE VERSUS CONTEXT

The second point—site versus context—further clarifies the power of inspiration. The dynamic of site versus context can be demonstrated in our use at Hyde of a high ropes course, an effective and powerful character-development site. The high ropes course fosters courage, risk-taking, and trust. Let's take the case of sixteen-year-old Debbie, who has climbed the rope ladder to accept the challenges offered by the course. It demands that she place her trust in a peer who stands on the ground thirty feet below holding her safety belay line. Thus, her life is literally held in the hands of her partner.

Now, what happens after Debbie descends from the ropes course, unfastens her harness, unstraps her helmet, and talks about the experience with her family? Let's assume that her parents do not value courage, risk-taking, and trust. Perhaps her family is highly dysfunctional. Debbie cannot possibly reap the maximum benefit of the ropes course if she spends most of her time living in a context that does not reinforce its lessons. If Debbie's parents are not striving to develop their character, it is doubtful that she will continue to seek out the kind of challenges necessary for her own character development.

As teachers or parents, we are being arrogant or foolish or both if we believe that the power of our character *sites* will overpower the dynamic of the daily *context* of the lives of our students. Thus, we must nurture that context with the same vigor that we currently apply to developing our learning sites. Think of the benefit to Debbie if her parents were to experience the ropes course *with* her. Then both site and context would be working in concert for Debbie's benefit.

Both of these points—the power of inspiration and the idea of site versus context—add up to the same conclusion: Parents need to be critical players in the development of their children's character.

While this idea does not break new ground, the 10 Priorities will often test parents in ways they might not expect.

In preparing to write this book, we decided to spend some time exploring the shelves of various bookstores. We naturally assumed that this exploration would begin in the psychology or education sections. Much to our surprise, most major bookstores today have separate sections for parenting and family. We very quickly came to understand why this is so—there are so many books on the subject! We read a number of them, and many of them are very good. Some gave us ideas on how we might improve our own parenting. However, our book differs from those in a significant way. Most books offer prescriptions for how parents might change behaviors in their children; we intend to help parents change behaviors and attitudes *in themselves*. Many of the parents we have worked with over the years have been so preoccupied with the behavior of their children that they have neglected to address their own character. As the story in the following chapter about a typical student-parent-teacher conference suggests, this can have a very negative effect on family dynamics and morale.

"You're a Bright Kid
Who Doesn't Apply Himself"
and Other Hollow Phrases

Over the years, we have conducted hundreds of interviews with teenagers and their parents. A typical session finds us in a room mediating with an anxious mom and dad counterbalanced by an indifferent or unwilling teenager. Mom, usually taking the lead, and Dad are concerned because their child has begun to show signs of one, some, or all of the following:

- Declining grades
- Discipline problems at school or at home
- Hanging around with a bad crowd
- Refusal to help around the house
- Insubordination or lack of respect for authority
- Suspected (and sometimes proven) drug abuse

They are anxious because they have heard stories of remarkable transformations and turnarounds that have happened with teenagers at the Hyde Schools. Perhaps they have seen the stories on television portraying such turnarounds. Their hope is balanced by the fear that Hyde's rapidly growing waiting list may prohibit their "Johnny" from enrolling. Johnny, on the other hand, often hopes he won't be accepted to the program. Having caught wind of the fact that the Hyde program is demanding, Johnny may try to sabotage the interview. "After all," Johnny reasons, "Mom and Dad are overreacting anyway."

We always begin by speaking to the teenager first. It often goes like this:

> US: How are you doing in school?
>
> JOHNNY: OK.
>
> US: Would you say that you are working up to your potential?
>
> JOHNNY: Probably not.
>
> US: So, you think you could do better?
>
> JOHNNY: I guess so.
>
> US: Why should you?
>
> JOHNNY: Huh? . . . Um. Why should I what?
>
> US: Why should you do better?
>
> JOHNNY: Well, uh . . . I don't . . . (Thinks: "Is this a trick question?")
>
> US: Did you ever think that this you-need-to-do-better-in-school-now-so-you-can-have-a-good-life-later bit is just some scam cooked up by parents and teachers in order to keep teenagers in line?
>
> JOHNNY: Well, now that you mention it . . .

At this point in the interview, Johnny cannot figure us out. Our serious and deliberate tone does not indicate that we're on his side. On the other hand, we're not playing to his parents either. In fact, we're not paying any attention to them at all. Chances are he has even heard us cut them off when they tried to step in and answer a question on his behalf. Johnny's eyes light up at the word *scam*. While he may not regard us as "cool," he does sense that we understand that he will never be motivated by those forced hollow phrases of encouragement adults like to throw around:

- You're a really bright kid; you just need to apply yourself.
- We don't care about your grades, just so long as you try hard.

- We don't care if you become a manual laborer, so long as you're happy.

We regard Johnny's confusion as a good sign. At least his guard is down. This can be a good place for him to begin a turnaround of his own. Let's return to the interview:

US: So, who says you need to do better, anyway?
JOHNNY: My parents.
US: Why do they say that?
JOHNNY: I guess they think I'll mess up my life if I don't.
US: Why do they think that?
JOHNNY: I don't know. Why don't you ask them?
US: Oh, we plan to. But right now we're trying to get *your* assessment of your situation. Do *you* think you'll mess up your life if you don't do better?
JOHNNY: I'm not sure.

As we're talking with Johnny, we observe Mom's and Dad's body language and general demeanor. How have they been doing with our expectation that they remain silent while we're talking with Johnny? Do they allow Johnny to speak for himself? Do they blurt out a response when he hesitates on a simple question like his date of birth? When we ask Johnny what his parents do for a living, will Mom and Dad resist the urge to edit or clarify his response? (Will they act dumbfounded or perhaps angry when they learn that Johnny is a bit uncertain about what they do for a living?) If we ask a harder question—like how he might evaluate Mom and Dad as parents—will they become defensive? Then we turn to Mom and Dad and ask, "At this very moment, who is the person in this room *most* concerned about Johnny's progress (or lack thereof)?" (With a nervous smile, Mom now either points to herself or repeatedly points her forefinger back and forth between Dad and herself.) "OK, now who in this room is *least* concerned about Johnny's progress (or lack thereof)?" (Now, Mom and Dad assuredly point their fingers at

Johnny, whose response typically runs a gamut from sheepish grin to angry defensiveness.) Sometimes sparks fly as public manners collide with private feelings to produce some explosive displays of raw emotion. In fact, over the years we have developed a condition we call "Immunity from Astonishment." "Until these roles are reversed, your family will be a 'day late and a dollar short' as you chase an endless mirage of ineffective solutions."

As we delve deeper into the family dynamics, it becomes clear that Mom and Dad are doing a lot of worrying about Johnny. Mom, usually more so than Dad, is spending a lot of sleepless nights wondering what they did wrong. She tries to fall asleep by counting the possibilities:

- We were too soft.
- We were too strict.
- It's a genetic fluke. (After all, our older kid isn't like this!)
- Maybe we need to consider some type of medication.
- Maybe he's just in a stage he'll grow out of.
- I wish he had a different biology teacher.
- If we could just get him in with a different crowd.

Meanwhile, down the hall, Johnny is sound asleep in a comatose state, oblivious to his mother's anguish. As a first step, Mom must shift the burden over to Johnny. Not only is her current approach ineffective with Johnny, it is wreaking havoc with her own peace of mind. She is willing to do almost anything to help Johnny grow up right. Intuitively knowing this, Johnny chooses to sit back and let Mom do all the work. Mom needs to replace her focus on Johnny with a focus on herself. As things currently stand, she's doing Johnny's worrying for him. She's part of the problem, not the solution.

As the years pass, we observe an ever-increasing number of mothers and fathers consumed by uncertainty, sometimes anguish. Life in their homes has not turned out as they had dreamed or imagined. Many have lost confidence in their parenting capabilities. Many are angry. Because very few possess a game plan for raising children, they usually fall victim to one of two extremes. One extreme finds them attempting to referee a black-and-white world of concrete hard-and-fast rules. This strategy generally fails because the children end up going through the motions of minimally acceptable behavior with lackluster enthusiasm, all the while never letting go of negative attitudes. The other extreme may find the parents swinging the pendulum clear over to the opposite pole where a vague, ineffectual philosophy is followed at the expense of genuine discipline and structure in the home. Both extremes invariably lead to parents reacting to the behavior of their children, typically feeling as though they are always one move behind. Neither leads to that feeling of fulfillment to which nearly all parents aspire.

As we have observed parents rendered ineffective by these two extremes, we have begun to believe that we can help them by sharing what we have learned through trial and error, perseverance, and our belief in the founding principles of the Hyde Schools. At face value, these principles are simple, even obvious. They borrow heavily from time-honored wisdom and do not pretend to break new ground. But they do dig deep into the core beliefs of what it means to be a truly good person. An understanding of the Hyde philosophy and program will serve to put the 10 Priorities in perspective.

The Hyde Schools:
Our Laboratory

Every individual has a unique potential that defines his or her destiny.

Malcolm's father, Joseph Gauld, founded Hyde in 1966 in Bath, Maine. A highly regarded mathematics teacher and varsity basketball and football coach in the fifties and sixties, he was inspired to start the school because of an experience in the advanced calculus class he taught. One member of his class was the brightest student he'd ever had. However, the boy exhibited very little genuine curiosity, relying almost exclusively on his innate abilities. Furthermore, he demonstrated little concern for the progress of his peers. Joe Gauld responded in the only way he knew how: He told this young man that he needed to test himself with more challenging extra work and that he needed to take a greater interest in his peers. Then he turned around and gave this student the highest grade in the class.

Another student in the same class was the classic "plugger." Although he had considerable difficulty with the material, he embodied all of the qualities and virtues schools should espouse: curiosity, strong work ethic, compassion, honesty, and so on. Gauld praised him in a heart-to-heart talk and then reluctantly gave him the lowest grade in the class. Distraught that neither student was best served by the traditional grading system, Gauld rebelled against the status quo and decided to start a school that would operate under a different set of priorities. (Incidentally, decades later, Gauld checked up on both students. The "genius" had been through a succession of jobs and had never really connected with either success or fulfillment. The "plugger" had become a noted engineer with a loving family.) He was in search of a new approach to education, one that consciously prepared students for life rather than merely preparing them for college. Instead of building his curriculum around five subjects, Joe Gauld decided to focus on five words—courage, integrity, leadership, curiosity, and concern—and began to explore ways to apply these words within a school curriculum.

Since its founding, Hyde has been engaged in an ongoing effort to teach and develop character. In the beginning, the school assumed a few core beliefs. Among them:

1. Every individual has a unique potential that defines his or her destiny.
2. The key to this destiny lies in developing character.
3. Character development requires a commitment to high principles—*virtue* as opposed to *values*.
4. Character development requires us to search for a deeper purpose in life.
5. Character development asks us to strive to leave the world a better place.

More than thirty-five years later, the Hyde Schools are a family of schools and programs striving to honor the Statement of Purpose we adopted in 1990 to articulate our commitment to our founding ideals. It is signed each year by all students and faculty:

Hyde School Statement of Purpose

Each of us is gifted with a Unique Potential that defines a destiny. A commitment to character development enables us to achieve personal excellence and find fulfillment in life. To paraphrase Martin

Luther King Jr., we strive for a school where the members of our community will be judged not by their inherent talents or native abilities but by the content of their character.

Our primary goal is the personal growth of Hyde's students, but our experience has taught us that all constituents—students, teachers, and parents—must strive for personal growth in order for Hyde's teenagers to achieve it. As we narrow the gap between what we want to foster and how we foster it, we continue to believe that our successes are due more to an adherence to a belief system than to a set curriculum. The cornerstones of that belief system are the Five Words and Five Principles.

The Five Words have adorned the school's shield since its founding:

Curiosity

Courage

Concern

Leadership

Integrity

The Five Principles were adopted by the entire community in 1988:

Destiny: Each of us is gifted with a unique potential.

Humility: We believe in a power and a purpose beyond ourselves.

Conscience: We achieve our best through character and conscience.

Truth: Truth is our primary guide.

Brother's Keeper: We help others achieve their best.

We value these words and aspire to reflect these principles in our individual and collective endeavors. Our respect in this community and that which we accord our peers is a direct reflection of these efforts.

In a kind of miniature version of the Statement of Purpose, the Hyde logo features three words in small print—*character family edu-*

cation. The words are integral to the daily lives of our students, our parents, and our teachers.

HYDE

Education Character Family

CHARACTER

Character permeates everything we do at Hyde, and everyone involved—students, parents, and faculty—strives to develop their character honestly and openly. The Five Words and Principles are at the forefront of nearly all daily activities and discussions. For many students, the most profound personal growth occurs when they are pushed by peers and faculty to take on challenges outside their comfort zones—when the football hero tries modern dance or when the computer whiz joins the wrestling team. Not only do such students discover new facets of their character and uncover hidden talents, they contribute to a school culture that places great value on such risk-taking. By graduation, a Hyde student will have:

- Completed a rigorous college preparatory academic program.
- Played on multiple interscholastic athletic teams.
- Performed a vocal solo in front of the entire school.
- Addressed the school community with both extemporaneous and prepared speeches.
- Participated in community service projects.
- Camped, canoed, and hiked in the Maine wilderness.
- Exercised leadership among peers.
- Participated in faculty and peer evaluations.
- Completed the Family Education Program with parents.

This same risk-taking is expected of the faculty, all of whom are challenged to teach and/or coach something outside his or her expertise.

FAMILY

Hyde parents also find themselves venturing into new territory as they experience our family program. The parents do not come merely to support the work of the faculty, they also participate and develop their own character. All parents practice and develop the 10 Priorities of the Biggest Job program.

EDUCATION

Part of the reason for Hyde's national reputation stems from the success we have had in college preparation; some of our students arrive at our doors with little hope of gaining admission to any credible college or university, much less a competitive one. Whereas many so-called turnaround schools may succeed in instilling positive attitudes and in bringing families together, few can match Hyde's record in college placement. More than 98 percent of Hyde's graduates gain admission to four-year colleges—a rate that has remained constant for more than thirty years. During the 1990s, Hyde graduates were enrolled at Bates, Bowdoin, Bucknell, Carleton, Carnegie-Mellon, Chicago, Colby, Colgate, Columbia, Cornell, Davidson, Duke, Georgetown, George Washington, Middlebury, Northwestern, Vanderbilt, Washington, and Wesleyan.

MIXED BLESSING: "THE ROLLS-ROYCE OF TURNAROUND SCHOOLS"

In the early days, Joe Gauld knew that potential applicants might feel like guinea pigs for an experiment, particularly in New England, a cradle of prestigious prep schools. Thus, he set his sights on the "underachiever," believing that success with this niche of students would ultimately result in a flood of applicants from top students who saw

35

Hyde as a better way to learn. However, the better Hyde's work was with so-called troubled teens, the more it became perceived as a school exclusively for this niche. Hyde began to receive national media attention in the seventies for its dramatic success in enrolling offtrack, misbehaving teenage underachievers and sending them to competitive colleges. Such shows as *Today, Donahue,* and *David Susskind* portrayed this story, as did national newspapers and magazines. Although we take pride in these accomplishments, we sometimes feel this reputation is oversimplified and limiting in much the same way that a serious musician might feel unfulfilled as a result of acquiring widespread recognition based on the popularity of a single novelty hit song. Today, a number of educational counselors and experts regard Hyde as the very best turnaround school in the nation. In fact, one referred to Hyde as "the Rolls-Royce of turnaround schools," a distinction we regard as a mixed blessing for two reasons.

First, not all students who attend Hyde come with problems. While we have a deserved reputation for enacting great turnarounds, we are also a school with a challenging and unique approach to education, one applicable to all types of kids. It is an education we deeply want our own three children to experience. Since we began working with parents in the seventies, we have enrolled scores of siblings of these so-called troubled teens—more than fifty of them in 2000–2001. These siblings typically come from families that initially sought Hyde out motivated by a problem with a son or daughter. Once the family embraces the Hyde program, the parents are apt to think, "Wow, this is great! We want all our children to have a Hyde education." They then send a second or third child. These students, their families, and a number of other students feel more than a bit insulted at the characterization of their school as one for troubled teens.

Another reason why Hyde balks at the "Rolls-Royce" idea is of a deeply philosophical nature. While we do believe that schools and families are in need of deep change, *we simply do* not *believe that the kids are "the problem."* Many of the kids who get good grades and perform well harbor the same issues troubled teens do. It's just that they are able to hide them better or their parents and teachers have chosen to avoid seeing them. One recent Hyde graduate, a National Merit semifinalist, wrote:

> Unfortunately, an education system valuing only achievement can make it extremely easy for test scores and awards to lure the "good kid" into a false sense of fulfillment. This fulfillment is false because it founds itself on the static expectations of someone else, like grades and rules for behavior, and not on standards for one's own potential. Many students can meet the standards set by teachers or a school's curriculum, but remain apathetic children, too lazy or cowardly to risk challenging themselves much beyond the status quo of their own boredom. Hyde has pushed me beyond that malaise, and I firmly believe in its relevance to both achieving and well-behaved teenagers.

A number of the so-called good kids come to resent the education they have received prior to attending Hyde (see Priority 5, Value Success and Failure). They feel they have been taught to avoid meaningful challenges that might threaten their grade point average. Ironically, the effort to embellish reputations for college applications can end up compromising critical character development. One girl writes: "All I could think of before Hyde was a dead spirit, filled with grades and manners and smiles, but at Hyde I gained an ability to let friends know me and my weaknesses." A Hyde freshman puts it quite simply: "I knew that if I stayed at my old high school, I would have become even more shallow and fake. Now, instead of wanting to look perfect, I want to be happy with who I am."

We believe our nation's current educational system actually plays a major role in the very creation of "troubled teens," that the preoccupation with innate talent is so debilitating to adolescent morale that it fuels the negativity of the current youth culture. Although we believe our book can help parents and teachers address some of the effects of this problem, our deepest motivations stem from a desire to shed some light on their causes.

In 1993 we founded the Hyde Leadership School of Greater New Haven (Connecticut), a public magnet high school enrolling 175 inner-city students. We "cloned" our boarding school model in 1996 when we founded the Hyde School of Woodstock, Connecticut. Hyde opened a public charter school in September 1999 with the founding of the Hyde Public Charter School of Washington, D.C., a school that will eventually enroll a thousand students in grades K–12. Our experiences working with students and parents in urban public schools convinces us that the Hyde promise possesses a universal quality, one that appeals to parents from a wide variety of racial, ethnic, and socioeconomic backgrounds. We envision future public and private schools based on the Hyde model in other parts of the country.

A map and compass are ineffective if we don't know our exact location. As we begin this journey, it will be helpful to have some sense of the terrain on which we will be traveling and have some sense of "why things are the way they are."

Why Things Are
the Way They Are

We often hear about how things "used to be," how children "used to act." Grandmothers talk about a lack of manners, college professors lament poor skills, and as parents, many of us remember having the fear factor with our own parents, which doesn't seem to exist much any more. Are these assertions about the past really helpful? Do they move us forward?

In our workshop, we talk about some of the influences and issues facing our children and our parenting. In trying to understand the framework that affects our families, we touch on four points:

1. Spokes on a Wheel and the Pact of Indifference
2. The Cult of Self-Esteem
3. We're All Trying to Fix Our Families of Origin
4. The Myth of Quality Time

Think about your own parents. Try to imagine the challenges they faced in raising you. Try to imagine their degree of parenting difficulty. Now, think about your challenges as a parent. Imagine the degree of difficulty you face as a parent. Who has had the tougher job: you or your parents? We have asked this question to hundreds of parents across the country. Consistently, more than 80 percent of any gathering of parents will claim they face a tougher job than their parents faced. Teachers seem to feel the same way. Perhaps you have seen the famous survey that contrasts teachers of the 1940s with those of the 1990s. When asked to name the biggest problems they faced in schools, the list assembled by the teachers from the 1940s seems quaint: tardiness, gum-chewing, and late homework. The list by the teachers from the 1990s is downright frightening: drugs, pregnancy, guns, violence. The problems can seem overwhelming.

In recent years we have visited scores of schools: public, private, parochial, nonsectarian, urban, suburban, rural. Regardless of the type of school or its location, we have become disheartened by a lack of a creative spark that cuts across all categories. Too many kids simply seem not to care. They share what we've come to call a "pact of indifference" in regard to exploring their own potential. Why?

American families and schools have been glued together in a spiral of decline for at least four decades. What began with curious symptoms like lower test scores and rising divorce rates soon evolved into a troubling collage of divorce, absenteeism, alienation, drugs, and violence. Recently this decline has even descended into sheer terror, featuring gun-toting teenagers in once anonymous, innocent towns like Jonesboro, Littleton, and Santee. As educators and parents, we are convinced that today's kids are simply responding to a culture they inherited from us, a culture to which we desperately cling, apparently oblivious to the irony of its debilitating side effects.

The bottom line is simple: *We have created a system in which our students do not believe that their best efforts will be respected.* Though parents continue to say things like "Just try your best," their children's grades too often reflect an end product, not the work that went into it. Given that our teenagers cannot be held responsible for a culture they have inherited, their parents must lead the creation of a new one. Before we can create such a culture, we must be aware of the pertinent problems surrounding the current one. Malcolm delineates four here, beginning with one we call "Spokes on a Wheel."

SPOKES ON A WHEEL
AND THE PACT OF INDIFFERENCE

Those of us born in the middle of the baby boom were not educated by the single institution of school so much as we were influenced by a vast network of agencies comparable to the spokes of a bicycle wheel. School was one of those spokes. Some of the others were sisters, brothers, parents, friends, friends' parents, the neighborhood, church, Boy Scouts and Girl Scouts. My barber talked to me about current events. I remember the Little League baseball coach who came out to the mound after I allowed seventeen runs before the first two innings were complete. With a sigh, he said, "Malcolm, your teammates just aren't supporting you today." I remember another coach who publicly reamed me out for throwing my glove in disgust after committing an error. (I also remember my mother permitting that reaming to occur without interruption—a rarity these days.) I even remember being introduced to the protocol of romance during my first dance at a New Hampshire Grange hall.

SPOKES ON A WHEEL

Experiences like the following hallway banter I recently had with a group of high school students suggest that many kids today have not benefited from this same "wheel." As I walked down the hall, I noticed a group of four or five freshmen who were good-naturedly needling one of their peers. Deciding to enter the fray, I caught their eye and announced, "Let he who is without sin cast the first stone." They all paused and kept their eyes glued on me with a curious stare. Finally, one exclaimed, "Boy, Mr. Gauld, you sure have a way with words!" After admitting that I was not the author of this phrase, I proceeded to give a brief explanation of its origin.

In all of the heated debate about prayer in schools, we seem to have either missed or intentionally avoided the obvious: Kids today know very little about the most basic Judeo-Christian principles that long served as guides to help teach Americans how one is supposed to live. When we began teaching, we discussed the merits of celebrating Hanukkah and/or Christmas. Those debates served to heighten tolerance and respect for differing views and beliefs. That's the good news. The bad news is that these gains were accomplished at the expense of a true understanding of those beliefs. In other words, most teenagers today know the importance of showing respect for both Hanukkah and Christmas during the winter holidays. Yet far too few have any comprehension of what either is about. The result? In the words of a respected college president: "Kids are ethically unformed. It's not that they don't have ethics. It's more that they don't possess a certainty of what their ethics are."

This is not a nostalgic call for a return to the good old days. Maybe there never was such a time. But before we are too quick to criticize the decline of the American school, we need to remember that there was never a time when school "did it all." The other spokes on the wheel played critical roles. We believe it is futile to expect school to "do it all" in the future. It is time to rebuild the wheel, beginning with the two most critical spokes: school and family. This change is more cultural than educational. The 10 Priorities can allow any family to begin this process.

THE CULT OF SELF-ESTEEM

Absent an effective culture, many families and schools have become locked in the debilitating grip of what we call the "Cult of Self-Esteem," a prevalent mind-set in our homes and schools suggesting that kids need to feel good about themselves all the time. The premise behind this mind-set says, "If we make kids feel good about themselves, they will do great things." We believe it's time to peer through the other end of the telescope: *If kids do great things, they will feel good about themselves.*

Kids were not meant to feel good all the time. The journey to gain genuine self-esteem requires that they endure difficulties and overcome obstacles along the way. They will likely feel a dearth of self-esteem before the journey ends. Although self-esteem is not a gift bestowed for the asking, once earned, it can never be taken away. We believe that the Cult of Self-Esteem has directly contributed to many of the specific problems we have in our schools today—from absenteeism and cheating to drug use, guns, and violence. In effect, these behaviors have become the substitutes for the effort, sacrifice, and hardship necessary for cultivating authentic self-esteem.

WE'RE ALL TRYING TO FIX
OUR FAMILIES OF ORIGIN

Which has been the stronger impulse in your parenting:

A. The impulse to parent the way you were parented?
B. The impulse to parent differently from the way you were parented?

We have asked this question to parents across the country at Biggest Job workshops. Regardless of demographics or geography, we would estimate that 80 percent of the parents we encounter choose B. (Consistently, the breakdown will mirror the audience's response to the earlier question that asked whether we or our own parents had the tougher job of parenting.) Most parents are motivated by an impulse to parent differently from how they were parented. Some are surprised to discover that they lack a coherent vision of how they should parent. They lack this vision because they have been consumed by a mind-set of how they should *not* parent. Some examples:

- They may have attempted to cultivate a sense of leniency to offset the strict upbringing they remember.
- They may strive to maintain an atmosphere of informality in reaction to the stiff interactions they remember.
- They may want to counterbalance the highly reserved father or mother they remember from their youth with a jovial and emotionally charged atmosphere in the home.

Some of these arrangements may have some positive outcomes for families. (An example of what Malcolm called "accidental offense" in his coaching days.) However, going out of your way to be the opposite of someone is no better than going out of your way to copy someone. You're not being yourself in either case. And in both cases you're allowing someone else to determine your parenting agenda. We have encountered many families who appear to labor under a mind-set that says, "If I do everything the opposite way my parents did, everything will work out." If it were that easy, we wouldn't call it the Biggest Job.

Rather than measure our actions against our memories of our parents, we need to measure them against a thoughtful vision for our own parenting. All parents at the Hyde Schools explore this and other issues in a three-day program we call the Family Learning Center. Despite the fact that most parents arrive motivated by a desire to improve relations with their children, we begin with a simple question: "Have you let go of your own parents?" At first they think, "Of course!" By the end of the first evening, many parents discover that they have yet to begin. By using the 10 Priorities, parents can establish a comprehensive starting point where they can begin to let go of the past and set a new vision for their families.

THE MYTH OF QUALITY TIME

We have also met many families who believe that an all-purpose key to family improvement exists in the form of "quality time." The solution of "more time" will not prove all that helpful to a family unsure of its vision or principles. In some cases, more time can even have the unintended effect of solidifying unproductive attitudes and behavior. We hesitate to mention a notion like the Myth of Quality Time because we do not want parents to conclude that they are justified in spending less time with their children. We urge you to assume that you will be unable to carry out the Biggest Job without committing a great deal of time and effort to the cause. However, this time must be spent in accordance with a set of principles that reflect a thoughtful vision for the best in your family. More time added to a shaky values system will not carry you far. Time alone will not get the job done.

Unique Potential—
the Key to Our Destiny

Your primary purpose is not *to have a relationship with your children. Your primary purpose is to help your children connect with their unique potential.*

The underlying premise of the 10 Priorities is that every individual has a *unique potential* that defines his or her destiny. This concept is central to this book. By unique potential, we mean a personal destiny that awaits each of us, and we believe that we must strengthen our character and connect with our conscience in order to enhance our chances to connect with this destiny.

Nearly all parents are fond of the well-worn phrase of encouragement for their children: "If you work hard, you can be anything you want in life." We at Hyde believe this statement actually feeds a number of problems we currently face as a society.

We see two problems with this well-intentioned and innocent message. First, it isn't true. For the sake of argument, what would happen if all the sons of the parents who read this book shared the goal of playing quarterback for Notre Dame? What if all the daughters of the parents who read this book wanted to become the first woman president of the United States? Still not convinced? What if all the boys and all the girls exchanged their goals? These things simply could not happen. When parents offer this and other phrases of encouragement, they are often trying to reassure themselves as much as their children. Their children almost always see through this. To them, it may look like: Mom and Dad like to make things up so that I won't get bummed out about my shortcomings. I wonder, Do they really believe in me for who I am? I also wonder, What are my true capabilities and how can I realize them? For more on this subject, see Priority 5, Value Success and Failure.

Second, this statement tends to be divorced from the notion of having a purpose in life. (Were we really put on this earth simply to do whatever we want to do?) In Malcolm's case, he has struggled with his Unique Potential as a teacher. He began teaching with the idea that his time in the classroom would be a temporary, personally enriching experience before heading off to a more lucrative and prestigious career, perhaps in law or business. Feeling the desire to achieve material success, he initially resisted the very idea of perceiving himself as a teacher. During his twenties and early thirties, there were times when a teacher was not what he wanted to be. Questioning the wisdom of remaining in a career with limited financial rewards, he left teaching for a few years in the corporate business world. Although he valued this experience, he came to discover that a teacher is what he is.

When our destiny calls us, it sometimes speaks in a language we do not want to hear. Yet we need to listen. We cannot expect our kids to hear destiny's voice if we have closed our own ears to it. An exciting date with destiny awaits each of us provided we prepare for it. Thus, the development of our character becomes a means to an end rather than an end in itself. (We will explore this in Priority 4: Set High Expectations and Let Go of Outcomes.)

When we ask parents how things are going in their families, they tend to respond with a comment about the state of their relationship with their children. They will invariably say something like: "Oh, lately we've all been getting along great!" or "In our house right now you could cut the tension with a knife." (In the interest of full disclosure, we have probably used both explanations to describe life in our own home at various times in the past few months!) We would challenge parents, perhaps beseech them, with a blunt proposition:

Your primary purpose is *not* to have a relationship with your children. Your primary purpose is to *help your children connect with their Unique Potential.*

To face this challenge, parents need to know that there will be times when they will need to risk the relationship in order to pursue the Unique Potential. Likewise, failure to put the relationship at occasional risk will likely diminish the child's prospects for realizing his or her Unique Potential. One of the most disappointing family dynamics we encounter exists in the form of the parent who is so risk averse that the family remains locked in a holding pattern of mediocrity. Such parents have consciously or unconsciously entered into a pact where they choose the devil they know over the one they don't know. In exchange for the illusion of a guarantee that nothing truly bad will happen (e.g., tumultuous arguments or a runaway teenager), they essentially guarantee that nothing great will happen. Unique Potential will not allow us to play not to lose. To place Unique Potential front and center in a family, each family member must understand that he or she is on a journey to discover his or her best. We cannot control this journey, we can only control the attitudes and effort we put into it.

Do You Live on the Right-Hand Side of the Page?

Think about your kids. Visualize a picture of them in your head. Now picture them twenty years from now. What principles do you hope they will honor? What qualities do you want them to possess? What kind of people do you hope they will become? Take a few minutes and make a list of your answers.

In 1998, after twenty-plus years of working with teenagers and parents in school settings, we began conducting family workshops for parents across the country. Titled "The Biggest Job We'll Ever Have," these workshops have been designed to help parents recognize, connect with, develop, and act upon their natural child-rearing instincts. We begin each workshop by asking the questions above. Then we get out a marker and write the responses on an easel pad in the front of the room. Regardless of geography or demographics, the lists are similar wherever we go. They invariably include terms like:

Respect for others
Be happy
Be fulfilled
Character
Employed
Honesty
Courage
Resourceful
Integrity

Confidence
Leadership
Peace of mind
Humility
Willingness to take risks
Communicator
Trusting
Self-esteem
Parenthood
To be excited about life
Loving people
Socially active
Responsible

If you're like most parents, your list includes some of these qualities. Our experiences demonstrate that parents across the United States share common ground in their hopes and aspirations for their children. As parents, we certainly hope our own three children will come to reflect these qualities. We also hope they will possess a confidence that will cause them to imagine and pursue exciting dreams, that they will have the courage to feel as though the world is their oyster. As parents, we also struggle with what we ourselves know is true about these qualities: We cannot give them to our children. Very often we need to get out of the way and let other people give them to our children. Sometimes we need to get out of the way and let them earn them by themselves through their own initiative. We can, however, work on these qualities ourselves and model a powerful message for our children.

Since beginning our work with families, we have been amazed to discover the qualities our own parents instilled in us, qualities that we don't remember discussing with them. They seem to have been absorbed through daily living, suggesting that talking to our kids about what is important may not be as effective as showing them what is important.

WHO AM I?

Parenting is a monumental challenge. To magnify this challenge, parents face a constant cultural pressure that suggests they possess magical instincts to guide their every move. This can cause panic, self-doubt, and a reluctance to ask for help or to admit that problems exist. Throughout, there is this constant, nagging reminder: "But I'm supposed to know what to do in this situation!" In an effort to lift this pressure, in the Biggest Job workshops we do a five-minute exercise called Who Am I? We begin with a comment from the best-selling book *Tuesdays with Morrie,* by Mitch Albom. In his book, Albom returns to the bedside of Morrie, his former professor, to learn about the dying man's wisdom about death and dying. In the end, Albom learns far more about life and living. At one point the professor says, "Our culture values the wrong things and you have to be strong enough to say that if the culture is not working, don't buy into it." During the Who Am I? exercise, we ask the audience, "When you think about the culture that surrounds us every day, where achievement and success reign supreme, what are some of the ways in which we are evaluated in that culture?" Though we intentionally avoid providing further explanation, we consistently receive the same answers from parents regardless of the geography. See the box on page 54 for the Achievement Culture answers given by workshop participants.

We then ask, "Now, let's look at character. How would we be perceived in that culture?" A typical list also appears in the box.

We then examine the two lists together and ask, "What do they say to you?" Think about how we operate in our daily lives with these two very different paradigms.

Next we ask participants to pair off with someone they do not know and take turns talking about themselves for two minutes, without referring to anything in the Achievement list. We typically specify, "You cannot talk about what you do for a living, where you vacation, or what kind of schooling you have had. Most important,

53

Achievement Culture	*Character Culture*
• Salary	• Attitude
• Job title	• Effort
• Education	• Service to others
• Your house	• Community service
• Your neighborhood	• Integrity
• Your car	• Courage
• Places where you vacation	• Role model
• How your children are doing	• Faith
• Where they go to school	• Passion
• Appearance–clothes, weight	• Perseverance
• How you speak	• Humor
• Birthday parties	• Dreams

you cannot talk about your children." (Experience has shown us that this last requirement is often especially tough on moms, who are often intensely focused on their kids and are fond of talking about their ages, their names, their idiosyncrasies, etc.) To lighten the mood, we ask, "Starting to freak out a bit?" (Most people shift noticeably in their seats at this point.) "Need some direction? Here's what you can talk about. . . ." We then list the following:

- *Kid:* What were you like as a child?
- *Strengths:* What are your personal strengths?
- *Obstacles:* What things hold you back, what things do you struggle with?
- *Likes:* What are the things you like to do? (So long as they're not included in the Achievement list.)
- *Vision:* What are your dreams about your life and future?

In the workshops, we usually ask one of our facilitators to model this exercise. This tends to cut the discernible nervousness in the room. Here is how Laura modeled the exercise at a workshop:

My name is Laura. I am forty-two years old. I think I have a strong sense of commitment. When I was a kid, I was a tomboy who liked to climb trees and make forts. My father died when I was young, so I built my own little fantasy world to which I would retreat at certain times. In my family I played the role of the clown, trying to make everyone laugh even when there was fighting. I have a sense of humor still. I also think I have an ability to see an overall vision of things. My obstacles are more hidden than they are "out there." I tend to get defensive when family members point them out. I appear more confident on the outside than I really am. Certain areas, like technology, bring out poor learning attitudes. I try to encourage others to ask for help, but want to do things by myself. I like to read and I also walk every day. That is one thing I do for myself and I feel good about the commitment I've made to that. I used to draw a lot as a kid and want to do more art. I love to look at all kinds of art. One of my dreams about the future is to have a real impact on . . .

"Times up!"

After the audience members have been off in pairs for two minutes, we yell "Switch!" The chatter resumes for two more minutes. When we reconvene and ask the participants about this exercise, they universally agree that their own priorities as parents and as people are not as clear as they might have expected. Common comments:

- "Although I never have met this person, we share more than I thought."
- "I felt instantly closer to this stranger than I do to many of my friends."
- "I wish I could talk like this to people in my everyday life."
- "I learned about myself in new ways."

These comments are typical. A few memorable ones from past workshops are:

- A father from New York City: "I actually listened to someone for the first time in ages!"

- A mother from Kankakee, Ill.: "There usually is this dance of deception we as adults engage in about how our kids are doing and how everything is going just great in our homes. It was refreshing not to do that."
- A father from San Francisco: "Although I tell my kids that the most important things in life are those qualities listed on the right-hand side of the page [the Character Culture], I have to admit that I live most of my life on the left-hand side of the page. I guess I show my kids that achievement is more important. After all, that is where I spend most of my time and effort."

Think about this comment from the San Francisco father. His observation speaks to our primary motivation for writing this book. There is no way we can reasonably expect our kids to live on the right-hand side of the page if we do not strive to live our own lives in accordance with those qualities. Although it might not be advisable for us to walk around engaging in the Who Am I? exercise with total strangers, we can start to talk to our children and close friends with more honesty and less image. Laura notes, "When I do this exercise in front of a workshop audience, it never fails to make me nervous. My voice is not the strong, confident voice that begins the workshop. The vulnerability we model when we truly talk about who we are actually reveals the foundation of the best of our parenting." For much of our lives, especially the professional side, we may have learned to expect success by relying on our confident, capable selves to steer the course. Raising our children takes a deeper set of navigation tools. It involves a journey in which we commit to learn about and better ourselves. It also involves the humility and courage to expose ourselves to the people we love most.

To return to the list at the beginning of this chapter (i.e., those qualities we hope our children will possess twenty years from now), as parents, we do not add qualities like honesty, respect, concern, and leadership to our children. Rather, we help them draw those qualities out of themselves. Like the flower reaching toward the sunlight, the most natural behavior of our children will be to copy the behavior we model. James Baldwin once observed, "Children have never been very good at listening to their elders, but they have never failed to imitate them." Therefore, if we are to inspire our children, we are going to have to expect to get involved by consciously modeling the very attitudes and behavior we hope to instill.

Notice how the list under the Character Culture closely resembles the What We Want for Our Kids list.

Character Culture	*What We Want for Our Kids*
• Attitude	• Respect for others
• Effort	• Be happy
• Service to others	• Character
• Community service	• Employed
• Integrity	• Honesty
• Courage	• Courage
• Role model	• Resourceful
• Faith	• Integrity
• Passion	• Confidence
• Perseverance	• Leadership
• Humor	• Peace of mind
• Dreams	• Humility
	• Willingness to take risks
	• Communicator
	• Trusting
	• Self-esteem
	• Parenthood
	• To be excited about life
	• Loving people
	• Socially active
	• Responsible

Now, let's turn to the 10 Priorities and begin to synchronize a culture that leads to the qualities we ultimately want for our children.

PART TWO

THE 10 PRIORITIES

Priority 1. Truth over Harmony
Priority 2. Principles over Rules
Priority 3. Attitude over Aptitude
Priority 4. Set High Expectations and Let Go of Outcomes
Priority 5. Value Success and Failure
Priority 6. Allow Obstacles to Become Opportunities
Priority 7. Take Hold and Let Go
Priority 8. Create a Character Culture
Priority 9. Humility to Ask for and Accept Help
Priority 10. Inspiration: Job 1

Get Your Priorities Straight

The 10 Priorities are offered as concepts to think about, to struggle with, to laugh about, and most important, to apply to our daily lives. We have found that they can help parents bring their natural child-rearing instincts to the surface for the benefit of their children and their families. As parenting can often seem like an overwhelming obligation, the 10 Priorities break this obligation down into bite-size chunks. Each chapter includes excerpts from personal stories written by teenagers, teachers, and parents we have worked with over the years. Each chapter is also accompanied by individual and group exercises designed to help parents and/or children put each Priority into practice. In addition to the exercises, journaling questions are presented for families to use as guides for the personal journals described in Priority 8.

The Biggest Job workshops evolved out of our motivation to distill the Hyde family program into a four-hour experience for parents. While their children are enrolled at Hyde, parents are engaged in a comprehensive program designed to help them stay focused on the "right-hand side of the page." As we set out to offer a four-hour experience on the road, we kept wondering, How can we help parents keep their priorities straight? The 10 Priorities proved to be the answer.

These 10 Priorities are not presented as a foolproof response to every challenge or difficulty we encounter in our homes. The choices of parenting cannot be made so unequivocally. But the 10 Priorities can offer a framework to guide our efforts. As a parent in Washington, D.C., said, "I have learned a system of articulation and practicality." They can help us decide where to put "the weight of our foot." For example, in offering Priority 1, Truth over Harmony, we do not suggest that parents focus on truth instead of harmony in their homes. Rather, we encourage parents to favor truth when they encounter uncertainty.

In offering the 10 Priorities, we urge parents to struggle with the distinction between philosophy and method. Just as a map and compass have separate functions as navigational tools, philosophy and method serve two different purposes in the parenting process. The methods must be carried out in the spirit of the philosophy. In helping kids live up to high standards, we find that we must constantly emphasize the need for kids to honor both the spirit and the letter of the law. Otherwise, they sometimes follow our rules but continue to hold on to negative attitudes. Thus, the 10 Priorities come with a warning: Parents hoping for a can't-miss, surefire recipe for child-rearing will be disappointed. The reader will be expected to struggle with the subtleties of these steps. This struggle begins at the outset with the first three Priorities: Truth over Harmony, Principles over Rules, Attitude over Aptitude.

We must be clear: Harmony, rules, and aptitude are not inherently bad objectives. We do, however, call upon parents to stand more firmly on truth, principles, and attitude. Put the weight of your foot there. Consider them *Priorities*. Anytime we tackle a complicated challenge, we often need to be reminded to "get our priorities straight." Nowhere is this prioritization more important than in our role as parents. The 10 Priorities show us how to begin and can serve as a guide in our efforts to continue.

EXERCISES AND ACTIVITIES

Each Priority is accompanied by exercises and activities that help to reinforce the Priorities. They are intended to encourage discussion and family interaction. The family might choose to address these exercises and activities during the weekly family meetings described in Priority 8, Create a Character Culture. Each of these has been tested with families at Hyde and with those who have attended Biggest Job workshops.

JOURNALING

Each Priority is accompanied by journaling questions. These questions can be used in two ways. The reader might write responses to them after each chapter, or the entire family can address them during the weekly family meetings discussed in Priority 8, Create a Character Culture. In either case, journaling provides clarity as we apply our best efforts to the 10 Priorities. It offers each family member a way to explore personal experience as a resource for reflection on feelings and attitudes. Taking the time to listen and to be in touch with this core of our lives, we discover new ways to view ourselves, our connections to others, our families, and our destiny.

Journaling can be incorporated into the weekly family meetings outlined in Priority 8. The facilitator, a rotating responsibility, simply asks a variety of questions, usually organized around a specified theme. There is typically a two- to three-minute pause after each question is asked while each family member writes a response to the question. Following the questions, anyone is invited to share his or her writing with the group. Through this sharing of unique experiences and perspectives, we connect to others who might have similar responses. This process offers creative possibilities for personal growth and change. Journals remain the personal property of each individual and can serve as confidential personal histories to be reviewed in the future.

STEP-BY-STEP JOURNALING PROCEDURES

The following steps are recommended procedures to follow in accordance with the journaling questions presented at the conclusion of each Priority:

1. Find a space/atmosphere in the home that allows for quiet and thoughtful reflection.
2. Read each question twice in a clear, distinct tone.
3. Allow for two to three minutes of writing per question.
4. *Everyone* in the session needs a journal. Expect each participant to take the session seriously.
5. All should feel that what they write is private and need be shared only when they choose.
6. During response time, the facilitator asks if anyone wants to share what he or she has written. Encourage each family member to participate in the discussion. If no one seems anxious to share, be patient—sometimes silence is better than a trivial response.
7. Begin to get each family member involved in both writing the questions and leading the sessions.

It's one thing to point out the problems. It's another to work on the solutions. Raising and teaching kids to be the best they can be is a huge job. Time's a-wastin'. Let's get started.

Priority 1,
Truth over Harmony

The truth shall set you free, but first it will make you miserable.

—Sign at entryway of each Hyde School

This Priority is the foundation upon which all of the 10 Priorities rest. It speaks to our core as individuals, as partners, and as family members. Putting the weight of our foot on the path of honesty is a lifelong challenge and journey. We learn great lessons when we exercise the courage to trust the truth. We can also learn them on those occasions when we recognize that we have actually been guided by harmony.

Susan, a Hyde mother of two, talked about her role in Truth over Harmony:

> Before we went to Hyde, my husband, Walter, used to lose his temper a lot. And I used to do everything in my power to make sure that he wouldn't lose his temper, so I was always backing away. I can remember my son, really in anger, saying to me, "Mom, you are so afraid of Dad! All you ever do is back away and support him instead of saying what is really happening in our family." As soon as Walter showed any hint of getting angry, I immediately backed away from everything and didn't care about the truth at all. I just wanted to keep things level so that he wouldn't explode. And our son told me that

I was doing that; he told me I was being dishonest. It affected the dynamics of our family because I wouldn't stand up for anything if it appeared there would be conflict.

Walter, her husband, responds:

It has always been important for me to see myself as an honest person. When I've done things that I wasn't proud of, I would often just block them out entirely. I can remember certain instances when Susan and I were having conflict and we'd be arguing about something, and she would say, "Oh, do you remember when you did the following thing?" and I'd say, "I never did that." And we'd talk some more and after a while I'd say, "I did do that, didn't I?" I wouldn't confront the fact that I had actually done that.

As a parent, ask yourself: Which holds a higher value in my family: truth, dealing honestly with each other, or *harmony,* getting along with each other? Remember, the question is not which of these two ought to hold higher value, but which of these two is, in fact, valued more. This is a tough one. Many parents who believe they place their highest value on truth end up discovering that they work even harder to maintain a role as peacemaker in their families. Whether expressed as honesty, integrity, or conscience, this chapter stresses the importance of placing truth front and center. We urge all families to regard truth as their ultimate anchor.

The reader may be wondering, How does one get truth? We're not sure one ever truly "gets" it. As you will hear from many parents in this chapter, we move closer to the truth by having the courage to listen to and then give voice to that silent message deep in our souls. If we do not feel great about how our families are operating, we need to consider "more truth" as the first prescription. Our experience has been that most people would like to be honest. However, competing values result in confused priorities. One common competing value is what we call "harmony." Our tendency to rely on harmony often originates in experiences we had with our families of origin.

One father, a doctor, talked about coming to grips with the truth about an issue in his family of origin:

The first thing I realized when I started to look at myself was that my family never talked about failure. Although I could tell my kids things like flunking out of college in my first year, I began to wonder, Why is it that I can't personally admit to failure? Why is it that truth won't become the center of these things? Then I think about my father. He was a coach who talked about the wins and not the losses. I was raised in a loving family and yet when I really start to talk about my parents honestly, as I learned to, I realized that there were dishonesties. My father was one of eight, raised on a farm in Oklahoma. He was blind in one eye. As a child, I was always told that Dad got his eye injury playing football. And it turns out he got it in a fight with his father on the farm and his father had hit him. This was the reason he lost his eye.

My mom and dad are dead now and I never had the opportunity to really talk to them that much about what went on in the family, but for the most part, when you talked with them, everything and everyone was happy. And as Hyde taught me, "The apple doesn't fall far from the tree." I put myself up on a pedestal with my own kids. I mean, I'm sitting up there doing nothing wrong. It really goes back with me to my upbringing. The truth is, we were always a truthful family, but we didn't have the deep truth. I just wish that I'd had the opportunity to realize that before their deaths, to be able to sit down and talk like this with them. I can do it now with my own children.

A Hyde teacher and mother talks about the harmony that she didn't trust as a child and how that affected her later:

Growing up in an alcoholic home, the constant message was that everything was okay. What we were seeing and experiencing was not harmony, but that was the message. I know that I grew up not trusting my instincts. I was trying to filter the information because the stuff that I was being told didn't match up with what I was experiencing.

Later, as a teenager, in order to avoid negative consequences, I did not tell my parents the truth. That kept things nice and easy. I was holding it together and looked like a responsible person. Even later in my marriage, I tried to maintain the idea that everything would work out. Finally I got to the point where I chose truth for the sake of my son. I didn't respect the marriage. There were truths that we both needed to face. I was fighting the idea of divorce because I wanted to maintain the ideal family picture for my son. I realized that Nick would see through it and that I would be modeling a falsehood, settling for a life of pretending.

At the Biggest Job workshops, we tell parents, "Treat your children as if they were someone else's kids." After all, we tend to see our children as so incredibly unique and special that our support for them can often drown out the truth of their behavior and actions. Indira Gandhi once said, "The world is not your mother." We need to remember that one of our primary responsibilities as parents is to teach our kids that they are ultimately accountable to life, not to us. Truth over Harmony can help us by providing us with an instant check: "Am I telling the full truth? . . . Why am I *not* telling the full truth? . . . Am I really willing to see and hear the truth about myself and my family?"

When we reflect on our own childhoods, we don't remember our parents being as concerned about having a relationship with us as we seem to be about having one with our children. In our professional roles it does seem as though today's parents are preoccupied with communication and rapport at the expense of truth and discipline. One explanation relates to the fact that nowadays both parents are working. Today's parent often acts as if to say "I know I've been working too hard. Now I need to overcompensate with some real quality time." This approach can be a problem when guilt overpowers truth as a motivator. Parents lose their effectiveness when discipline is put on the back burner.

In our youth, we watched adult parties from behind the spindles of the stairwell. If we were lucky, we were allowed to take coats and perform certain tasks before being sent upstairs to our rooms. We could count on being expected to introduce ourselves at some point during the evening. ("Make sure you look them directly in the eye and give them a firm handshake," Malcolm's mother would tell him.) Today's parents tend to bring their children to most social functions, where they sometimes command center stage even when they are acting out. At these times, our preoccupation with harmony can keep us from seeing the real truth about our children. Let's call them parenting moments of truth. These are times when we need to put the relationship on the back burner and do what our better selves know to be the right thing. It happens every day in all of our families. Laura writes about an incident with our oldest daughter:

Mahalia was struggling with a bad attitude—or rather, she wasn't struggling much at all. The rest of us were suffering from her attitude toward her younger sister and her disrespectful tone of voice. While all the details of the actual incident are fuzzy, it had something to do with not doing her chores and lying about it to the baby-sitter.

She was planning to attend a performing arts event with her sister and friends. I remember sitting down in the living room (our quiet place where we try to limit activities to music, reading, and conversation) and thinking about what needed to happen. I thought about the special night out and how much we had all looked forward to it. I knew in my gut that the right thing to do would be to keep her home, but I kept thinking about ways to get around that truth.

On the "truth" side, Laura weighed the factors:

- Her actions are part of an increasing pattern of negative attitudes and inappropriate behavior.
- This kid needs to feel some accountability for her actions.
- This pattern doesn't seem to bother her.
- In fact, we are definitely more upset about this than she is.

- Our "gut" feeling is that keeping her home is the right thing to do.

On the "harmony" side:

- It would be enriching for her to see the show.
- Her friends are planning for her to be there.
- Maybe there is an alternative measure of disciplinary accountability.
- If she stays home, we can't go as a family (i.e., one of us will have to stay with her).

After thinking it through, I finally decided that she needed to stay home and focus on neglected chores. While I was nervous about the fallout from telling her this, I did feel a certain calm in the knowledge that this was the right thing to do. When I told her, there was crying and stomping around the house. But this reaction didn't last as long as I had feared. After everyone left the house to attend the performance, she came down and started working on her chores. Oddly, she seemed almost relieved. We even had a good talk about attitudes later that evening.

Sound familiar? Most of us experience the Truth over Harmony tension daily in our interactions with our children. The simple effort to "know the truth" can be the first step, followed by the courage to give voice to that truth.

Was that one incident a life-changing moment in our daughter's life? We'll probably never know. What it did do was reinforce to us the importance of trying to let the truth of any given situation lead us as parents. It also showed that our family takes time to fully address such matters. While these examples involving our daughter might appear quaint, the same dynamic of truth versus harmony can manifest itself in critical and major ways regarding issues such as alcohol abuse, anger, and family lies. (In Priority 2, Laura will introduce her example of the "Family Life Raft" as a metaphor for how many families face, or don't face, these issues.) Sometimes families don't confront the truth, preferring instead to try to "live and let live" in order to keep the peace at home. Not only does this approach prevent families from reaching the truth, it also creates a much deeper problem with the messages it sends the children in the family by teaching them that serious family issues will be swept under the carpet. No matter how we may construct our version of the truth, our children will absorb the dishonesties in the family even if they do not have the specifics.

Another father talks about the lies his family of origin lived:

> When I think about Truth over Harmony, it brings back memories of my family: My father and all of his brothers were alcoholics. Never once has he recognized or acknowledged that there was a drinking problem in the family. My parents always presented this picture of perfection, which ultimately was a dishonest thing. Unfortunately, I followed suit and put harmony over truth many times, and it's affected our family. Even when I have employees I need to call on the carpet, I can't seem to do it. Truth is still a difficult thing for me.

First, we must want to know the truth. And in order to know the truth, we must make ourselves vulnerable and ask for it up front. It takes courage to say to our families and friends, "I want to know your true thoughts and feelings, especially when it comes to the strengths and obstacles of my children. Give it to me. I may not always act like I want to hear it, but I want and need it." Unless we genuinely ask for it, people will give us only a watered-down version. (Saving the full version for gossip!) The truth will not provide us with answers so much as it will provide a road to travel as we try to be good parents and good people. As we stay on the road of truth, the correct direction becomes clearer.

In our professional lives, we can use a clear set of skills and approaches. It becomes a whole new ballgame when it comes to home and family. Raising our children requires a deeper set of navigational tools. It involves a journey where we commit to learn about and better ourselves. It also involves the humility and courage to expose ourselves to the people we love the most. John, the father of three, all of whom graduated from Hyde, talks about the journey to make himself real to his family:

As I think about the Truth over Harmony issue, I think back to my dishonesty with our children, particularly when they were younger. My approach to them, when I was around them, was to fabricate an image of myself, an image of someone who had always done every-thing the right way and someone who had never encountered any major failures. Of course, the reason I had never failed was because I was so circumspect and smart. I was able to slip into this great person who now and again came home. I think what I basically said to them in so many words was "You should be like this fabricated image of me." When they weren't, when the kids screwed up or things didn't go well in one way or another, I always managed to bring this in. If I didn't say this directly, I implied it.

Finally, our oldest son, Henry, our first child to attend Hyde, had actually given it a try to be like this fabricated image. Of course, he couldn't (no one could) and he finally just blew up, as there was no way he could articulate this dishonesty at that stage in his life. But I still didn't get it. Later, with our second child, Rebecca, we were sit-ting in a family seminar at Hyde. Rebecca was clearly struggling with this issue of being able to try things where she might fail. She wanted to do everything just right. She wanted to be first, she wanted to be out front. One of the mothers turned to me and said, "You know, your daughter is really afraid to fail. And just listening to you, it seems to me that she probably thinks you've never failed at any-thing. Maybe that is something you need to think about."

When it came time to write our letters to each other, I wrote her a letter about a patient I had had, a young woman, who had a signifi-cant problem. We elected to do a procedure. Things didn't go well and this woman died. It was an utter failure. I think that even before I wrote that letter, I was going through my usual rationalizations—it was a terrible thing, one thing and another—but when I wrote the letter to Rebecca, it was one of the first times that I was completely honest about how I failed, how I had been afraid to do certain things, how I later realized some things about the case that might have made a difference. I think Rebecca realized that the "if you can't be perfect, fake it" approach had led me to faking quite a bit in my life. The interesting thing to me is that it was a kind of release, it seemed that Rebecca felt freer to fail, freer to try things and to realize that she could learn from them. I think for me it was a release from my own persistent dishonesty that was affecting my family.

When we talk about Truth over Harmony, the word *perfection* seems to creep into much of the discussion. A Hyde father, a former businessman, shared his thoughts:

I learned a long time ago: If you're not perfect, for God's sake, fake it. And then I realized at some point, everyone's faking it. We were in a discussion with some parents in our Hyde region and some man was talking. For some reason, I didn't like him. I'm not sure I even trusted him. It was a great lesson for me because we were talking about perfectionism and he came up with a quote that has stayed with me ever since: "You know, what brings people together is not their perfection, it's their imperfection."

Another father, a successful lawyer, had a moment of truth when he "got real" with his son:

I had about a hundred reasons why I had to act in ways that were inconsistent, such as being dishonest, valuing harmony over truth because having disharmony was something I couldn't deal with. I've always felt bad about myself inside—my conduct outside was 180 degrees. If you just looked at my work, listened to my words, and looked at the way I acted, you'd think, "This guy has it all together." Of course, people didn't like me all that much, as I came across as arrogant and egotistical.

I will never forget the moment when I began to move toward putting myself in sync. The first step was becoming honest about the things I had been dishonest about. One of these was taking my son's bar mitzvah money to cover some debts. It was a turning point to first become honest with myself—"This is something you need to say"—and then to share this with my son. It opened up a whole new relationship between us when he said, "Dad, all you had to do was ask me. I would have given it to you." I'll never forget those words.

Another dad shares what he learned about shielding his son from the truth:

I practiced harmony over truth when twice in my older son's early childhood I was in situations where I badly mishandled situations at work and ultimately got fired for it. Yet I kept coming home and whistling a happy tune to my kids. Everything is cool. Dad decided to change jobs—better opportunity, better this, better that, life goes on. It was years later that I realized that I wanted to protect them from being worried. As we talked later, my son's image of me was of someone who always succeeded and never failed. However high-minded my outward objectives might have been, I really didn't want to admit that I had failed and I was scared. And in not doing this, I deprived him of a piece of my life, a piece of real-life experience that he needed, because I was practicing harmony over truth.

THE APPLE DOESN'T FALL
FAR FROM THE TREE

Although every human being is unique, the strengths and obstacles of kids and parents often mirror each other. When we see our children act inappropriately, it is important to look at ourselves. Where am I with that? How am I dealing with that in *my* life? This does not let our children off the hook—they need to feel the consequences of their actions—but their deepest growth will occur when they see us tackle our own versions of that issue. Laura writes:

When our oldest daughter was about seven, she went through a lying phase. Not only was she lying about minor details, she was also getting her sister in trouble by attempting to put the blame on her. She took a ring off my dresser and said that her sister had taken it. I was going back and forth between giving out consequences and losing my cool: yelling, grimacing, and such.

At one point, I asked myself, Where are you with honesty? Are there any areas where you need to get more honest? At the time, our youngest child was diagnosed with some delays in his speech and development. We were both frightened and motivated to work intensively with him. My days were spent marching forward with a warrior-like demeanor, while the nights brought me to my knees with fear and worry.

There were many nights when Mahalia would see me with red eyes and ask, "What's the matter, Mommy?" I would use that time-honored mantra of motherhood: "I'm OK. Mommy's tired." It certainly made sense to me then. My daughter was too young to lay this burden on her. She didn't need to have this added to her life. I also knew that if I shared this with her, I would cry and how would that help her? One night, I found myself in the same situation. I sent her to bed with my "Everything's fine. Mommy doesn't feel too well." After she went into her room, I was faced squarely with my own emotional dishonesty.

I made a pact with myself: If she is awake when I go in, I will share some of my feelings with her. She was awake. I sat on the bed and said, "Mahalia, Mommy's feeling sad. I am worried about Harrison." Of course, the careful words stopped and the tears came. We sat in silence for a few moments. She reached up, put her hand on my shoulder, and said, "Harrison is going to be all right."

She was ready for more truth than I was giving her credit for. I also learned an important lesson about trusting my kids with truth and asking for help. Her lying didn't change overnight, but it did begin to dissipate. Once again, when I focused on myself, a ripple effect was started in the family that had more impact than all the yelling, screaming, and manipulating of outcomes.

THE RIGHT FRAME OF MIND

In getting on track with Truth over Harmony, it may be helpful to consider two concepts: love + truth = true love, and the weight of your foot.

LOVE + TRUTH = TRUE LOVE

A deep respect for truth lies at the heart of each of the 10 Priorities presented in this book. Whether expressed as honesty, integrity, or conscience, the Biggest Job calls upon parents to place truth front and center. Truth over Harmony may strike some as a departure from the more conventional focus on love. Although essential to parenting, love can also be misunderstood. Certainly there are places in the world today where love is sorely lacking. However, if you have read this far in this book, chances are that lack of love is not a problem with you or your family. In fact, it may even be true that an abundance of love has led to an unhealthy division of responsibilities and expectations in your family.

At a Biggest Job workshop, a mother once asked, "Are you saying that I need to choose between love and truth in interacting with my kids?" It may feel like that for a while. Ultimately, in the healthiest of families, love and truth go hand in hand. If the choice of love or truth feels too stark or unpalatable, think of the idea that the two are actually inseparable: Love demands that I be truthful with my children and all of my family members. If *true* is the root word of truth, then *true love* must demand that we be truthful. The deepest love of a parent for a child is expressed in a parent's commitment to raise his or her children to honor their best and to better their world. This commitment demands that we be truthful with our children, our spouses, and ourselves.

THE WEIGHT OF YOUR FOOT

We do not suggest that harmony is necessarily a bad thing. Certainly, there are times when we may do well to consciously choose harmony over truth to maintain the best course of action at a given moment. However, let's do so consciously and not as the result of denying or avoiding the truth. Have the courage to say to yourself, "I choose harmony."

When is it appropriate to choose harmony? As a teacher, we might emphasize a positive feature of a student's academic work as an act of encouragement. As a parent, we will praise our daughter's progress on the clarinet as she practices in the living room even if the sound coming from the room includes a lot of screeches and squelches. There is a difference between encouraging the best effort of our children and tiptoeing around their negative attitudes. We call upon parents and teachers to follow a simple rule of thumb: "When in doubt, bet on the truth." If we have the courage to err on the side of honesty with those around us in an effort to help others be the best they can be, in the long run, they will thank us. There is no way we can expect to build strong families and schools if the foundations of both do not rest on a commitment to honest relationships.

HARMONY OVER TRUTH = FAMILY DYSFUNCTION

The term *dysfunctional* is thrown around so much these days that it has lost some of its true meaning. If we accept the idea that a dysfunctional family is any family that does not operate in an optimal manner for the maximum benefit of all family members, then we would probably have to conclude that all families are dysfunctional. It is obviously a matter of degree. Furthermore, any family with high expectations will eventually encounter dysfunction. (If not, then the expectations probably aren't all that high.) As families strive to stand against the challenges and difficulties of the big, bad real world "out there," our natural parenting tendency is to create a warm, nurturing artificial world "in here" to protect our children and other family members. That world at home can become so artificial that it begins to bear little or no resemblance to the outer real world that our children must ultimately face. We can offer too much protection to those family members experiencing difficulty with functioning productively in that outer world that lies beyond the threshold of our front doors. Such a family can be on the road to becoming seriously dysfunctional if it has not already arrived.

In his book *The Fifth Discipline*, Peter Senge tells "The Parable of the Boiled Frog." Place a frog in a pot of boiling water and the frog will predictably try to scramble out of the pot. However, if you place the frog in a pot of water at room temperature and then turn the heat all the way up, the frog will put up little or no resistance, and descend into drowsy indifference. Ultimately, the frog will sit in the pot until it dies. Why will it seem to willingly accept its impending death? This is because the frog is only capable of responding to wild fluctuations in its environment.

A mother writes:

When my son first started to self-destruct, I couldn't let my friends see what was happening with us. I figured that if I just kept everything contained, we'd get over this and nobody would ever know what had happened. I justified that I was trying to protect my son, when in fact I was terribly embarrassed that I had failed him as a mother. So, when I was talking to my friends who had kids the same age as Kirk, I would hear all about their successes and that caused me to withdraw more and more. It was painful to hear how well their kids were doing knowing that mine was doing so poorly. Yet I couldn't open my mouth and lie about what he was doing. While I couldn't lie, I also couldn't verbalize the truth of what was going on in our situation. So I socially isolated myself to maintain some sort of harmony. At one point I was able to put truth over harmony and tell people what had happened.

Each time I did that, it lost some of its power over me. I was amazed at how accepting and supportive people were who I had been pushing away.

Many families function like the frog, especially when it comes to interacting truthfully. We generally don't consciously choose to lie. We usually get caught in a virtual spider's web of conflicting emotions and mistakenly believe that well-intentioned dishonesty can set us free. For example, parents might very well react aggressively if their child, in a single marking period, went from straight As to straight Fs. However, the same parents will likely react more passively if this change occurs over a period of two years. Let's assume that the child reacts angrily when the parent first expresses concern over declining grades. The parent may well choose to remain silent as the grades decline further during the next marking period. Eventually, the parent may unconsciously "lower the bar" of expectation and begin to convince him- or herself that the decline either is "not so bad" or will reverse itself. In such a case, the family's collective understanding of what is normal is changing so gradually that the change is not perceived. The result is that a new understanding of "how we're going to deal with each other" sneaks up on the family. Although this new understanding is never actually expressed, it is understood and accepted in the form of a silent pact. This new understanding of what is normal is also almost always accompanied by lower standards of expectation. The gradual decline continues and the family dysfunction grows.

Mary, a Hyde alumni parent, talks about her family's descent into harmony over truth:

Thinking about Truth over Harmony, it was insidious in the way harmony crept into my parenting. It started early on with our son, Bill. For instance, the bus would come to pick him up at the end of the driveway. He started to go out early to get there on time. But soon, he would come running back and say, "I have to go to the bathroom!" How are you going to tell somebody that they can't go to the bath-

79

room? Over time, I realized, "He's not going to the bathroom, he just wants to miss the bus so that I'll take him to school." And sure enough, I would do that! Or he would call me from school and say, "I forgot my homework." Far be it for me to say "Too bad!" or "*You* missed the bus. Walk!" I just could never bring myself to do that. It was really dysfunctional.

As Bill got older, there was more. He would say to me, "I have to be at school at seven in the morning for chorus." In the beginning that may have been true, but over time I realized he didn't have to be there at seven in the morning. He just wanted me to take him to school early so he could run across the street to a friend's house and smoke marijuana. It was a sick sort of enabling. There was definitely harmony over truth: no confrontation, no words, no ugliness. I had a physical reaction to that sort of thing. I just couldn't do that.

Today, Bill jokingly refers to his mother back then as the "harmony queen":

Things started to go downhill for me in ninth grade. One day I skipped school with a friend. We were hitchhiking back to his house. My mother was out power walking and caught us. We tried to hide behind a tree, but it was too late. My mother knew that I was already in trouble at school and this would probably mean suspension. So I'm thinking that I'm dead. We went home to wait for my dad. I heard my mom on the phone in the back room saying, "Unfortunately, Billy cannot come to school today, he's sick." I don't think we ever told my dad.

Later, when Bill's substance issue forced the family to get outside help, Mary had a powerful "moment of truth":

Bill was in rehab and had come home for his first overnight. He was fifteen. We had been given all these restrictions. One was that a parent had to be in the room with him at all times, or he couldn't be out of a parent's sight. When he went to bed, I paid close attention to where he had placed his sneakers at the back door, almost like I drew an invisible line around them.

When I got up the next morning, the sneakers were not where they had been when I had gone to bed. My husband, Doug, had gone to work. I can remember standing in the kitchen and I said to Billy, "You went out last night, didn't you?" "What are you talking about? Of course I wouldn't do that." I could feel my heart starting to race. I said to myself, "You can either take this where it's going or you can take him at his word and you know he's lying." I was an absolute wreck. I said, "I know that you snuck out last night! Your shoes . . ." and we went through the whole thing. He knew he was caught and he started to pound his fists on the refrigerator to the point where I didn't know what was going to happen. The rehab had said to us, "If they break the rules, they have to come back." I could feel myself getting closer and closer to saying "I'm taking you back." I can remember saying to myself, "Can you say this?" Bill was beating his fists on the refrigerator and I said, "Get your stuff together. I'm taking you back."

I don't think he believed that I would ever do it. I called Doug and he came home and we took him back together. To this day, Bill still talks about that being the first time that his mom ever stood up to him. I was mostly scared. As Bill said to me at that time, "You know, Mom, I was probably just begging you to stand up to me and you never could." That was one of the first times that truth took precedence over harmony with my son.

Mary's son went on to deal with his substance issue and eventually got sober midway through his college years. He went on to excel in athletics, graduating from his college as Athlete of the Year before playing sports at the professional level. This success was the result of his having learned one important lesson about having to honor his own truth: being true to himself in the face of peer pressure. Bill writes:

I was chosen to play lacrosse on a team in Australia. One of my biggest fears about going came from stories I had heard about the legendary drinking culture on the teams "down under." I was twenty-four years old and had been sober for three years. It had been tough getting sober in college. There were many nights in my college dorm where I would be playing Nintendo while everyone else was out partying.

When I got off the plane, there was a big party to introduce me to the team and their families. There were probably two hundred people there. At one point, someone got up to give a toast to the "only American on the team." *Me.* They began to sing a traditional drinking song. Everyone raised their glasses and looked at me indicating that I was supposed to chug the pint of beer in front of me. I was terrified of what people were going to think. I was terrified I wasn't going to fit in. There was a moment when I had to make a decision. Instead of picking up the pint of beer, I grabbed my can of soda and began to chug it to a chorus of boos and taunts of "send the Yank back home." Eventually I earned the respect of the team. I also learned that I am tougher on the inside than I thought and I am not going to compromise who I am for other people. That's being truthful.

It is often when times are the toughest that we cling to harmony. This mother can now laugh about her total denial of the truth when her son was acting out and she chose to deal with it by hoping harmony would eventually sort it all out:

I really struggled as a parent to be the perfect mother. I read all the books. I had the idea that praise and positive encouragement were the only answers. I thought I could love my children enough so that everything would be okay. It became very dysfunctional. When my son, Neil, was at his worst and his behavior was a nightmare, I did something that was incredible. I don't sew, that's not my thing, but I cross-stitched a pillow that read "To have a son like you is a dream come true." The pillow is still in his room! I mean, this was when he was at his worst! We get a good laugh about it now.

We have seen many parents heap congratulations on children who are exhibiting the most minimal effort. The following vignette was written by the mother of a teenage girl:

When my children lied to me, and I knew in my heart that they were lying, I chose to believe them because it was easier and I was afraid to deal with the truth once I heard it. Once, when my husband and I returned home from a business trip, it was clear people had been in our house. Our daughter lied and covered it up. In my heart I knew there was more to the story. For the first time, I didn't let her off the hook. It was a long, tearful, and fearful evening. I told her the truth would set her free. It was an eye-opening experience for me. I look at her differently now, more realistically. Once the truth was out, we could and did deal with it. We held her accountable for her actions and her lying.

Another Hyde alumni parent was an early "soccer mom." Her story hits home with us:

Neither one of our boys was aggressive (our daughter took on that role in our family). When Henry played soccer as a little kid, he would go out there and be so polite, he didn't kick the ball if the other kids wanted to kick it. He would just run with the other kids up and down the field in a cloud of dust. There were many times when he finished a soccer game and he had never put his foot on the ball, because he just wasn't sure he could do it. At the time I was reading all this stuff about giving your kids self-esteem, and I would say, "Great game, Henry! That was really good!" And so he had this idea that he was doing a great job, and as a result, he never got any better. He was getting all the praise he needed. As we got more honest as a family, I handled it differently when our youngest son, Charles, played. He had the same problem: He would run after the ball but not kick it. And so he would run over at halftime and say, "Well, how did it go?" I'd say, "Well, you know, Charles, part of the deal is that you kick the ball." It wasn't that I needed to hit him over the head and tell him he was playing a crummy game, but I did need to be honest with him about what this was about.

We have continually seen three causes at the root of family dysfunction. Dysfunction is prevalent when a family (1) lacks a shared vision of its best, (2) lacks an objective measuring stick of its performance against that vision, or (3) loses truth as a priority and shifts to harmony. We challenge all families to keep their eyes firmly fixed on number 3, the Priority of maintaining truth as its primary guide. (When you think about it, how effective can we be in acting upon a shared vision with only a halfhearted commitment to truth?)

The Truth over Harmony Priority implies that parents can rarely go too far in teaching their children to respect the truth above all else. At our school, signs of this effort are everywhere. One of the Five Principles of our school states:

Truth is our primary guide.

One of the guidelines for our daily interactions with each other states:

When in doubt, I will bet on the truth; still in doubt, I will bet on more truth.

Suffice it to say that it is not easy for any of us to make truth our primary guide. That is why there is a sign at the entryway to each of the Hyde Schools that reads: "The truth shall set you free, but first it will make you miserable."

We have worked with many families who came to us with a desire to work on better communication among all family members. As discussed earlier (the Myth of Quality Time), these parents typically assume they need to spend more time with their children. We often surprise them when we suggest that they suspend their preoccupation with time and replace it with a focus on truth. Our experience demonstrates that more truth tends to result in better communication. (Even if it initially results in family members refusing to speak to each other, try to trust that this will be a temporary phase on your journey to the deepest relationships imaginable.) Still, all the "quality time" in the world will never compensate for a halfhearted commitment to the truth. While a commitment to truth offers a promise of long-term serenity and happiness for your family, there is no question that it will also involve some short-term heartache.

Considerable family dysfunction normally results when a family espouses truth as its primary guide but actually acts in a manner where harmony is valued more than truth. Professor Lee Bolman of the Harvard Graduate School of Education calls this contradiction "Espoused Theory versus Theory in Use." We believe that very few families exist today that could not be improved by leaning a little harder on the truth side of this choice.

Some families slip into an unbalanced valuation of truth and harmony without even knowing they're doing it. A mother writes:

> I was asked, How do you feel about your son's ambition to be a truck driver?
>
> "That's fine," I said. "I just want him to be the best truck driver he can be."
>
> Months later I was asked: What are your family issues?
>
> I said, "Honesty is a major one."
>
> I was then asked: What role do you play in this issue?
>
> My response: "Who, me? I'm an honest person."
>
> After a restless night, I pulled my son aside the next morning and said, "Son, I have not been honest. I really don't want you to be a truck driver."
>
> That experience taught me several things:
> - I'm often dishonest about my feelings.
> - Honesty is an issue for our entire family.
> - The apple doesn't fall far from the tree.

The intention here is not to be disrespectful to truck drivers or any other occupation. The intention is to simply point out that this mother realized that she had been parroting hollow phrases to her son to express the way she thought she was supposed to feel about his future. Such parroting may have been well intended, but it was not honest.

As we have seen, many parents are afraid to confront negative attitudes within their children. (We remember one family where the parents used to flip a coin in the morning to see who drew the ugly assignment of waking Johnny up for school!) But just as many are afraid to confront issues with each other. A mother writes:

> I was in my third year at Hyde. My son was OK, dealing with his own issues. So my husband and I could no longer focus on him, we had to deal with each other. I had a lot to say about the marriage and I was scared to death. I was very unhappy and recognized that my needs were not getting met in our relationship. I knew I had to say many things to my husband that he would resent, be angry about, or possibly hate me for saying. I felt my truths had to be voiced. His truths came back and we really got to a low point in our relationship. From there it was either get out or "re-up," as they say in the military. Since then I view our marriage somewhat like a rubber band that is constantly being stretched to the limits. Today our marriage is more truthful and more significant for me. Being honest in all my relationships is now an important goal in my life.

When parents avoid the truth, their children will often emulate this same avoidance. We can often see where and when our children are taking shortcuts with honesty. Our own example can be fuzzier and will require a commitment to identify it. Our desire to help our children can lead to manipulations and half-truths, all done with the best of intentions. This only models another form of dishonesty. Committing to honesty is not always pleasant in the short run. Before truth can work its wonders, we must be vigilant in maintaining pure and genuine motivations. One slogan to keep in mind: "Never kid a kid." Although our kids may fail to remember whether we told them to be home by nine or ten, they will never misread our true motivations in dealing with them. They almost always correctly read our bottom line.

One of our favorite family stories comes from Laura's sister, Claire, when her son Jesse was six years old. Claire asked Jesse to accompany her on some routine errands and he asked, "Can we stop at the toy store?" (He then had a fixation on Ninja Turtles.) Claire responded with that classic parental fix-all: "Maybe. We'll see." Off they went. The errands went off without a hitch. After the last stop, Claire turned the car in the direction of home and away from the toy store. Jesse asked, "Mom, aren't we going to the toy store?" Claire responded, "Jesse, it looks like we'll not have time today." Silence from the backseat. Jesse crossed his arms, vacantly looked out the window, and simply sighed, "Another lie." We recount this story often to remind ourselves that our kids always know what we aren't willing to admit. We try to remember that story when we hear ourselves say "maybe" to our kids in similar circumstances. We usually say this as a preference over disrupting familial harmony by saying "no." As the struggle between tension and harmony can be ever present, we now try to use phrases like "no" and "probably not" instead of "maybe." Yes, even turning down a simple request like going to the toy store can require courage.

When we take the time to really think about it, we find that we can usually speak the truth to our children about simple requests like stopping at the toy store. In fact, this basic level of honesty becomes a habit. Although this may seem like an insignificant step on our journey as parents, we never want to forget that the everyday actions are the ones that may matter most. After all, they are the actions we will carry out (or not carry out) on the only day we can truly impact, *today*.

The most important truths are the ones we discover or uncover about ourselves. The following are stories from three moms who had to face their own issues of Truth over Harmony instead of looking to the rest of the family.

It took me a long time to figure out my part in the basic dishonesty of our family. We were good people of character, but we got offtrack and it was highlighted when our oldest son was a teenager. I was busy blaming my husband for being a workaholic and absentee father. As I look back, my dishonesty began when the children were young and during the process that led us back to the hometown of our youth.

By mutual decision, we had moved to the Southwest. I loved living there and had begun to build a life that I thought we would have forever. But the job situation didn't work out for Tom. He really missed home and his roots. I couldn't believe that it was happening and felt angry and resentful. Yet I felt that my job was to do what other people needed me to do, you know, to "suck it up" and go along with it. I kept thinking two contradictory things: (1) "This isn't really happening," and (2) "If I do what other people need me to do, then that's what will make me happy. Surely everyone else will then be happy."

I was never really honest about this and, of course, it leaked out as resentment in all sorts of ways. So for years, there was this basic dishonesty in our relationship that certainly our children were aware of. We weren't fighting, yelling, screaming, or anything like that. It was just a tenor of emotional dishonesty that was there and built huge resentment in me for years.

The second mom writes:

I grew up around harmony, and while I differed from my mother, I was still very busy trying to fix everyone's stuff and make everyone comfortable at my expense. I did not acknowledge my own truths.

At one point I realized that my son wasn't as nice a person as I wanted him to be. He had never had to consider anyone's reality but his own. The more I tried to satisfy him, the less respect he had for me, and ultimately himself. If you can visualize a limbo bar, I was lowering the standards and expectations of him and cutting him off at the knee. As he began to venture out into the world more, he lost respect for me.

I realized that I needed to include myself in this equation and started to ask him to consider the larger reality of the family. I took my rightful place in the family and began to honor some of my own needs. Initially, this brought out anger in him toward me, but that turned into respect for both of us.

The third mom shares:

We were living the fantasy of harmony over truth, but the harmony was for other people to see. The turmoil was turned inward. I always wanted to protect my children. I didn't want to tell them things that would upset them, so I would manipulate situations to make everything fine.

When I shared things about myself that I was ashamed of, I was just astounded by their acceptance and respect for me. I have learned the lesson that if I am true to myself, then I can be true to people I really care about and love.

Finally, whether we are sixteen, forty-two, sixty-seven, or eighty-one, we all have the potential to uncover past truths and discover new ones. It is an ongoing journey and it is never too late to share the truth with our children and grandchildren. The search for the truth is not free. It will exact a fee, but the resulting liberation is priceless and will create ripples throughout your family. Begin with yourself.

FAMILY EXERCISES AND ACTIVITIES

Who Am I?

Materials: Easel, pad of paper for chart, marker, watch
Time: 15 to 30 minutes
Explanation: This exercise is explained in Part One of this book. Draw a line down the middle of a large piece of paper. Ask the fam-

ily, "How are we evaluated in the Achievement Culture?" Write down all the answers on the left side of the paper. Then ask, "How are we evaluated in the Character Culture?" Write those answers down on the right-hand side of the paper. Next, ask each family member to talk about themselves for one to two minutes (depending on age of children) without mentioning anything listed on the left side of the page. They can talk about:

- What they were like as a kid.
- What strengths they have.
- What obstacles they have.
- What things they like to do.
- What dreams or visions they have for their life.

Time each person. After the exercise talk about the idea of being yourself. How does that connect to our honesty?

Public/Private Exercise

Materials: Large (3+ feet wide) pieces of roll-out paper, markers
Time: 30 minutes
Explanation: Have each family member lay down on the paper and draw the outline of their body with marker. Have each family member decorate the body as they wish. (If you don't have large paper, you can just draw a body outline on regular-size paper.) Then ask family members to write words outside the body outlines that reflect the public image that you present to the world. Then write the words inside the body outlines that speak to the private self that you may or may not share with others. (Some of the words may be the same.) For example, public self: *confident, strong, funny, loving, angry, caring, not interested;* private self: *unsure, caring, holds resentment, outgoing, faith.*

After each person is finished, hang up the outlines and spend time looking at each one. This is a great opportunity for parents to talk to their kids about some of the differences between their public and private qualities. (Many parents do not share enough of their struggles with their kids.)

Family Solo

Materials: Journaling questions, paper, pen.
Time: 45 minutes
Explanation: This activity can be done anywhere—at home, on vacation, and so on. Look at the journaling questions on Truth over Harmony and choose several to write about. (With younger children, fewer questions are more effective.) Have a family member read each question and allow five to ten minutes for everyone to write down his or her thoughts and feelings. Then share your answers. You may decide to hear everyone's answer on each question or have each person read through all his or her answers. After hearing from everyone, ask if there are any comments.

The "7-Eleven" Dilemma

We came up with the "7-Eleven" Dilemma over a decade ago and have presented it to hundreds of students, teachers, and parents.

First, *the facts:*

You drop in to a 7-Eleven to grab a quick snack. After settling on a Coke and a bag of chips, you head for the cash register. As the third customer in line, you notice that the attendant behind the register is a bit flustered by all the activity in the store. She looks as if she's already had a long day. She is trying to keep her eye on two young teens in the back of the store who she suspects are trying to steal some beef jerky. The customer in front of you is rudely interrupting the transaction in front of him by brusquely inquiring about the directions to the local shopping mall and another customer is angrily waving the gasoline pump nozzle because he can't get it to pump any gasoline.

Then it's your turn and the attendant tabulates your purchases. Your purchase totals two dollars and you give her a five-dollar bill. Amid the confusion, the attendant takes your five and says, "OK, that's two dollars. Here's your three and here's your five. Next." Due to her divided attention, the attendant has made your visit to the 7-Eleven a very profitable one. You walked in with five dollars and you are leaving with a Coke, a bag of chips, and eight dollars. Furthermore, she is now dealing with the two teens, relieved that they have decided to pay for the beef jerky. It is clear to you that she is oblivious to her blunder.

The *Dilemma*:

1. What would you do?
2. Do you think there is a right thing to do in this situation?
3. Why? Or why not?
4. How does your answer to question number 1 square with your answer to question number 2?

Commentary on the "7-Eleven" Dilemma: The answers we have heard over the years can be broken down in a manner that resembles the work done by Harvard professor Lawrence Kohlberg in his book *Levels of Moral Development.* Here's how the most common answers break down in order of degrees of moral character:

1. *"I'd keep the money."*

    Students who give this answer might rationalize their decision as just consolation for past experiences when they have been overcharged by cash register attendants (i.e., "It all evens out"). Others feel that the store pays the attendant to count change properly and believe that correct change is not the customer's responsibility. A few will claim that it's the only thing to do in this dog-eat-dog world.

    Those who would give the money back would do so for a variety of reasons, each reflecting different levels of character:

2. *"I'd give the money back because . . . with my luck she'd realize her mistake by the time I got out in the parking lot and I'd look like a lowlife sneak when she called out to me to reenter the store."*

This is a case of "right answer, wrong reason." The next response, although on a higher moral plane, is an example of the same:

3. *"I've worked in a store and I know that the attendant will have to make up the five-dollar shortfall out of her own paycheck at the end of the day when the receipts are totaled up."*

This response is more encouraging than response number 2, but it is still morally shaky. We ask, "If the attendant were not charged for her error, would you keep the money and feel good about it?" The student then generally shifts uneasily, heart in conflict with her head.

4. *". . . my parents value the truth above all else and are absolutely intolerant of any dishonesty."*

This is a notch above response number 3. However, it is accompanied by a fear of what would happen if the student were caught keeping the money. That fear is competing with the individual's conscience. It may be a more moral response than response number 3, but it does raise some doubts. Fear is a poor substitute for conscience.

5. *"I don't know why. I just would."*

This response is music to our ears. When pressed for a reason, this student is often unable to explain why he would give the money back because, with this individual, the response to give the money back is one born of habit. This says that some great parenting and/or teaching has been going on.

Follow-up: After each family member gives his or her response, begin a discussion on truth and personal integrity. Return to the question "Do you think there is a right thing to do in this situation?" The fact that some will answer "no" is perhaps a reflection of those in our society who have come to hold subjective perceptions of right and wrong to be resolved in the "eye of the beholder." We respond with our hope that each individual will eventually develop his or her character a step beyond response number 5. After all, the answer to this question is quite clear to anyone who has accepted the premise that "the truth is my primary guide."

Journaling Questions

1. How was the concept of "truth" handled in my upbringing?
2. How did I handle the "truth" as a teenager?
3. Describe an important lesson I learned involving the truth.
4. How honest are we today with members of our family?
5. What gets in the way of being totally honest with each other?
6. If I had a major life issue, would I tend to share it or keep it from my children? Explain.
7. Do I tend to make a distinction between major dishonesties and "little white lies"?
8. How do I feel about the level of honesty and integrity I see in my children?
9. What is one specific action I could take to improve my personal level of honesty?
10. How could we bring more honesty into the family?
11. Where have I been inspired by my honesty?
12. Where have I been inspired by the honesty of my family members?
13. Do I tend to lean toward truth or harmony in the family? Explain.

Priority 2,
Principles over Rules

Rules may be like putting new tires on the car, whereas principles offer the realignment that will enable the vehicle to go the distance.

Although parenting seems to be on everyone's mind these days, the focus most often centers on getting our kids to do what they are supposed to do and keeping them safe from the harm that exists *out there*. This is understandable, and yet despite all the considerable issues facing our children—drugs, alcohol, anorexia, teen pregnancy, violence, teenage suicides—we still need to resist the temptation to assume that the solutions need to change from the outside first. While external influences must be addressed, we cannot control the timetable. Instead, we can commit to our own personal growth as parents. We can raise our children to prepare for a higher purpose in their lives. We can instill in them a sense of principles. We can inspire our children to commit to a life based on their highest ideals.

When we travel around the country talking with parents and grandparents, someone inevitably exclaims, "These ideas are more common sense than anything else. Heck, you're just reiterating those things my parents tried to teach me!" Exactly. But if these ideas are so basic, why then do we move so quickly from the rhetoric of "principles" to the quick fix of the problem at hand? This is because focusing on principles is hard work. It requires us to try and practice principles with ourselves as well as with our families. It demands that we practice what we preach.

This Priority will help you find ways to put principles first. Once the foundation of principles is laid, the whole family naturally begins to take part in the ownership of these family principles. As a first step, we must take an honest look at ourselves. If you're like us, it takes about two seconds to come down from the mountain of lofty principles and get sucked into trying to control the household once life veers off course. Usually, when things go wrong, we tend to yell out another rule: "OK, from now on there is no more eating in *that* room! Does everyone understand this now?!?" As we stomp around, we may know deep down that a total focus on rules will not take us where we want to go as a family. Even worse, such a focus can move us away from the importance of individuals in the family taking responsibility for the solutions. Rules are not unimportant but limited. They may be like putting new tires on the car, whereas principles offer the realignment that will enable the vehicle to go the distance.

First, we need to have the courage to face the truth about where we are as a family. Let go of how things "should be" and acknowledge how "they are." There is an energy that comes from fresh honesty. Start with the essential question, What's at the center of our family? Before considering an exercise focused on this question, give some thought to a typical daily scene at our house as seen through Laura's eyes:

It ought to be the middle of the night. I groan as I hear another small body hurl itself onto our bed. Glancing at the clock, I see that I only have thirteen minutes to "sleep" before I need to get up and meet my friends out in the frigid February air for our daily walk. From the moment my feet hit the floor at 6:10 A.M. until the last child heads out the door two hours later at 8:10, there is nonstop movement in our house:

- Lunches to be made.
- Various forms of breakfast (some of suspect nutritional value) to be administered.
- Lost shoes to be found.
- Tangled hair to be unsnarled and brushed.
- Teeth to be checked.
- Arguments to be refereed.
- Permission slips to be reconstructed.

Then I take a few minutes to pull myself together and head out the door to face the workday.

At 4:00 P.M., there is another shift in the day and home becomes a place to greet faces, drive to soccer practices, listen patiently (extremely tough on many days) about classroom projects, and keep the young one awake so that his nighttime schedule is not thrown off. If I am moving on schedule, the kids are in bed relatively close to their 8:00 P.M. bedtime and I then have ninety minutes to myself. If I have made the mistake of stopping (I liken the parent to the shark; both must keep moving to survive!) to grab a quick catnap, chaos is sure to erupt. There have been many nights when I am unable to lift my body up from the bed and the kids are running around at 9:20 P.M. happy as young pirates in Never-never land.

You may identify with this description and you certainly experience your own unique family chaos as you move through each busy day. It is hard to stop and ask, What's at the center of our family?, and yet that is where we need to start. After asking this question for several years to parents and kids, it became clear to us that there were three basic options for families to choose. See where you are as a family.

WHAT'S AT THE CENTER OF OUR FAMILY?

Take a look at these circles:

Choose the option that seems to fit best *right now:*

1. Person: For the most part, our family revolves around the attitude and actions of one person. If this person is having a good day, then we're all having a good day. Likewise, if this person is offtrack, everyone is affected. This person may change from time to time, but the effect is basically the same. Often, in this situation, other people (usually parents) worry about this person and their "worry" is disproportionate to the person's own concern about his or her actions.

2. Principles: For the most part, we have articulated a set of principles we hold to be sacred as a family and that act as the moral compass for our family's direction. We share a consensus in our belief in this set of principles. We talk about these principles often and they have real meaning to us. They are not just flat words on the wall, but a living, breathing dynamic throughout the family.

3. ???: If we are really being honest with ourselves, we are not sure what is really at the center of our family. Mom may have one idea, Dad may have another, but we are not sure that everyone understands and acknowledges the family's core principles.

Consider the three options and decide where you would put your family. Don't think too much. Go with your gut instincts. Don't worry about where you *should be* as a family. For what it's worth, when we ask this question at Biggest Job workshops, very few parents choose Principles. Some choose Option 1, Person, but the vast majority of parents choose ???. As Laura says, "No matter what you choose, you'll spend time at all three positions on a never-ending pursuit of Option 2. Always remember that honesty can only move you forward." Now think about your answer. How do you feel about it? Now consider each of the three possible responses.

If You Chose Option 1: Person

If this is the category that you chose, who is the person in the center? Is it a powerful mom who directs the whole family? Is it a workaholic dad whose anger has everyone walking on eggshells? Or is it a child whose attitude and behavior affects the entire family? It may be all three at different times. The Raft Exercise is one we utilize to illustrate the effect of having a person at the center.

The Raft Exercise

Have one person stand on a rug or on a taped-off section of the floor. Tell this person to imagine that he or she is floating out on the open ocean in this raft. Lacking a keel, the raft is very tipsy. Tell this person, "You can go anywhere and do anything you want on this raft." Wait ten to fifteen seconds, then add another person. Say to this person, "You have one job to do and that is to balance the raft. You also may not talk to each other." Wait another ten to fifteen seconds to see what happens. Now, before adding a third person, restate the roles of the two people on the raft. The first person has carte blanche. She can go anywhere and do anything she wants. The second person must balance the raft. The third person must help balance the raft. Give them about fifteen seconds to work on this and then add a fourth person. This fourth person is told nothing more than: "You take whatever role you feel you need to take on the raft." Wait fifteen more seconds. Then sit down and discuss what happened.

While every group adds something unique to this exercise, there are usually several common themes. Often, the first person will do very little when he is the only one on the raft. When the second person (the primary raft balancer) is added, the focus changes. This person is so intent on balancing the raft, he barely looks up to see where "the boat is going." The third person (the secondary raft balancer) is usually equally helpless. While the second and third people move in tandem around the "carte blanche" character, they are not really working together and are more focused on the disruption than even making eye contact with each other. The fourth person can assume many roles. She could find a quiet corner and "hide." She could add to the disruption, or she could join the efforts to balance the raft. Even though balancing the raft was the original goal, that raft has long since capsized with this system.

If you have a child at the center of the raft, it is nearly impossible to maintain a focus on Principles over Rules. While everyone is running around worrying and manipulating outcomes for the child, the child may actually be having a "good time" relaxing and doing whatever he or she wants to do. Often the parents lie awake at night worrying about that child while the child sleeps soundly down the hall. We are not referring here to the generic "worrying" that comes with the territory of being a parent; we mean the constant attention that only reinforces the vicious cycle resulting from having a person at the center of the family.

If the person at the center of the family is not a child, and the effect is a negative one on the family, then you must take real action to address the situation. Some issues can be addressed in the family meetings discussed in Priority 8, Create a Character Culture. If these issues are of a deeper, more serious nature (rage, alcohol, abuse), summon the courage to seek professional help. As discussed in the previous Priority, all growth begins with the courage to seek and face the truth about our families. There is one very important lesson to know about truth, one summed up in a popular Hyde slogan: "Once we know the truth, we cannot *unknow* it."

If You Chose Option 2: Principles

Obviously, this is the one we want to be working toward. Having a set of principles is one thing; truly operating your family in accordance with them is quite another. Regardless of how deeply we believe in these principles, it is easy to get offtrack in their day-to-day practice. The analogy of a sailboat tacking back and forth against the wind as it seeks its destination symbolizes our efforts to stay on the course mandated by our principles. Once the principles are established, the real work begins. While rules are not unimportant, too much of a focus on them tends to box parents in. There is only so far one can go with rules.

Principles can be a powerful tool for parents who are trying to teach the deeper lessons of life through the daily struggles of life. For example, let's assume that you place your consuming focus on basic rules: curfew, dinner at home twice a week, homework before television, and so on. It is conceivable that your child could follow these rules and still have an unacceptable attitude. This circumstance finds you caught between the fact that the rules are being followed on the one hand and that your child is giving you that "Whatever" look on the other. This is what happens when our children follow the letter of the law but not its spirit. But when you place the weight of your foot on core principles, your range is limitless. You suddenly have enlisted a cavalry of principles supporting your family: truth, concern for others, doing your best, courage. Thus, sometimes we need to challenge family members with the truth of their attitudes: "Yes, you are here in body, but not in spirit. Your lack of concern and/or enthusiasm is unacceptable. We need to stop and address this."

Likewise, principles can also be celebrated, sometimes even in the toughest of family conflicts. The following is a personal story, one that represents one of the most important lessons Laura learned as an adolescent:

In my family, two important principles were honesty and responsibility. My stepfather came into my life when I was eight, after my real father died. The entrance of this very strict disciplinarian into my family, along with a geographical move from the South to New England, jolted my world. For a long time I had a "business relationship" with my stepfather. He had a job to do: to raise me to be a responsible human being. Often his unyielding approach to his principles seemed ridiculous to me.

During the summer after my sophomore year of high school, I got my driver's license. My stepfather spent an entire day with me, teaching me how to use the stick shift. Sitting with him in a cramped VW bug, listening over and over to the relentless instructions, was not my idea of fun. At the end of the day, he announced that while I had made some progress, more lessons were needed.

A few days later, my parents were planning to leave us alone for an overnight. As they were giving out final instructions, my stepfather reminded me that I was not ready to take the car by myself. I agreed, and meant it. After my parents had gone, friends came by and urged me to head off to the beach. Not wanting to look "uncool," I agreed. Soon I was grinding the gears, jerking my stepfather's car down the street. At one point, I went down a one-way street and tried to turn around. I hit a parked car. Someone yelled, "Take off!" and I did, without thinking for myself. We drove home. Of course, someone spotted me and reported the license plate and soon I was summoned home by my stepfather. Busted!

We drove together to the police station and while I do not remember all the details, I vividly remember some. My parents did not go into the station office with me. Rather, they waited in the vestibule, sending the clear message that I needed to face this myself. Afterward, as we were driving home, they said something to the effect of "We were proud of your honesty." That remark floored me because I knew they were angry and disappointed with my actions. (Here was an example of principles being celebrated in the face of obstacles.)

Later, at home, my stepfather handed me the Yellow Pages and told me, "You will need to call a lawyer." I called a lawyer, set up an appointment, and then spent the rest of the summer dealing with this situation. At the end of the summer, I had less than twenty dollars in my bank account after covering all the costs of the lawyer, traffic fines, and so on. Most important, what might have been some "jam" that my parents handled and I could brush off became a lesson seared into me because they demanded that I be held accountable for my actions. If I had been alone, I never would have driven off in that car. My actions were motivated by a shallow desire to look "cool" in front of a group of kids whose names I'm not sure I could recall today. My big issue in high school was genuine confidence and this incident showed me what I compromised in order to be accepted. It wasn't worth it.

While there may have been times when Laura's parents didn't handle things so well, this was one of their finest parenting moments. (They were Hyde parents at the time.) They stepped back and allowed her to face her burden, one of her own creation, alone. While they may have worried about a permanent legal record resulting from this, they didn't sneak behind the scenes to micromanage the situation. They also did not check in with the lawyer, staying in the background throughout the process. What started out as a horrible situation for Laura turned into a confidence builder: She realized that maintaining an image wasn't worth the trouble she was in, yet she was extremely proud of the way she handled the circumstances.

Allowing our children to handle as many of their problems as possible gives them the opportunity to learn indelible lessons. Putting principles at the center acts as a constant reminder that all moments can be learning opportunities, from the small, relatively benign incidents of daily life to the larger "big holes" into which kids can fall.

IF YOU CHOSE OPTION 3: ???

If this explanation rings true for your family right now, take heart. You have the courage to admit what's *not happening* and that is the first step toward addressing what needs to change. Too often we choose to live with a general fuzziness as long as no disaster is occurring. We start to shift to a position where we are keeping the family from its worst rather than focusing on and pushing for its best. Meanwhile, the frog continues to boil right before our eyes. Stop everything and take the steps to move toward principles. It won't happen overnight, but every step you take in that direction will have an impact on the future of your family.

The family raft is such a vivid image that we often use it to bring some humor into our dysfunctional moments: "This raft is sinking!" someone may shout to remind us that we need to refocus. It's hard to establish our own principles without first exploring those that we learned, consciously or unconsciously, while growing up. Our own upbringing is a defining and powerful force in our journey. Coming to terms with our parents and our childhood "moments of truth" are essential if we are to connect with our natural child-rearing instincts. Laura writes:

> My stepfather introduced the whole concept of jobs to me. Not just jobs, but inspections. In our home, the job was not complete until it passed his inspection. In fact, the back door of our kitchen was covered with job assignments and rotations. Many times I would try to leave it open so that my friends wouldn't see how strict my stepfather was. I fought with my stepfather for several years, but eventually there was a turning point.
>
> Today I am thankful for the lessons my stepfather instilled in me. I also accept that there were things my parents were not able to give me. I have forgiven them for their own issues that may have gotten in the way of them following their better instincts. Yet the most powerful emotion I have today is complete and total gratitude to them for raising me with high standards of excellence and a belief that principles are more important than anything else. I hope I can do the same for my children.

HOW DO WE PUT PRINCIPLES
AT THE CENTER OF THE FAMILY?

First, have a family meeting where the important ideals and principles are discussed (see Priority 8, Create a Character Culture). What's important to us? What do we hold sacred? You may begin with only one or two principles. It is most important to start with something that is clear and undiluted. You will probably find that if you talk about this, the most important principles will emerge. Give every family member the opportunity to speak, yet remember that you, as the parents, may initially need to take the lead and set a proper tone. Write your principles on a piece of paper and display them in a prominent place. (Index cards are ideal for displaying on the corner of a bathroom mirror.) You may also create family slogans to support your principles. Ask everyone to identify one, and then display them for all to see. Some examples we have discovered in our Biggest Job parent workshops:

- "Return with honor"
- "Best effort over achievement"
- "Begin with belief"
- "Welcome and learn from obstacles"
- "Move forward with faith"
- "Give more than you take"
- "Leave it better than you found it"
- "Know thyself, be thyself"
- "No such word as can't"
- "Only failure is the failure to try"
- "E.I.M. (everything in moderation)"
- "We always show up; we never quit"

A popular Hyde saying notes, "If you cannot define the goal, you cannot attain it." Our families will not live principle-centered lives if we are vague about the principles we hope to honor. Be as explicit as possible. As described on page 32, all Hyde students and faculty sign the school's Statement of Purpose at the beginning of each year. Central to this statement are the Five Words and Five Principles. The act of signing the statement heightens the level of commitment for all. Immediately upon signing the statement, students are virtually bombarded with reminders. For example, the auditorium at each Hyde school features twenty-foot-high banners emblazoned with the Five Words on one wall and the Five Principles on the other:

Five Words	*Five Principles*
Curiosity: I am responsible for my own learning.	*Destiny:* Each of us is gifted with a Unique Potential.
Courage: I learn the most about myself by facing challenges and taking risks.	*Humility:* We believe in a power and a purpose beyond ourselves.
Concern: I need a challenging and supportive community in which to develop my character.	*Conscience:* We achieve our best through character and conscience.
Leadership: I am a leader through asking the best of myself and others.	*Truth:* Truth is our primary guide.
Integrity: I am gifted with a unique potential and conscience is my guide to discovering it.	*Brother's Keeper:* We help others achieve their best.

The placement of these banners enables the community to consider and apply the Words and Principles to issues as they arise. They can be discussed at any school gathering.

Recently, a Hyde parent observed, "I get it! You are essentially overwhelming these kids with character!" In many respects this is true. We choose to err on the side of being overly explicit in what we mean by character. We recommend that parents choose to be firm with a few principles, rather than to be flexible with a long list of them.

Once the family principles are identified, think about the areas in your life where you need to strengthen your efforts to honor them. In order to have any real meaning to our children, these principles must be reflected in our daily actions. This is the point made earlier about site versus context in relation to character development. Suffice it to say that our daily actions speak louder than any words we speak.

A mother writes:

> Things would start to get a little out of control in our family, so we'd make a rule—you can't do this. Then something else would go wrong and we would put another rule on top of that rule and another until everything got really rule heavy. There were no principles under the rules other than I didn't want the boat rocked. I was making rules to keep the boat stable. It had little to do with the purpose of the boat.

Her husband talks about how the family now functions:

> I teach mathematics. When students come to a subject like trigonometry, there's a long list of identities that one needs to study. I never memorized those trigonometric identities. I tell students there are three that are fundamental and everything else can be derived from them.
>
> Principles over Rules are like that for me. There are a few basic things that are fundamental—always go back to those places and ask yourself, "If we start here, where do we get to?" That is what we do in our family now.

He goes on to describe an example of how this worked recently:

> I took our daughter back to school. We got there the night before she was expected on campus. Naturally, she wanted to catch up with

friends. I told her that I really wanted to get to bed early because I had a long drive the next day and then told her the time I wanted her to be in. She said, "Dad, this is really important to me." And I said, "OK, I hear you." We talked about it and came up with a time that she felt comfortable with and I felt good about. It was great! It was a situation where we focused on the principles of respect and caring instead of a fixed rule. We were able to come to an agreement together.

Along with establishing our family principles, the Raft Exercise teaches us to take a hard look at the roles we fill in the family. Every time we do this exercise at a workshop, there is hearty laughter, the kind that comes from a direct hit. We all know the drill. Sometimes we even think we are being effective as we spin out of control, trying to manipulate the family and maintain balance. We ask the question, How many of you have played the role of the "primary raft balancer"? Many hands are raised, usually more women than men. Next question, How many have played the role of the "secondary raft balancer"? Again, many hands. Has anyone been in the middle of the raft at some point? More hands. In our family, it is usually one of our children whose behavior is at the center. We have asked hundreds of kids about this situation and most of them have spent some time in the center. When we ask them, How did you feel being in the center of the family? the response goes something like: "I didn't like . . . (pause) . . . and I liked it." They didn't like the pain their behavior caused family members and yet there was no denying they enjoyed the ultimate power that being in the middle gave them. We also asked siblings who were not in the center how it felt to watch from the sidelines. One younger sister writes:

I felt neglected and started to act out. I didn't do drugs or drink like my older sister, but I'd steal or lie. It was obvious things so that my parents would see and would take some attention off her. They were both so busy dealing with her, I figured if I did something wrong, I'd get their attention.

Most kids we have worked with do not want to be in the middle. Yet they probably won't change their position on their own. Likewise, parents can get caught in a good cop/bad cop scenario. One parent may believe, "I am obligated to come down hard on this behavior because I know you will let him off the hook. You always do." We remember a kid once saying, "When I want to get out of the house by nine P.M., I start things going around seven forty-five. Eventually, my parents will turn on each other, and at some point in the battle, I will get 'thrown' out just in time to meet my friends. I've got it timed like a science." It's easy to get into a corner. Like the boiled frog, we may wake up one day and discover our own straitjacket. Laura writes:

> I have definitely played the role of the "primary raft balancer" in our family. As a child, I watched my mother play that role in our family. If you are always the "go to" person, you become the strength as well as the obstacle. I tend to exhibit the strength because I usually hold the highest vision for our family and I probably hold the deepest desire to see us realize that vision. I have been the obstacle, because I take care of too much in the family, enabling others to sit back.
>
> I call this scenario the "flying wedge." This is where Mom is out front with her purse dangling off her flexed arm and the rest of the family is following behind in V-formation. Whether heading into the YMCA for swimming lessons or taking a trip to the shopping mall, the flying wedge is in full operation. One day, when I realized that we were in this formation, I stopped. Guess what? Everyone else stopped, dead in their tracks. I said and motioned to Malcolm, "Go ahead." Puzzled, Malcolm responded, "Oh no, you go ahead." No one would move forward until I did! My tendency to take charge and make things happen can work against me with my own family. I keep learning that the more I "shut my mouth," the more other family members offer suggestions and solutions. I also find that the less I take charge, the less resentment I stockpile.

HOW DO WE CHANGE OUR ROLES?

First, as in Priority 1, Truth over Harmony, we must face ourselves squarely with the truth. Why am I playing this role? If I were to let go of this role, what would happen? Mom's "flying wedge" is often based on the fear that the house of cards will fall down if she steps back. And it may. Yet, given its flimsy foundation, it is bound to fall anyway. Remember this rule of thumb: *As long as our motivation to keep things from getting worse outweighs our desire to make them better, we may never find the courage to discover our greatness as a family.*

Asking our children for help in getting out of our boxes is also effective. Ask your kids, "What do you see as my strength and what do I need to work on?" Then close your mouth—*really* close your mouth—and listen to your children. Don't respond after they finish. If you have to say something, try "Thanks."

When you move a person out of the center of the family, you need to fill the void with principles. They are sacred and nonnegotiable. When our raft is floundering in the waves, our principles will show us the way home. We return to them by asking the right questions:

- What is the right thing to do here?
- What aligns with the principles of this family?
- What role do I need to take in honoring our principles?
- How many times have I been truly sorry for having done the right thing?

We ask parents in the workshops two questions about principles: (1) What principles do you remember in your upbringing? and (2) What is important to your family today?

Some of the responses include:

- We didn't talk a lot about principles, it was more about rules.
- Principles were stated but were not followed with action.
- Some of the principles were positive; some were for appearances.

- We have principles, but we need to talk about them more.
- There are vague principles, but we spend more time on the rules.

One mother talked about the different messages she received:

I was brought up in a family where there were clear principles, like giving back to your community and being useful. These were articulated and I am grateful for that. There was also an emphasis on appearances. It was important that things look right for other people. That was also communicated. I'm probably not as grateful for that.

Another parent writes:

My dad would always say, "Don't do a half-baked job." That phrase echoed throughout my childhood. I knew that was some sort of principle. In our home today, one of the things we agree on is the principle of best effort. Every morning when John gets out of the car, I say, "Have a good day and best effort."

Two mothers talked about the need to realize that total focus on just one principle may not lead one to a clear direction:

I was raised with the principle of perseverance. My father used to say, "If at first you don't succeed, try again!" I used that with my marriage and needed to have more humility to finally let go. In terms of our family's principles, there was love and concern, but the center was more mushy. I had a list of rules that needed to be followed, but those didn't work. We have come to the principles of honesty and respect.

The next mom writes:

My mother had breast cancer and a heart attack and that molded a huge need in me to never give up hope that things could get better. When things in my marriage became very painful, I was determined to never give up, so I held on. It wasn't until I realized that I couldn't single-handedly save my marriage and it needed two people to make it work that I found some humility. One principle exclusively doesn't always keep it right for me. I need a balance of all the principles I hold dear.

One family shared a hilarious story about how a family principle got expressed through a rule involving a battle of wills:

In our family, the dinner hour was something that we valued a great deal and we tried to instill that value in our two boys. It was a time to be together and reconnect, talk about the day, life, dreams, etc. When the kids were young, we did just that. Then they hit adolescence and suddenly everything turned chaotic. The traffic in the house was constant and the phone rang off the hook. It would create arguments back and forth between Roger, myself, and the boys. We decided enough was enough. We needed to do something. So we made up a rule: You can't talk on the phone at dinner.

The response was, "Why? It could be someone calling about something important!" That lasted a couple of days. Soon we would be sitting at the table and the phone would ring. Inevitably, the fighting would erupt. We saw the rule needed more teeth and so we tacked on another layer: You can't talk on the phone at dinner. And if you do, you will be grounded.

Again, this didn't last long. The phone would ring and the warning would be stated: "Remember, if you answer that, you will be grounded." The fighting continued. So Roger and I—the two geniuses—got together and came up with a smarter plan: We are going to take the phone off the hook. The phone will not ring and the problem will be solved.

Of course, the kids would see us getting ready to prepare the meal and they would put the phone back on the hook. The phone would ring and we were back at square one. You get the picture.

The grounding did not work; the phone off the hook did not work. Sometimes we would be sitting at the table and the phone was back on the hook and the boys were grounded and the tension mounted. We actually started to hide the phone. The boys responded by pressing the intercom button to locate the phone. (The receiver would beep.) This was all as we were trying to get a meal ready. By now, most people would admit that this approach was not working, but we were in serious denial. Thus, we decided that the plan needed further revision.

We thought, "OK, we'll show you two who's boss!" We got this bright idea and conspired to implement a secretive plan: Each night before dinner we would disconnect the phone.

One of us would creep out the side door, sneak across the lawn to the other side of the house with a Phillips-head screwdriver, open the phone box, disconnect the line, and then screw the cover back on. We'd return to the house pretending nothing ever happened. The boys would come to us and say, "Mom, Dad, the phone isn't working." We would play dumb. I said something like, "Really? We'll have to call the phone company."

Basically, we lost sight of the original message, what we were really trying to do. Our focus had shifted from working to establish an important principle to feeble and futile attempts to enforce a meaningless rule. We ended up engaged in a dishonest struggle for control and power. We needed to spend more time talking about the principle.

A couple of years ago we were telling family stories and we shared this with the boys. They laughed when we told them, but the extremes we went to in order to enforce the rule will always stay with us. Whenever I get critical about other people's parenting, I think about that story and it puts me right back on track.

Principles force us to aim high. We will not always live up to them, but the journey to honor them will elevate our daily actions in both minor and major moments of family life. Laura writes:

As I look back on it now, there were little things that reflected the principles. We were never allowed to cheat at the movies or when buying tickets for anything that required fudging our age. Working hard

113

and doing a job well was important. Writing a thank-you note was important. Calling up someone and apologizing when appropriate was expected. It essentially became a sense of doing the right thing. I am trying to instill much of the same with my family.

We believe that working on the daily moments prepares us for the "biggies." The major moments are never scheduled. They have their own timetable and we cannot control when and from where they come. We need to be ready to face them with our best. Sit down as a family and talk about the principles that are sacred to you. Live, breathe, work them.

FAMILY EXERCISES AND ACTIVITIES

Family Mottos

Materials: Paper (rectangle sign shape); crayons, markers, or paints; books of quotations; books with favorite themes
Time: 15 to 30 minutes
Explanation: This exercise may help you create family mottos that will be "keepers" in the family for years to come. Spend a few minutes talking about mottos and their meaning. Give some examples. Share some of the ones in your upbringing. If someone has a favorite book or movie, ask them to sum up the message in one sentence. Give everyone some time to work on creating a family motto in a few words or a sentence. Afterward, gather together and explain your creations. The family may decide to take one or two and try them on for a while. (A motto works if it resonates with family members and gives a sense of pride and excellence.) Some examples are:

- "We show up and we do not quit"
- "Everything in moderation"
- "Risk and respect your uniqueness"

- "Begin with belief, learn from obstacles, move forward with faith"
- "Birds in a nest"

Family Shields

Materials: Large easel, pad of paper, crayons or markers, tape
Time: 30 to 60 minutes
Explanation: In our workshops, parents consistently give this simple exercise high ratings. It helps define the family and brings out the creativity and wisdom of each member. Start with a few questions:

- "What are the principles that are sacred to all of us?" (Examples: truth, doing your best, concern, courage.)
- "What is important to this family?" (Examples: family, God, reaching out, exploration.)
- "What shared experiences have shaped our character?" (Examples: summers at the lake, visiting grandparents, skiing, reading, telling family stories.)

Spend some time talking about these questions and then jump in. Take a large piece of paper and start with a shield design. Then add the principles, core values, and shared experiences that make up your family. Draw pictures and symbols to elaborate. Some families designate one family member as the artist and give her the input. Other families take turns adding to the shield. (You may want to do a practice shield and then a final draft.) Hang the final product up in a prominent location and spend some time over the next few months talking about the shield.

Draw the Family

Materials: White paper; pencils, pens, or markers
Time: 30 minutes

Explanation: This is a great exercise for a family meeting. Ask everyone to draw a visual representation of how they see the family and their role within it. The drawing can be symbols, stick figures, anything basic. (The goal here is not a piece of art.) Then have each family member share their picture and explain its meaning. You can either respond or give people some time to think about the pictures and talk about it in next week's meeting. Try to avoid reacting too quickly to family members. If a natural discussion develops, talk about the "roles" people take on and what "boxes" they might get into. Action steps can also be established geared toward changing an unproductive role.

JOURNALING QUESTIONS

1. What were the principles or core ideals in my upbringing?
2. What did and did not seem positive in my upbringing?
3. What are the important principles in my family today?
4. Where in my life do I compromise my principles? Explain.
5. Where in my life have I stood up for my principles? Explain.
6. What gets in the way of placing principles at the center of our family?
7. If there is a person at the center of the family, what steps do we need to take to move that person or persons out and principles in?
8. What roles do each of us play on our "raft" (primary raft balancer, secondary balancer, bystander, etc.)?
9. What could I do to get out of the "box" I am in within the family?
10. How will we evaluate our progress in adhering to our family principles?

Priority 3,
Attitude over Aptitude

It's time for new priorities:
attitude over *aptitude,*
effort over *ability,*
and character over *talent.*

Sometimes the deepest wisdom is expressed in old adages. After all, in order for any adage to stand the test of time, it must offer something genuine and it must also pass the cultural test of being time-honored. One of our favorite adages speaks to the core principle behind Priority 3, Attitude over Aptitude: Nothing can stop the person with the right attitude; nothing can help the person with the wrong one.

America was established and built by enterprising pioneers, people who faced challenges with a "can do" attitude. However, our schools have chosen to relegate these qualities to casual by-products, often burying them in high school yearbooks on a few pages devoted to "Senior Superlatives." Meanwhile, that pioneer spirit lies dormant, awaiting a vibrant reawakening.

Over the course of our careers, we have worked with students of widely varying capabilities. Whether labeled "gifted and talented" or "special needs," we remain convinced that our national preoccupation with aptitude is failing American kids. During our time at Hyde, 98 percent of our graduates have gone on to attend four-year colleges, and many of them came to us with a variety of learning differences and disabilities. In scores of cases, parents have wondered whether their son or daughter possessed the skills or capabilities to meet with success in our program. Our experiences teaching this population of students have cemented our belief that a philosophy and program truly committed to the Priority of Attitude over Aptitude will work for any student. This belief was tested and forged by two memorable examples.

In the first case, we admitted a student with serious learning disabilities. As both the parents and the school were uncertain whether Hyde was ultimately the best placement for this student, both parties agreed to enter into the first year on a trial basis. The student enrolled and had predictable difficulty with her academic work throughout the year. At the end of the school year, the school and the family agreed that a school specifically focused on learning disabilities would be more appropriate. As the student made plans to enroll in another school, her parents made a point to thank us for performing a critical function. They felt we had separated their daughter's attitude from her disability. Their daughter had always performed poorly in school and had always had a bad attitude about it; they had just never been sure how much of the problem was aptitude and how much of it was attitude. The year at Hyde had separated the two factors and the girl then went to a more specialized school where she met with success.

The second student's story was one of the most moving experiences we have had as educators. This student, a sixteen-year-old girl, came to our five-week Summer Challenge Program with some of the most severe learning differences we have encountered. All parties began the program with the understanding that this girl would not be enrolling at Hyde as a full-time student in the fall. The hope was that she would have a constructive summer and then transfer to a school designed for students with learning disabilities. Although she went on to experience the expected difficulties with our academic program, her overall confidence blossomed while she was engaged in some of our co-curricular activities: athletics, performing arts, wilderness trips, and such. At the end of the summer, we sat down with the family prepared with a list of potential schools that this girl might attend. Before Malcolm could begin to describe the first school, the mother interjected, "We want to be at Hyde." Malcolm went on to explain his strong doubts about the girl's chances for ever graduating from Hyde, much less her chances for ever gaining admission to college. At this point the mother said, "We are prepared to accept the idea that she may never graduate from Hyde and that she may never go to college. However, we feel that the potential benefits of thriving in this community outweigh any of the potential downsides you describe." Then she challenged Malcolm on how strongly Hyde believed what it preached about things like commitment and character. ("I thought Hyde was for any kid and family willing to make a genuine commitment," she stated.)

After reiterating the risks to the family, we gave this girl a chance. Not only did she attend Hyde that September, she ultimately graduated from Hyde two years later. She even gained admission to college. This girl taught us something very important. Prior to her enrollment, we had grown accustomed to proving the experts wrong when they predicted that student "A" could not meet with success at Hyde. However, here was a student who proved *us* wrong. Like the adage says: Nothing can stop the person with the right attitude.

In the Biggest Job workshops, Malcolm introduces Priority 3, Attitude over Aptitude, by telling his own story, one he has told scores of times to hundreds of students:

> I got off to a good start as a solid elementary school student in rural New Hampshire, where I enjoyed sports and the benefits of a caring and close family. Early in the seventh grade my grades sank like a stone as I became fascinated with what I kept hearing was the "wrong crowd." The more my parents cautioned me, the more fascinated I became. I remember numerous parent-teacher conferences during which the adults would tell my parents that I was "a bright kid who doesn't apply himself." I began to perceive this characterization as a polite adult smoke screen. (I always wanted to ask, "If you truly

thought I just couldn't cut it, would you tell me that?") I began to form a negative perception of school and performed accordingly. As my grades continued to decline, it seemed to me that school was becoming an exercise in futility. I believed that school was "rigged." I believe this today.

I remember watching schoolmates receive awards at school assemblies with full belief that no matter how hard I tried, I would never receive one of those awards. I felt that everyone knew this was true but no one would say so. It was an unwritten rule. I even believed that if I studied as hard as I could, I would wind up a two-way loser: First, I'd spend a lot of time performing tasks I'd rather not perform; and second, I wouldn't do appreciably better anyway. My cynical disposition eventually dominated my efforts and I wound up in the lowest academic track, the non-college-bound program.

I wanted to do well in school, but I was not interested in being an also-ran. I responded to my dilemma by rebelling against my teachers, intuitively reasoning: If I can't be among the very best, I'd prefer to be among the very worst. If I can't win the game, I'd rather lose in grand style. Wanting to make some kind of mark, I went the route of an educational saboteur.

Our view from the "other side of the desk" strongly indicates that many students take the same path Malcolm took. There will be many more as long as school in America maintains its oppressive focus on variables that are not within the control of the students, as long as schools persist in valuing aptitude over attitude, ability over effort, talent over character. The "Aptitude Culture" fails to grasp that every student wants to "be somebody."

Malcolm's story has a happy ending, an ending that began in 1968 when he enrolled at Hyde School as a freshman with feelings of resignation and defeat. He writes:

My teachers immediately focused on my effort . . . or lack of it. It was as though they were saying:

- "If you work hard, you'll do well."
- "If you don't, you won't."
- "You'll get no privileges for any raw abilities you possess."
- "You'll get no penalties due to any you lack."
- "Here, you'll truly get whatever you deserve."

Although I didn't like everything about the place, I had to admit, "This place is fair." I began to excel. I became fascinated with the very notion of excelling. Four years later, I was admitted to Bowdoin College, a highly selective school. I eventually received a master's degree from Harvard. Prior to Hyde, I was certainly not a kid headed to a Bowdoin or a Harvard. Hyde didn't do it *for* me. Hyde created a level playing field, one that provided genuine challenge and encouragement. It really is that simple.

Malcolm recently attended a weeklong seminar of fifteen experienced school heads. Although the group represented a cross section of schools—public, private, Catholic, elementary, secondary—the participants were united by a fervent desire to teach kids how to build better communities tomorrow. How should we teach? How should we parent? All participants quickly realized that the questions were a lot easier to formulate than were the answers. Eventually the seminar turned to a discussion of Martin Luther King Jr.'s "Letter from a Birmingham Jail." When one high school principal described Dr. King as "the most inspirational leader of our lifetime," all heads in this room full of baby boomers nodded in agreement. Discussion then focused on Dr. King's efforts in the 1960s. What was it he was able to do that so inspired the nation? How could we rekindle that inspiration today? The answers crystallized:

1. King was deeply committed to his cause.
2. He was able to crystallize an either/or issue that forced people to come down on one side or the other.
3. He was able to inspire people to imagine and work toward a better way.

Our memory of those times is in black and white, not because we were actively involved in the civil rights movement but because we watched it on television in the days when a color television set was coveted and rare. "Bull" Connor's fire hoses presented such sharp contrast to the moods conveyed by *Lassie*, *Leave It to Beaver*, and *The Ed Sullivan Show*. We joined the millions of American families who watched the horror of those fire hoses literally blowing those black Americans down the street. Although too young to appreciate Dr. King's inspiration, our generation could easily understand the either/or issue at the heart of the civil rights movement: Should freedom and opportunities be granted or denied on the basis of skin color—yes or no? After helping to clarify the critical issue, Martin Luther King Jr. came along with an inspirational dream for a better way.

Today, the problems inherent in child-rearing and teaching in school seem harder to define. Either there is no discernible fire hose or the spray seems so omnipresent that we cannot find its source. There doesn't seem to be a leader of Dr. King's stature to show us the way. Rather than wait for the leader, perhaps we would do better to crystallize the issue. Consider similar times more than two hundred years ago when the American colonists began to move toward independence. As the struggle heated up, there were many issues raised. Some cried, "No taxation without representation," while others felt lucky to be part of the British Empire. The die was eventually cast and it came down to an either/or proposition: Either you are for independence or you are not.

Consider the notion that we as parents and teachers face an either/or proposition as critical to our work as did King before us and the American colonists before him. As teachers and parents ourselves, we might consider a simple choice: Either we believe that attitude is more important than aptitude or we believe that aptitude is more important than attitude.

Our experience has been that most people will profess to believe that attitude is the more important of the two. ("Honey, I don't care about the grade as long as you try your hardest.") Yet many of today's schools and families actually operate as though they value aptitude more than attitude, whether they intend to or not. We frequently ask high school students if they know any students at their schools who do very little academic work and yet consistently make the honor roll. Not only do they acknowledge that this practice is common, the way they acknowledge it is more than a bit disheartening: "Sure, that's the way it's always been. Some kids just 'have it' and school rewards them." Many point admiringly to the student who is able to get the A with next to no effort.

As educators and parents, we have come to believe that the valuation of aptitude over attitude is crippling our schools and our families in ways we don't even realize. The bright kids know they don't really need to work hard, and the average to below-average ones don't believe their efforts will be rewarded in any significant way. Furthermore, we live in an age when our entire country is concerned with test scores and national standards, and yet little attention is given to the rampant cheating exercised by all types of students to get the precious results. How could we possibly believe that we can inspire genuine learning or character development in a system where our students do not believe that their best efforts will be respected? Instead, we have schools, families, and communities populated by teenagers characterized by a general lack of a creative spark.

Most students want to learn; they want to do better. Yet far too many are simply caught in a system where they believe that their effort is ineffectual, perhaps even futile. Many of these students believe that a high IQ or SAT score promises a bye in the game of school, regardless of their attitude. Meanwhile, too many parents and teachers either cannot see or do not want to see how many signs support this belief. In any case, we have worked with many teenagers who operate as if they believe that the attitude of a saint will get you nowhere if you don't have the right test score. Whether this perception is true or not, we believe it's time for parents and teachers to give serious consideration to the idea that students believe it is true.

TWO POLES OF SCHOOL REFORM
AND THE FORGOTTEN MULTITUDE
IN THE MIDDLE

Since educators began aggressively talking about reform in the early 1960s, American schools have focused their energies on addressing the needs of two groups served by our schools, two groups at opposite poles. At one pole, the high-achieving end, there are numerous programs for those students deemed "gifted and talented." In most American high schools, the top 10+/- percent of the student body receives a rigorous program, preparing them for selective and prestigious American colleges and universities. Every June, local newspapers tout the accomplishments of these students and broadcast the prestige of their intended postsecondary destinations. At the other pole, a range of so-called LD (learning disability) programs has exploded in the last two decades. Proponents uphold such programs as having significantly advanced the cause of learning for young people; however, others believe that they have merely served to create an overflowing alphabet soup of ineffective expensive categories of students—ADD, ADHD, LD, and so on. In any case, both sides acknowledge the importance of considering learning differences among students.

Left out of our reform efforts have been the vast majority of students who quietly exist between these two poles, the teeming multitude of teenagers who often seem to be passively punching a time clock between 8:30 A.M. and 3:00 P.M. Watching them mark time in the corridors of our schools, a riff from a Pink Floyd song plays in our heads: "All in all, you're just another brick in the wall."

We have spoken with scores of high school principals who openly acknowledge that the needs of this group are not being addressed in any coherent or systematic way. It is an accepted fact that this group is not at all excited about school. All of this makes sense when one considers the notion that analysis of and preoccupation with aptitude has fueled the reforms at the two extremes. Those with high aptitude have received gifted-and-talented programs, while those with low aptitude have received specialized extra attention. Yet those with average aptitude often don't even receive average attention. In fact, it has become common for parents of students deemed "average" to try to prove that their children actually possess *lower* intellectual capabilities than school authorities state. They do so because they believe that a lower classification will enable their children to receive more focused, qualified attention. School in America may be the only place where a parent would try to prove such a thing.

ATTITUDE OVER APTITUDE: BEST FOR SOME, BEST FOR ALL

If Malcolm's story can speak for the forgotten multitude in the middle, let us consider the two poles. We recently asked a group of students, What do you think would happen if Ray Charles or Stevie Wonder enrolled in an American school today? One replied, "They would get stuck in classes for the visually impaired and we would never hear from them again." Whether or not this student's observation is true, suffice it to say that LD programs often focus on disabilities at the expense of dreams. Stevie Wonder and Ray Charles each had a dream of being a musician and then realized that they needed to address and overcome the disability of blindness in order to honor that dream. Blindness was and remains a challenge to both men. Yet their dreams took precedence over the disability and they went on to become seminal figures in American popular music. Preoccupation with the Aptitude Culture can cause the dream to get smothered by the disability.

As debilitating as the Aptitude Culture can be for those on the lower end of the testing totem pole, the effects can be equally insidious at the other end of the spectrum, the gifted-and-talented category. How often have we heard of the student who will drop a class, taking an incomplete, rather than struggle through and face the dreaded consequences of a lower GPA as the result of receiving a B or C in the course? Most disturbing is the fact that in many of these cases it has been the adults—the teachers or the parents—who have encouraged the student to drop the course. Although it may never be spoken, it is clear to all concerned, especially the student, that one's GPA is more important than the development of character that might occur as a result of struggling through the challenge of such a course. No matter what we tell students about the virtues of "best effort" and "character," they usually know quite clearly where we really stand. As teachers and parents consider their roles as the molders of the men and women of tomorrow, how can they possibly believe such an approach could work?

THE SEDUCTION OF ABILITY AND MEDIOCRITY: GOOD KID/BAD KID

How many times have we observed a rebellious or disrespectful teenager and heard someone say, "Boy, that kid has an attitude!" A popular saying at our school is "He has an attitude that could choke a horse!" In general, it is obvious when someone has a bad attitude. However, it is important for parents to stop and try to give some serious and unbiased thought to just how high the bar is on attitude in their families. Many families are content to demand little more than the expectation that the attitude not be bad. One of the reasons is that we fail to realize the extent to which ability or attitude is coloring our perception. Malcolm remembers a time when he learned some important lessons in this regard during his time coaching women's soccer:

> Remembering back to that first year, a winless season (0–8), I regularly echoed the usual sayings: "It's not whether we win; it's how we play the game." "Try your best and accept the results." "Let's demonstrate the best sportsmanship in the league." "We may be outplayed; we will never be outworked."
> I believed these things as I said them and I believe them today.

However, I found that I wasn't bellowing them across the field as much in subsequent seasons after we climbed out of the cellar and into the hunt for the league championship. In other words, I discovered that it was relatively easy to focus on effort and sportsmanship when there was little chance of victory. (After all, what else could I have focused on?) Then, as we began to win, I became seduced by the fun and feeling of accomplishment that came from "the thrill of victory."

The combination of ability and success can often camouflage our perceptions of the attitudes in our families. We end up focusing on attitude only when the behavior is bad or the performance is low.

One example of how this seduction can camouflage a family's perception of itself occurs in a dynamic we call "Good Kid/Bad Kid." We frequently encounter a family dynamic where mom and dad are concerned about the attitude and behavior of "Johnny." Let's assume he has a very negative attitude and his parents are consumed with trying to find ways to address and change it. Let's say he has a brother named Rick who does not cause the grief and turmoil in his family that Johnny causes. We have watched as parents heap accolades on the Ricks of the world despite the fact that Rick might do little more than refrain from being bad. Such parents do Rick a fundamental disservice because they do not measure him against a perception of his best. Instead, they measure him against the much lower standard of Johnny's worst. To Rick, the game sometimes looks like: "I don't have to do my best; I just need to make sure that I stay one or two jumps ahead of Johnny." Although Rick may play this game quite well at home, it doesn't prepare him for the higher expectations he will inevitably face once he leaves home. Meanwhile, Rick's parents let him off the hook, grateful that they do not have another Johnny on their hands. Parents must strive to see through the camouflage of ability and success. We must work to perceive each of our children as individuals, each possessing a different standard of personal excellence.

"NEVER NEGOTIATE WITH A TERRORIST"

One of the facts of life in a boarding school is that there are never enough telephones. As a result, any walking tour of campus will find students stationed at pay phones, engaged in conversation with folks from home. And it is not all that uncommon to find them engaged in very heated conversation where it is not unusual to hear disrespectful words and feel the tension in the air. As Laura likes to point out, "Whenever I come upon this scene, I generally assume two things to be true: (1) There is a parent on the other end of the line, and (2) that parent is probably paying for the call." Chances are such parents are falling into the trap we call "negotiating with a terrorist." Although we can't always insist on positive outcomes, we owe it to our kids to insist on positive attitudes.

Coming face to face with our own dysfunctional moments happens to the best of us. In Priority 1, Truth over Harmony, we referred to the world "in here" versus the world "out there" and how we try to compromise between these two worlds in our parenting. Many families lose sight of the wisdom embodied in another adage: We cannot control how others react to us; we can only control how we react to them. The mom on the other end of the telephone line may not be able to control the attitude of the child speaking to her, but she can control her reaction to that attitude. In fact, she has a number of choices at her disposal. She can:

- Refuse to accept the charges.
- Tell her son that she will not continue the conversation unless he changes his tone.
- Hang up the phone with the explanation that her son needs to put his own coins in the phone the next time he calls and that she will assess his attitude at that time before determining if and when she will pay for future calls.
- Hang up with no explanation, thereby placing the burden on him (where it belongs!) to figure out the next move.

Invariably her son is speaking with a disrespectful attitude for a very elementary reason: He is allowed to do so. The bad news: This young man's attitude will not change overnight. The good news: His mother's reaction to that attitude can change before night falls.

The moral of the story? Never negotiate with a terrorist! This is a basic rule of international relations and we would do well to adopt it with our children. Think about all the times our kids are exhibiting terrorist attitudes and behavior. What is our response? More often than not, we engage in various attempts to reason with them. What defines a terrorist attitude? As a Supreme Court judge said, "I know it when I see it." Although he was talking about pornography, we define terrorist activity the same way. It involves tone of voice, body language, and level of respect. When a child displays this attitude, adopt a simple rule: All bets are off! Whether we stop the conversation, leave the room, or walk out of the house, we need to take some action that communicates the message "Your attitude is unacceptable and I will not continue this conversation until it changes." Remember a simple phrase when in this mode: *The more you talk, the more you lose!* Your actions will speak much louder than any efforts to convince your child what needs to be done.

MOTIONS TO EFFORT TO EXCELLENCE— THE BUILDING BLOCKS OF ATTITUDE

If the seduction of ability and negotiation with terrorists are things to be avoided, what positive steps can we take as parents to avoid falling into these traps? One critical piece can be the weekly meetings described in Priority 8, Create a Character Culture. One concept to consider at these meetings is one we call "Building Blocks." It is a simple tool for self-assessment and the assessment of others.

The Building Blocks model consists of three phases:

- *Motions:* The individual follows the motions of responsible behavior.

BUILDING BLOCKS
of the Hyde education

- a chain reaction
- an evolutionary process
- culminates with a Hyde graduation
- ultimate goal: the Hyde Diploma

MOTIONS
taker

- The motions of responsible behavior.
- *Move the body and the mind will follow.*
- Expectations are set almost exclusively by the faculty.
- Sometimes an unpleasant phase.
- The foundation for the discovery of Unique Potential is set.

FOUNDATION

EFFORT
doer

- Beginnings of a positive attitude.
- *If I have to do this, I might as well do it well.*
- Expectations are shared.
- The student-teacher bond is formed.
- A partnership begins to evolve.
- Creativity begins.

FOUNDATION

EXCELLENCE
giver

- Concept of one's BEST.
- Student is *majority shareholder* in student-faculty partnership.
- *Prime the pump:* givers assume responsibility for the growth of the takers.
- Graduation—A commitment for the DIPLOMA.
- Faculty and parents *let go* of the student.

FOUNDATION

- *Effort:* The individual begins to take pride in meeting his or her given challenges.
- *Excellence:* The individual begins to pursue his or her best.

At the Hyde schools, students, faculty, and parents regularly rate themselves and each other in accordance with these phases. It is not uncommon to hear a student say, "Although I'm at 'excellence' in my chemistry class, I'm stuck at 'motions' on my soccer team." A student operating below "motions" is considered "offtrack."

All of us—parents, children, teachers, and students—travel through these phases within a myriad of activities. We might be at all three levels in different endeavors at any given time. Perhaps the model is easiest understood with an actual case study where we can follow the progress of a group of teenagers through the entire continuum. In this case, we will explore Malcolm's experiences as a coach of a high school women's soccer team. Although this story demonstrates that progress may not occur overnight, it does show how it can happen in a steady and sure fashion so long as we stay the course.

CASE STUDY: A HIGH SCHOOL WOMEN'S SOCCER TEAM

In the mid-eighties, Malcolm took over a high school women's soccer team mired in a deep slump. The program was in shambles. Not only did the girls not want to play soccer, but they had great disdain for the school's mandatory sports policy. Since playing sports had been second nature for Malcolm as a kid, he had a difficult time facing the negative attitudes he encountered.

When Malcolm went out for the first day of practice and saw the girls who would comprise the team, all he could ask himself was: What's wrong with this picture? It was easy to determine the answer as he scanned the playing field. Many of the girls wore jewelry and makeup. Most were not wearing cleats. Many were attempting to outdo each other in terms of fashion. Some had brought their

131

purses out to the playing field. He wasn't sure where to start, but his instincts told him the immediate focus would not be on the fundamentals of soccer.

He called these "athletes" together and said:

OK, I know that many of you would prefer not to be out here. I'm not going to waste my time explaining why this will be good for you or why I think you could begin to develop a love for soccer or athletics. For the next two months we are simply going to do the things that true soccer players do. What do soccer players do? They show up on time. They bring their cleats and leave their purses at home. They don't wear makeup; they don' t wear jewelry. All of you will be expected to wear special practice uniforms, which I will order. In short, I expect you to behave like soccer players and keep your attention on task while you're out here on this field.

MOTIONS

During that initial meeting Malcolm didn't talk about win-loss records or the strategies of soccer. He did institute what came to be known as the "no tee-hee" rule. This occurred after he noticed that several of the girls would flub a kick or completely miss the ball and then laugh about it. He outlawed this reaction without bothering to define it as the defense mechanism that it was. He told them he didn't care if they were completely uncoordinated or if they looked ridiculous trying to kick the ball, he only demanded that they take soccer practice seriously. He informed them that they would be done at 5:00 P.M. if the practice was taken seriously but that he would add increments of five minutes of extra running or calisthenics if he felt there was a lack of seriousness. It was clear that they still weren't taking him seriously. Even the threat of a special Saturday practice didn't seem to inspire acceptable attitudes.

That was where he started. These girls despised him and routinely complained about him to each other and to their parents. He was the butt of jokes emanating from different corners of the campus and he received scowls from these players when he met them in the hall. His strategy was simple: *Make the consequences of failing to follow the "motions" of a responsible soccer player more distasteful than those resulting from following them.*

In other words, the reason these girls were following the "motions" of responsible soccer players was because of the "ax" that would fall on them if they didn't. It was hard for Malcolm to play this unpopular role, as he had always had positive relationships with the teams he coached. His teams had done well; they had won a fair number of championships and he had always been able to engage in friendly give-and-take banter with his athletes. In short, he was in a new role, and at this early phase he didn't like it very much. His players didn't like it (or him) at all.

Malcolm writes:

> This unpleasant relationship lasted for a good part of that initial season. Our record was 0 and 8. We failed to win a single game! We didn't score a single goal until midway through the season, and it was clear that other schools wanted to schedule us on their Parents Weekends so they could be assured a win for the home crowd. As a coach, I found it humiliating. I don't believe the athletes cared. They didn't perceive themselves as athletes in the first place. Nevertheless, I believed that the approach I was taking was the only one possible under the circumstances.

EFFORT

Midway through the season a group of the girls took the step from the "motions" to the "effort" phase. Perhaps one experienced the euphoria of scoring a goal. Perhaps another was stopped in the lunch line and complimented on her fine play in a game. Perhaps one's parents were coming for a visit and she wanted to surprise them by playing in a game for the first time. For many, it was simply a case of the lesser of two evils. Many realized, "Well, this guy Gauld seems to have us beat. If we have to play, I have to admit it's more fun being out on the field than sitting on the bench." Thus, many found themselves competing for starting positions only because they didn't like sitting on the bench. Although they would probably still have said that they would rather not play at all (the rebel must always surrender reluctantly!), they did seem to be working harder in spite of themselves.

EXCELLENCE

By the end of that first season, a critical mass of the players were going out on the field each afternoon and at least exhibiting a minimum standard of enthusiasm, even if the motivation for this varied. That winter, when Malcolm was in the middle of his boys' basketball season, three of his soccer players came to see him in his office. They had heard about a local indoor winter women's league consisting of former high school and college players and wanted to know if he could enter them in it. Malcolm was both ecstatic and stunned by the request. It was clear that these three wanted to move from the "effort" phase to the "excellence" phase. They wanted to begin to pursue their best in the game of soccer. They played in the winter league, had positive experiences, and developed a desire to improve even more as soccer players. Malcolm wondered, "Could we have some positive momentum starting here?"

SYNERGY = MOTIONS + EFFORT + EXCELLENCE

The next fall Malcolm returned as soccer coach and began to steel himself for what he perceived would be another tooth-pulling first week of trying to convince students with negative attitudes to play a game they didn't want to play. He was surprised in several ways. For one, the three players at the "excellence" level began to serve as role models. (Two of them ultimately went on to become accomplished college players.) Second, a core of kids at the "effort" level wanted to compete for starting positions. There was actually a "critical mass"— that is, the number of players who wanted to do well outnumbered those who didn't want to be out there at all. The girls with the negative attitudes fell into step with a more positive norm. The tide had turned. They would now feel out of place with an outwardly negative attitude. The norm was to go out there and hustle and work hard for a couple of hours, and that's what 90+ percent of the players did.

Malcolm writes:

Perhaps the most momentous event occurred in the first game of our second season: We won! You would have thought we had won the Super Bowl. The players who had returned from the previous year were beside themselves with joy. They clearly preferred the "thrill of victory" to the "agony of defeat," and it was obvious they wanted more of it. Well, they got more of it, ultimately going on to win their league championship that fall. Several of the girls entered that same winter league and soon were applying pressure on other teammates to attend summer soccer camps. Several players did attend soccer camps and others played in summer leagues.

Success evolved into a tradition. In the following four years, the girls were state prep school champions three times, and twice went on to participate in the New England Prep School Soccer Tournament. Competition for starting positions was very keen, as there was a great deal of pride associated with simply being on the team. These young women proved that personal progress in individuals and in groups is exponential. The contention that nothing can stop the person with the proper attitude was supported. When we first set out on our soccer odyssey, I was already convinced that nothing could help the individual with the wrong attitude.

An exercise following this chapter offers the opportunity for all family members to apply the Building Blocks concept to themselves and each other. This continuum from "motions" to "effort" to

135

"excellence" can serve as a guide for us as we tackle a wide spectrum of challenges: from a math class, guitar lessons, or a sport to chores or club memberships. It is a good thing for us to continually find ourselves at all three levels. The one variable we cannot control is the timetable of our students' growth. All of us progress through the curriculum at different rates of speed. As we like to say, "You can't open a rose with a chisel." All journeys begin with a single step. Just as the sailor cannot control the wind, we cannot control the difficulty of the journey our challenges will require. Yet just as the sailor can adjust the sails, we can control the attitude we bring to the task every day.

Finally, accept the fact that, as parents, it is an ongoing struggle to keep the weight of our foot anchored in attitude. We get seduced by the potential aptitudes of our children and there are few statements that excite us more than hearing "Your child is bright." It's as if everything will turn out all right because they are bright! While there is nothing more joyous than taking pleasure in the gifts of our children, we need to keep the focus on what they can control. Look around at the most successful people you deal with in your life. Chances are they possess more of a positive attitude than an incredible aptitude. If our children are going to fulfill the potential of their aptitudes and put their lives together, they will need the right attitude. And so will we. Aptitudes are developed as long as we live and an attitude can be changed almost immediately.

We are fond of a piece on attitude written by religious leader Charles Swindoll. A parent sent it to us a few years back. It has been taped to our bathroom mirror ever since:

> The longer I live, the more I realize the impact of attitude on life. Attitude, to me, is more important than facts. It is more important than the past, than education, than money, than circumstances, than failures, than successes, than what other people say or do. It is more important than appearance, giftedness, or skill. It will make or break a company . . . a church . . . a home. The remarkable thing is we have a choice every day regarding the attitude we will embrace for that day.

We cannot change our past. . ∴. We cannot change the fact that people will act in a certain way. We cannot change the inevitable. The only thing we can do is play on the one string we have and that is our attitude. . . . I am convinced that life is 10% what happens to me and 90% how I react to it.

FAMILY EXERCISES AND ACTIVITIES

Chair Exercise

Materials: Chair (one you can pick up easily), paper, pen
Time: 30 minutes
Explanation: This is an exercise we do during many of the workshops. One parent should take the lead. Hold the chair over your shoulder. (You can do this by locking your arms through the rungs on the back of the chair.) Walk around the space in front of the family and ask them, "What do you think about me?" (Most of them will laugh and say they think you may be a little crazy.) Then ask the family to think about attitudes they carry just like you are carrying the chair. Ask them to write down an attitude they may be carrying that is unproductive. Some other questions that may be helpful are:

- "Do you think you need to carry this chair [attitude]?"
- "What would happen if you put the chair [attitude] down?"
- "What chairs [attitudes] do we carry as a family?"

Effort/Attitude Chart

Materials: Large piece of paper for each chart, marker, tape
Time: 15 minutes to set up; daily input for 1 month
Explanation: Have each family member come up with three areas

of aptitude they would like to improve upon. Create a chart for each person and decide on a time frame to chart (week, month, etc.). Then set up the chart so that one axis is the aptitude and the other represents the attitude/effort. Each day or week, make an entry about how each family member is addressing that skill or area of improvement. At the end of the time frame, sit down as a family and talk about the results.

Here are some questions to ask:

- "Did you find improving your attitude helped improve your aptitude?"
- "How did you improve your attitude?"
- "Can you carry this into other areas?"

"Family Risk Tree"

Materials: Paper and supplies to make a large tree trunk and a box of plain "leaves" to put by the tree
Time: 30 minutes to set "tree" up, then daily/weekly input
Explanation: This exercise helps encourage risk-taking as a key factor in developing attitude and aptitude. It may be helpful to first talk about risks and define the term: "What are dangerous risks to take as opposed to risks taken to encourage growth?"

Brainstorm some important risks:

- Speaking up in class or at work
- Meeting a new friend
- Learning a new move in sports
- Saying "no" to something that may cause rejection
- Singing a song
- Getting in shape
- Looking for a job
- Asking for more responsibility

Leave the box of leaves by the "tree." As family members take risks, they are to label their act and tape it to the tree. At the end of a week or month, the family can get together and review the tree.

Some questions to ask:

- "What did I learn from taking that risk?"
- "What has been difficult?"
- "Has my aptitude improved as a result?"
- "Has my attitude improved as a result?"
- "Has my family seen any change in me?"

JOURNALING QUESTIONS

1. How would I define my overall attitude toward life?
2. What are the strengths of my general attitude about life?
3. What holds me back in my general attitude about life?
4. What situations or which people bring out my worst attitudes?
5. When I have an "offtrack" attitude, who sees it?
6. Do I believe that my attitude is really more important than my aptitude? In what areas of my life do I question this?
7. How do I feel about the general attitudes of my family members? (Describe each family member.)
8. When and under what circumstances do I see my children struggle with their attitudes?
9. Describe an incident in which I was proud of the attitude I saw in someone in my family.
10. Is "attitude" important enough to me?
11. Where have I controlled my attitude?
12. Where has it controlled me?
13. Who among my peers might I acknowledge as having a positive attitude?

Priority 4,
Set High Expectations and
Let Go of Outcomes

Aim higher than you think you can reach. If our children give their best, they will ultimately feel good about the outcome whether or not they actually accomplish their intended goals.

Most parents and teachers today seem motivated by a desire to improve discipline in their homes and schools. As we discussed in Priority 2, Principles over Rules, sometimes this motivation causes us to focus on rules at the expense of principles. This tendency can give rise to a parent-child relationship in which our children may follow the letter of the law but not its spirit.

Just as parents might impulsively seize upon rules at the expense of principles during trying times in the home, they will often seize upon discipline at the expense of high expectations. Discipline is critical to establishing and maintaining a bottom line. However, discipline alone cannot open up the world of dreams to our children. The key to this door lies with personal accomplishments. Children need to "aim high" in order to experience accomplishment, and we cannot help them if we spend all of our time focused on bottom lines. When times are hard in our homes, we often reach for discipline as a consolation. (The parent thinks: "If we can't have a great home, maybe we can at least avoid having a really bad one.") This is not a long-term solution. As we like to say, "The goal of character development is not to keep people out of the gutter. The goal is to reach for the stars."

Discipline and high expectations must go hand in hand. Yet many parents commonly respond to the daily pressures of home life by focusing on discipline at the expense of expectations. Parents obsessed with discipline, those who have lost sight of high expectations, will often end up assembling list after list of "house rules," behaviors in the home that will not be tolerated. The forbidden activities typically include smoking, use of drugs and alcohol, certain types of dress, perhaps body piercings and tattoos. House rules may include a curfew and perhaps a chore or two. The problem with such lists is that they tend to center on minimum acceptable behavior and families wind up descending to the lowest common denominator. To the kid, it looks like: "You don't have to be a winner, just don't be a loser."

Another problem with an obsession with discipline is that our children will fail to take ownership of their own goals. If they learn to feel that their goals are always being set by others, they will ultimately rebel against any expectation of effort or accomplishment. A Hyde father of two writes:

> Our son really rebelled against what he thought was us setting goals for him, rather than letting him set goals for himself. Letting go of the outcome here was closely related to our fear that he wasn't going to be successful and the fear that he wouldn't be able to do things for himself. He did not feel empowered by us to be his own person.

Our experience has demonstrated that parents can become obsessed with discipline and treat it as if it were an end in itself. This is understandable, particularly when we become frustrated by teenage problems in our homes. We are drawn to discipline in the hopes that it might result in cleaner rooms, better dress, honored curfews, and decreased drug usage. Discipline, however, should not be viewed as an end; it is a means. It must be accompanied by high expectations and by tangible goals.

Sometimes we are afraid to set high goals for our children because we fear the inevitable letdown should they not achieve their goals. For example, if we encourage them to try out for soccer teams or school plays, they might not be selected. However, a different atmosphere, an inspiring one, can emerge if we can develop a healthy respect for best effort and if we come to accept failure as a learning experience (see Priority 5, Value Success and Failure). At the same time, we must avoid the common trap of encouraging our kids to "try to try." Malcolm remembers a student in his history class who submitted a careless, unsatisfactory essay. Required to rewrite the paper, the student merely submitted the very same essay a day later, only this time with flawless penmanship. Did the student *try* harder? Perhaps. Did the student earnestly strive to produce an accomplished essay? No way.

Sometimes parents are tempted to intervene to "lower the bar" when they see their children struggling. Not only does this fail to help kids meet their goals, it can have a long-term negative effect on parent-child relationships. A mother writes:

When my children were in school, I always thought that if they tried their best, that would be fine. But then, when they started getting grades and the grades weren't so good, I would start thinking, "Well, they weren't trying their best. If they were trying their best, they would get good grades." So I would start finding ways in which to manipulate the outcome so they could meet my high expectations. I realized that my expectations were all about how other people were evaluating my children. It wasn't about how I was evaluating them. I wasn't willing to let go of other people's evaluation and I was insistent upon pushing them to meet these expectations.

My children understood that this was not a truthful way to approach the world and my son rebelled. He absolutely refused to do the things other people set out for him to do and I was unwilling to let go of what he was doing with his life. I felt he had to do it the way I wanted him to do it and the way society as a whole dictates the way to do it. So, as I think about it today, I was good at setting high expectations, but had to pay close attention to everything they did on the way to getting to those high expectations. Even today, my son says, "Mom, you say you've let go entirely, but I can tell you're still paying close attention, you're still watching."

Focusing on high expectations can sometimes seem overly achievement-oriented. There is an ever-present danger of slipping into the "seduction of ability" described in Priority 3. In the effort to extol attitude, we do not want to disregard aptitude. After all, increased aptitude is the ultimate target of our efforts. It is the parent's and teacher's job to make sure that the effort is honest and fair. Parents must avoid the trap of discipline for discipline's sake, or effort for effort's sake, or character for character's sake. It is essential to aim high. Aim higher than you think you can reach. If our children give their best, they will ultimately feel good about the outcome whether or not they actually accomplish their intended goals.

Malcolm remembers how one of his high school teachers taught him to aim high. During his senior year, this teacher asked Malcolm where he hoped to go to college. Malcolm responded, "Well, I'd really like to go to Harvard, but chances are pretty slim of that ever happening." With a serious tone, the teacher asked Malcolm if he had yet to apply or interview. Malcolm responded with something along the lines of, "I'm smart enough to know that I shouldn't waste my time." At that point, the teacher presented him with a challenge: "Call the Harvard admissions office, set up an interview, and go down there and talk your way in." Probably for no other reason than his respect for the teacher, Malcolm agreed.

A few weeks later, he found himself in Cambridge, Massachusetts, for his interview. Entering the admissions office, he half expected someone to tell him that he didn't belong in the building. Once the interview began, he made his case. At the conclusion of the interview, Malcolm shook hands with the admissions officer and then exited the building with an odd sense of accomplishment. On the one hand, he didn't believe he had any better chance of being admitted to Harvard than he did before the teacher offered his challenge. On the other, he felt a sense of pride that he had made a case for himself. He felt great.

Today, Malcolm knows that he would never have had that Harvard interview had his teacher not challenged him with high expectations. The short-term outcome of the interview was the rejection letter he had predicted a few months later. But the lasting impact was the genuine self-confidence that resulted from aiming high. The interview had no adverse effects on his self-esteem. Indeed, his self-esteem was dramatically enhanced. As an educator, Malcolm has since counseled many students with their college plans. He tells all of them, "Don't get your self-confidence from the schools that ultimately accept or reject you; get your confidence from who you are."

PUTTING AIMING HIGH
INTO PERSPECTIVE

Although our focus is on Attitude over Aptitude, the Hyde Schools have gained national attention due to some fairly remarkable accomplishments in the classroom, on the stage, and on the athletic field. Since our school was founded, 98 percent of our graduates have enrolled at four-year colleges. Many of these students arrived at our school with weak transcripts and little hope of moving on to higher education. In the performing arts, groups from Hyde have performed at the Kennedy Center in Washington, D.C., and the Circle in the Square Theatre off Broadway. This is all the more amazing when one considers that very few of our students have had any prior experience with the performing arts. Our sports teams have won a number of state and regional championships. These experiences have convinced us that academics, sports, and performing arts offer especially valuable opportunities pertaining to high expectations.

The greatest potentials of these opportunities will not be realized, of course, without great parenting, teaching, and coaching. Such

145

mentoring can create a powerful synergy, one that can transform an entire school community. Yet there is also a lot that can go wrong. We don't need to look far to see that some negative outcomes can occur with sports. Go to any high school basketball game and observe as the fans mockingly wave handkerchiefs at the opposing team's star player who has just fouled out of the game. (You can hear the chant in any gym in America: "Na-na-na-na. Na-na-na-na. Hey, heaaay! Goooooood-bye!") Some interscholastic conferences have banned the traditional postgame team-to-team handshake. Apparently this ban was the result of too many insults and skirmishes between the opposing teams. The problems can magnify at the college level.

Malcolm recently attended a college lacrosse game that happened to pit a prestigious liberal arts college, the home team, against a school of lesser reputation. He observed some very competitive lacrosse being played between two fairly evenly matched teams whose players exhibited positive sportsmanship and demonstrated respect for each other. Before long, he was distracted by the appalling attitudes and behavior of the home fans. After the visitors piled up a formidable lead, the home team's fans began to chant: "That's all right; that's OK! You'll be working for us someday!" As the professors and administrators in attendance apparently pretended not to hear, he wondered, "What are the qualifications for prestige?"

If it is indeed true that "the apple doesn't fall far from the tree," perhaps we should not be surprised by some of the astounding examples of deplorable behavior by parents supposedly observing from the stands as their children "play" in Little League baseball and Pee Wee hockey contests. In one recent infamous case, a Massachusetts father took his rage out to the parking lot, where he confronted another father, engaged him in a fistfight, and beat him to death as the victim's sons tugged on the man, begging him to stop. This incident did not occur at the conclusion of a championship game. It had been a practice session.

In our view, it is the adults who embody the most troubling aspect of this national decline in sportsmanship. It is one thing for a young athlete to lip off to a referee, get into a skirmish with an opponent, or throw a tantrum when mistakes threaten a coveted victory. It is another for coaches and parents to tolerate such behavior—tolerance as expressed by a lack of outrage. Then again, perhaps tolerance for these behaviors is the very reason why they are on the increase. Thus, this Priority calls for high expectations in the broadest sense. As teachers and parents, we must call for the highest standards of attitude, effort, skills, and sportsmanship.

Sports, if left unchecked, can also be a breeding ground for exclusive cliques. One reason cliques form around sports is that most American high schools actually limit the offer of sports to those students who are already good at them. It is difficult to imagine a seventeen-year-old junior going to the athletic office of a typical high school and being encouraged to simply ask, "I think I'd like to try football. Where do I sign up?" This student's opportunity to play would most likely be based on a coach's assessment of whether he could help the team. We at Hyde would stress that sports (as well as a wide variety of school activities) can be extremely valuable as learning tools *provided they're deliberately organized to deliver that outcome.* As they are typically organized in most schools—as an outlet for talented athletes or sometimes as a revenue producer—it can be difficult for sports to play such a role.

At Hyde, we have come to believe that sports should not be regarded as extracurricular, that they should be a co-curricular part of every student's education. In fact, we would go so far as to call into question the very notion of extracurricular activities. Sometimes, when people ask us what kind of extracurricular activities we offer at our schools, we shock them with our response: "Very few." What other schools would consider "extra," we consider "integral" to the program. Sometimes the students who learn the most from sports are those who feel the most ill-equipped to play them or who don't want to play them at all!

Before scoffing at mandatory sports, imagine how any school might respond to the student who said, "I really don't feel I'm suited to algebra. Do I have to take it?" As a nation, we offer blind allegiance to the premise that a student's intellectual development is to be required but we leave most other adolescent development up to chance in the form of a set of activities we have come to call "extracurricular." We openly challenge that assumption, as we believe that many learning opportunities can be missed.

IPSES

To keep ourselves on track, we have developed the acronym IPSES to symbolize the aspects of a person that education and parenting ought to address and develop:

I = Intellectual
P = Physical
S = Spiritual
E = Emotional
S = Social

We regularly assess the progress of each student, parent, and teacher using the self-assessment sheet presented on page 149. Students meet in any number of mixed groups—the sophomore class, a soccer team, a performing arts group, a dormitory—to discuss their overall progress. They give themselves a numerical grade (from 0 to 100 percent) in each of the five categories and sometimes write a few comments for each. Then they talk about their progress with each other, perhaps exchanging the charts for discussion purposes. We have discovered that the simple act of discussing these categories opens students to becoming more consciously aware of the need for overall personal growth. (You might discuss the IPSES concept during the family meetings discussed in Priority 8, Create a Character Culture.)

IPSES CHART

For:_____ Date:_____

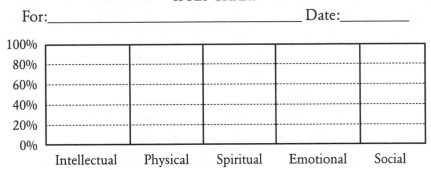

| | Intellectual | Physical | Spiritual | Emotional | Social |

Comments

Intellectual

Physical

Spiritual

Emotional

Social

WRESTLING: A VEHICLE TO HELP KIDS AIM HIGH

The one sport where we have seen dramatic opportunities occur for boys is wrestling. By wrestling, we don't mean the hyped "showtime" served up by the WWF, but honest interscholastic wrestling by weight classes. In this manner, wrestling is truly a democratic sport in which accomplishment is open to any athlete willing to "pay the price." Wrestling has been an important activity at Hyde since the school was founded. It is the sport athletes hate and the one the alumni invariably claim contributed the most to their character development. The success Hyde has experienced is little short of startling. Hyde, a school of 230 students, has long competed in a conference consisting of the largest and most prestigious boarding schools in the country, including, among others, Exeter, Andover, Deerfield, and Northfield–Mt. Hermon. Hyde neither recruits wrestlers nor offers a postgraduate program—a thirteenth year of academic and/or athletic seasoning in preparation for college—often utilized by superior athletes.

Perhaps the subtle distinction between setting high expectations and letting go of the outcomes is personified in the approach Hyde's wrestling coaches apply to their wrestlers as they begin the season, one that culminates in the Class A New England Wrestling Tournament. The coach does not say, "Gentlemen, we don't care about the outcome; we only care how hard you try." (Indeed, the wrestlers are fond of spouting off slogans like "Trying is lying.") The coach simply says, "This year, as always, our goal is to win the New England Tournament. Here are some of the things I think we'll need to work on in order to accomplish this goal." The wrestlers do try, and try very hard. There have been years when Hyde teams have been trounced, finishing at the very bottom of the standings. However, believe it or not, in the past twenty-five years, Hyde has won the championship four times. We have won it by having every wrestler on the team contribute his very best effort toward winning. In fact, the last time Hyde won it all (1994), we had only one champion among thirteen weight classes, whereas other schools in the tournament had four or five champions. Although there was only one champion, eleven out of thirteen wrestlers finished at least fifth, the lowest scoring position. Thus, enough points were scored to enable Hyde to win. Everyone in the gym was surprised by the fact that Hyde emerged as the champion—everyone, *including* Hyde! It was a true team effort.

The point is not that Hyde won. The point is simply that Hyde *aimed* to win rather than merely to try. Having watched these teams over the years, We know our coaches were just as proud of teams that finished dead last as they were of those who pulled off the unlikely championship. Yet the aim each year is to attain the ultimate goal of winning the championship, and that's what inspires the athletes. Think about the number of times parents or teachers have said, "We don't care how well you do; we just care how hard you try." When we offer phrases like that, sometimes we're trying to convince ourselves as much as we're trying to convince the kids. (Parent to parent: Is that phrase preceding the semicolon *really* true? You *really* don't care how well they do? Hey, we're parents, not saints!) In fact, the kids might actually be hearing something different from what we're saying. Our experience tells us that they actually may hear something closer to: "I don't think you can hack it; so I don't want you to feel too bad when you fail."

Our wrestling coaches have learned that when we treat our students like champions and expect them to act like champions, they tend to feel like champions no matter the outcome. In our experience, the end result has been a great deal of pride on the part of the athletes and the students in school. In fact, a sort of legend has evolved around Hyde wrestling that no matter how strong the other teams may be, they have come to believe that anything can happen when they wrestle Hyde. A reputation has evolved that Hyde wrestlers never quit. It is inspiring to watch the kids wear this reputation. At the same time, there is a fine line between aiming high and becoming obsessed with achievement. That is why we, as parents or teachers, must pay attention to the subtle distinctions in demanding high expectations as we let go of the outcomes. However, the incredible power in developing this Priority is worth the effort.

Gary Kent, the architect of the Hyde wrestling program since the mid-seventies, was recently inducted into the Maine Wrestling Hall of Fame. We were proud that the Hall of Fame asked to hold the ceremony at Hyde as a place symbolizing the best of wrestling. We asked past Hyde wrestlers to contribute stories and anecdotes about their experiences with wrestling. A number of former New England champions wrote in and thanked Gary for what he gave them. Our favorite letter, however, came from a young man who never distinguished himself as a champion on the mat when he wrestled twenty years before. He was someone who probably would have slipped through the cracks at other schools without ever having been encouraged to try sports. Here's what he wrote:

I was a mediocre wrestler, at best. Under Gary, though, I became the best mediocre wrestler I could be. He gave me an understanding of how to eat, train, and condition. I came to embrace the commitment that Gary had to us and to wrestling. For me, he became a tangible example of "real commitment." For the first time in my life I made a real commitment to do something.

If you have read any of the early works of contemporary writer John Irving, you will have a sense of how wrestling can get under your skin. Not everyone gets a chance to be that passionate about something in life. I got a chance to have that kind of passion—and that was a gift Gary gave me.

Of course, I didn't realize it then. Back then it was really hard and sometimes I hated it. It was only when I got into living my life that I realized what I had been given. I wrestled in college, the best mediocre wrestler on my team, and can give tangible testimony of how deep the gift I received from Gary was.

To break for a moment from this story, think about the writer's categorization of himself as "the best mediocre wrestler on my team." This young man's self-esteem was not damaged as a result of aiming high. Note his observation: "It was only when I got into living my life that I realized what I had been given." By willing to sacrifice short-term popularity for the prospect of long-term respect, this coach did some great teaching. Was long-term respect attained? This young man's testimonial to Gary is proof.

Gary taught us a drill used to escape from the "down position" at the start of a period. He called it the Ha-Ha Drill. You would be on your hands and knees and the idea was to fire up from that position in two moves—first, driving up with one knee and back with the opposite elbow to release the hand grip of the opponent; second, repeating the maneuver and standing—shouting with each step "ha!" We would repeat this drill for fifteen minutes in the heat of the wrestling room to end a workout. I can imagine an outside observer seeing this drill—a bunch of guys jumping up and falling down screaming "ha-

ha!" in unison—and wondering what the hell this was all about. It was during this drill that I realized I could go farther than I believed I could, if I just shut out the pain and exhaustion and did what I was told. I became known for this escape during my college wrestling, and shared the Ha-Ha Drill with my teammates.

As many of us have, I went through some very down times in my life. It was the memory of the Ha-Ha Drill that kept me going through the very worst of them. When you are down, you have to fire up and say "ha-ha!"

Thank you, Gary!

When we aim high, there are no guarantees that we will attain our goals. Yet more often than not, we will end up in appealing destinations.

PERFORMING ARTS: FROM STAGE FRIGHT
TO REAL SELF-ESTEEM

The performing arts is another arena where kids can learn to aim high. Each year, one or two Hyde graduates pursue performing arts in college. And many return years later and point to the performing arts as preparation for a successful job interview or as the beginning point to a better understanding of self. The following story tells of a young fourteen-year-old girl's experience on the road with our Performing Group, a group that might be considered varsity performing arts at Hyde. At the time (1990) we were presenting a series of shows in the public schools of Springfield, Massachusetts. The following account appeared in a monthly newsletter Malcolm wrote recounting the experiences of the performers:

"When I first came to Hyde I was very nervous about doing performing arts. Kind of like I am right now."

Thus spoke Sue Jenson on the stage at Van Sickle Junior High in Springfield, Massachusetts. She spoke for many in the cast. All could

153

sense that this crowd of students would not be as supportive as the one back at school. We were going to try to teach the Springfield kids about the Hyde education in a half-hour show. Moods in the audience were varied: guarded hope, cynicism, apprehension, suspicion, mockery. The Hyde performers had a few moods of their own. Many, probably most, were in a social setting for the first time where they constituted the racial minority. On with the show . . .

After just three notes of introductory instrumental accompaniment, the audience collectively realized that Sue was about to sing Whitney Houston's "The Greatest Love of All." We could feel the Springfield kids coming alive. Ah, our song selection would not hurt us today. Then Sue kicked in with the vocals. I wide-angled the audience for its reaction from my perch in the rear of the theater.

They laughed. Some laughed hard.

These kids wanted Whitney. They also weren't the least bit shy about showing that Sue's rendition was not quite the real McCoy. It seemed unfair. At this moment I felt for those performers who get booed off stage at Amateur Night at the Apollo Theatre. My protective instincts kicked in. What if that were my little girl up there? Why should the youngest member of the cast have the most pressure? Then my focus zoomed frontward and telephotoed Sue at center stage. How would she react?

She sang. She sang hard.

She stayed right with it, just as she had been taught. Her perseverance symbolized the point we were trying to make to our audience. She won them over! By the second verse it was almost as if the audience had collectively realized, "Hey, I get it! The point isn't to sound like Whitney. The point is to give it my best. Come to think of it, *I* don't sound like Whitney. But maybe I am capable of giving it my best."

It was a great moment. Our kids had worked hard: twelve shows in only three days. We set out to teach the Springfield kids something about Hyde. One cast member noted that they probably taught us more about ourselves.

Hyde gives every student the challenging experience of singing a solo in front of their peers. (Each member of the faculty does the same. Even parents do it!) We are all expected to take the risk to aim high. In the words of an old adage: Sometimes you have to go out on a limb; that's where the fruit is.

THE FRAGILITY METER

Many times we have found ourselves fantasizing about an imaginary device Malcolm calls the "Fragility Meter." These fantasies occur typically when we have been embroiled in controversies where we may have found ourselves at odds with parents regarding expectations we were putting on their children. Perhaps we are standing our ground on our mandatory athletics policy and one or both parents are holding a note from a doctor, stating that their child should be excused from sports due to an injury or a particular medical condition. In such cases, the air is charged with emotions, most of which are never actually expressed. A flavor of the mood is offered below. These unspoken comments occur at schools across the country. See if you can guess who is feeling which emotion: parent or school official.

- "Isn't it interesting how this kid has put more energy into getting this doctor's note than he has ever put into his studies?"
- "I heard they made another kid with the same condition play last season. He ended up needing a cast at the end of the season!"
- "This doctor is a soft touch for any kid who wants to get out of sports."
- "This coach cares more about winning than he does about my kid!"
- "I guess Doc cares more about his own malpractice liability than he does about this kid's long-term character development."
- "If they don't honor this note, I'm going to the school board."

- "If we honor this note, we'll be facing twenty more just like it by next week. If we don't honor it, do you suppose she'll go to the school board?"

A Fragility Meter would be capable of determining just how fragile someone actually is. We could connect electrodes to the student in question, get a reading, and then make a determination as to just how fragile he or she is. Of course, no such device exists. Thus, parents and school officials will have to continue to work out their disagreements as they negotiate proper expectations for children. We would submit a simple observation, one based on years of experience: "We don't know how fragile kids are, but we would bet the house that they are less fragile than their parents believe." By "fragile," we are not referring exclusively to their physical health. We also mean their emotional well-being. Kids are amazingly resilient, capable of bouncing back from setbacks and failures. Parents need not fear the notion of their children aiming high.

Recently, Malcolm accompanied a group of high school kids on a mountain hike in western Maine. They were scheduled to hike Old Speck, a four-thousand-plus-foot peak at the edge of the White Mountains. Although no technical expertise was required, the trail demanded a fairly steep four-mile scramble (each way) over rocks, logs, and roots. We floated it past our nine-year-old daughter and were startled by her immediate attraction to the whole idea. As we talked about it, Malcolm grew concerned that Mahalia would think of herself as a failure if we had to quit halfway up the trail. While Malcolm pondered the possible outcomes, she asked, "Can I bring a friend?" "Sure," Malcolm said, and began to mull over the downside of being stranded on a mountainside with two nine-year-old girls.

Shortly after nine o'clock one summer morning, they headed up the trail. They hadn't gone more than five hundred feet when Malcolm heard one of them say, "Boy, this is really tiring on the legs!" Although they weren't complaining, Malcolm didn't feel very optimistic about this beginning. Then the rain began to fall and continued steadily. Malcolm thought, "Maybe we'll see lightning in the distance. That way we could turn back and everyone could save face." He decided to keep them engaged in discussion as a way to keep them moving. Shortly thereafter, they started talking about a wager. The two girls proposed the following: "Since we had to listen to your CDs on the way here, how about this? If we make the summit, we get to listen to our music on the way home." They shook on it and headed up the mountain trail.

Although Malcolm hoped to make the summit, he was now beginning to perceive some benefits to turning back. They trudged upward, one step at a time. After three and a half hours, they reached the summit and gazed out on a panoramic view of the mountains, lakes, rivers, and ski trails of Maine and New Hampshire. As it turned out, they reached the summit before any of the high school students. While Malcolm had been worrying about the effects of not making the summit, these two nine-year-olds had been putting one foot in front of the other. At the top, their sense of accomplishment was evident. As they drove home to the sounds of Britney Spears and 'N Sync, Malcolm sensed that they probably would have been fine even if they had been compelled to turn back. They had *aimed* for four thousand feet, that was the important thing.

For parents and teachers, the challenge of "aiming high" and "letting go" is as tough a balancing act as there is. The Biggest Job workshops present two concepts that can help clarify this confusing Priority. These are called the One Thing and the Effort Savings Bank.

TWO CONCEPTS TO HELP US TO AIM HIGH

The One Thing

The One Thing is an abbreviated form of "the one thing I will do each day, not *try* to do." Most of us want to improve the quality of life in our families, our schools, our companies. Too often we are willing to settle for a vague commitment: "OK, let's commit to spending more time together as a family." When we make these commitments, we sincerely mean to live up to them. But then competing interests with very specific commitments (for example, the ones that keep us going from 9:00 A.M. to 5:00 P.M., Monday through Friday) encroach on this commitment, and we end up making another vague commitment a few weeks later.

The One Thing can keep us on track. It enables us to take control of our own progress. Consider the student having trouble at school. Students in this predicament often become overwhelmed with things that are out of their control:

- "I know the teacher doesn't like me."
- "I've created a bad reputation for myself."
- "I've fallen too far behind."
- "I just don't get this stuff!"

The student ends up focusing on what can't be done. We will ask that student, "Can you control whether or not Mr. XYZ will like you?" After we get the correct answer ("no"), we ask, "Can you control whether or not you show up for study hall five minutes early and leave five minutes late?" After we get the correct answer ("yes"), we reach agreement on the One Thing: "The one thing I will do each day is arrive at study hall five minutes early and stay five minutes late." Another prescription for the same symptoms might be "I will raise my hand at least twice (once to ask a question, once to make an observation) in every class." Rather than focusing on the obstacles to a destination, the One Thing helps us to visualize specific steps that can begin to take us there.

Malcolm remembers utilizing this concept when coaching women's soccer. After a few games, he analyzed the team's play and statistics and called a team meeting. To a girl whose shots frequently missed the net, he would say, "Twenty shots on net before every practice, that's your One Thing." Another student might be expected to do twenty head balls before practice and another might do twenty corner kicks. As the players began to endorse this system, it was common for them to discuss the concept routinely at team meetings: "I've messed up a lot of scoring chances lately, I'd like to switch my One Thing to twenty breakaways before practice." "Sally, maybe you should switch your One Thing to throw-ins." We kept records and each player could take pride in her progress rather than dwell on her shortcomings. The actual One Thing is not as important as the need for it to be publicly stated for all to hear.

The One Thing says, "Better to light a candle than to curse the darkness." When faced with a difficult challenge, a focus on the enormity of the obstacle before us can cause us to lose sight of the initial tangible action steps we must take before we can reasonably expect any positive momentum to occur.

As a boy, it was Malcolm's job to shovel the front walk of his home after snowstorms. He remembers his mother's advice: "Malcolm, never look ahead. Instead, look straight down and keep shoveling. Then, every once in a while, take a look behind you to admire the work you've done." The One Thing teaches us not to focus on the hardship that lies ahead. Instead, focus on what we're doing about it right now. Somehow, we will arrive at the right destination, be it the front door with shovel in hand, the end of a difficult task, or the beginning of a new view of ourselves.

THE EFFORT SAVINGS BANK

Malcolm literally stumbled over the concept of the Effort Savings Bank on a Brooklyn subway platform after having just dropped out of the New York City Marathon at mile thirteen in 1986. It was a disappointing day in many respects, but out of the failure came a valuable discovery. The concept behind the Effort Savings Bank is simple: Any effort I expend toward my best or toward helping others toward their best goes into an imaginary savings bank where it accrues interest and will be returned to me in the future, perhaps even when I least expect it.

The following story comes from Malcolm's personal journal, written shortly after he completed his first marathon, a year after he had dropped out in Brooklyn. He believes that the work he put into that first marathon paid off when he tackled his second. He reasons, "Even if I'm wrong, I'm learning that there is no harm in believing this." Here's part of the story:

I pressed onward past the Mile 18 marker. I was tired, but I got a burst of confidence from the knowledge that each step forward from that point would be a Personal Best of sorts. I had never run eighteen miles before. From here on, I would have the satisfaction of knowing that every step I took would mark the farthest I had ever run. It was exciting running with 25,000 colleagues. It was also around this point that I discovered a personal truth I believe is the key to the marathon.

Kurt Hahn, founder of the Outward Bound Schools, once said, "Your disability is your opportunity." The disabled runners at the NYC Marathon and the courage they displayed in pursuing the opportunity offered by the marathon were inspirations to me. I saw:

- Many wheelchair entrants.
- A woman with two artificial legs hobbling along on First Avenue.
- A man with a steel rod for a leg with a shoe attached at the end.
- A blind man being led by the hand of a volunteer. He would be led to another volunteer farther on down the road who would help him press on to another volunteer, and so on.
- The man who lost the lower half of his body in Vietnam who starts the race at 5:00 A.M. He wears heavily padded gloves and "runs" on his fists. He will finish four days later when he will be greeted at the finish line by NYC Marathon officials, afforded the same respect all finishers receive, nothing more and nothing less.

I saw the first wheelchair near the end of the Verrazano Narrows Bridge. I was struck by the extent to which the other runners, presumably veteran marathoners, went out of their way to cheer this woman on. I wondered if they might be making a mistake by sapping their strength. What I learned a few hours later was very much to the contrary: They were making an investment in their own marathons.

As the race continued I continued to be struck by the extent of the rapport between the abled and disabled marathoners. It was clear that the runners who were cheering on the wheelchair entrants were among the more confident participants in the race. I wondered to myself, "Am I missing something?" It then dawned on me that a reciprocity of energy was occurring between the runners and the wheelchair participants. Those in the chairs seemed to move their arms faster; the runners appeared to receive a booster shot of resolve.

The runners' words of encouragement seemed to say, "I respect you. Others have succeeded at what you're attempting to do. Keep pushing onward!" This encouragement served as an elixir for the efforts of the disabled and a reciprocal strength served of inestimable value to the runners. They became inspired by the courage of the disabled, who seemed to be saying, "If I can keep pushing this chair forward, you can certainly do the same with your legs." It was as though a bond of trust had formed between the two.

As I ran up First Avenue, I thought to myself, "When in Rome . . ." Thus, I began to go out of my way to encourage other runners and wheelchair participants. I watched the woman hobbling on her artificial legs and made a silent vow to finish the race in her honor. Simultaneously, I offered a few words of encouragement. I believe we helped each other finish.

Many other runners have told similar stories. A student of mine ran in his first marathon the following year in Boston. His confidence and his legs began to falter as he approached the seventeen-mile marker. At the very moment when he was going to quit a senior citizen pierced this eighteen-year-old's negative meditation. The senior citizen said, "I won't quit if you don't." An old salt of the roads, he sensed the weakening resolve of his younger colleague. They trudged onward through Wellesley and Newton, exchanging clipped phrases every half mile or so. About four miles from the finish, the old man turned to Ken and said, "I've got to drop out. You can go it alone. Finish for both of us." Ken understood. With tears in his eyes, he jogged on to the finish line at the Prudential Center, never to see his mentor again.

The concept of the Effort Savings Bank can release us from undue worry about the outcome of our efforts. We simply try to concentrate on the input and trust that good things will eventually result. If we try to do something and fail, we try to imagine that our efforts will materialize on some future endeavor. If we are successful at something, there's no harm in assuming that our success has been due, in part, to efforts on past endeavors, some that we may not even remember. The Effort Savings Bank has enhanced our lives considerably and has added value to countless numbers of student's and parent's.

We saw how it can play out with an experience our fourth-grade daughter had. All girls in grades 4–6 in our town had been invited to try out for a basketball travel team. Being a basketball town, scores of girls showed up. The local "buzz" said that it was unusual for a fifth grader, let alone a fourth grader, to be selected. Assuming our daughter would not be selected, we became concerned about the letdown she would feel. That's when we started touting a family motto around the house: "We always show up; we never quit."

The gym where the tryout was held was full of spirited kids, clipboard-toting coaches, and anxious parents. We were tremendously proud of the way Mahalia hustled from start to finish. Although she was not selected, we told her how impressed we were with her attitude and effort. It was obvious that she was not depressed. On the contrary, her self-esteem had been boosted by the day's activities and the knowledge that she had given her best. If that were the end of the story, this would be another nice anecdote supporting the Priority of "Set High Expectations." However, the story continues toward an even happier ending.

A few weeks later, we received a call from a local father who was assembling his own travel team. He had called the local high school coach and had asked if he knew any girls who might fit the bill. The coach, remembering her from the earlier tryout, suggested our daughter as one who was eager to play and willing to work. Our daughter joined this new team and had a great experience playing a sport she has come to love. In her case, the Effort Savings Bank paid off a dividend directly related to the effort she expended. Although she might dismiss this new opportunity as coincidence, we know she never would have gotten this call had she failed to show up for the earlier tryout. That's what can happen with the Effort Savings Bank when we aim high and let go.

As teachers, we have found teenagers to be quick to embrace the concept of the Effort Savings Bank. In school meetings, we will ask, "Has there ever been a time when you have put your very best effort into something only to find nothing good comes of it?" They will then raise their hands and offer several examples:

- I studied all night for a final exam, but I flunked it anyway.
- I put all my effort into making the team, but I got cut anyway.
- I memorized all my lines for the school play, but someone else got the part.
- I got up the nerve to ask a girl to the prom, but she shot me down.

Then we will ask, "Has there ever been a time when something really good came your way, but you clearly hadn't earned your good fortune?" The students might then respond:

- I wrote the term paper off the top of my head, and the teacher said it was absolutely first-rate!
- After not scoring a point the entire game, I threw a "Hail Mary" in the final seconds to win the game.
- I tried out for a "bit" part; the director gave me the lead role.
- I was sitting by the phone trying to get up my nerve and the girl of my dreams called me and asked for a date!

After we have a good laugh about some of the responses, we then ask, "Is there any harm in believing that these examples of good fortune are actually dividends paid off for the effort you put into those tasks that didn't work out as you had hoped?" They tend to get the point. A popular saying at the Hyde Schools reflects this thinking: "The harder I work, the luckier I get." The Effort Savings Bank can help kids aim high with a positive attitude and genuine effort.

The One Thing and the Effort Savings Bank are concepts that can help "put us in play." Furthermore, their value is not limited to teenagers. A Hyde father talks about a "moment of truth" in his early teens when he learned the value of staying in the game:

> One of the things about outcomes is that we never really know what the outcome is. We can think, if we do this, this will happen, but we never really know. One example comes back to me. I was in junior high and I was a dweeby kind of kid who played in the band (not that the band was bad) and wasn't very tough. I finally decided that I needed to polish my image. One day the answer came as they announced football tryouts over the loudspeaker. Tomorrow the city bus was going to take anyone who wanted to go down to the stadium for practice. I thought, this was the thing for me! So I went down and went through all the spring training. I remember the bus started out with forty kids, and by the end of the spring there were eight kids. Everyone had quit. I was not a big kid and I was getting knocked around pretty well. I certainly was not used to being treated that way.
>
> Then summer practice started. It started in June; in July we started putting on the helmet and hitting the pads. In August you went out twice a day. I was making this enormous effort. Our coach had laid out the deal: No one was going to get cut from the team. If you stuck it out, you would get a jersey and dress out. So we worked our way through summer practice and one morning I woke up and said to myself, "I don't need to get beat up like this. I can't do it. I am going to quit." So I went downstairs and told my dad. My dad didn't really say anything. We had a car pool and he said, "Well, today's my day for the car pool and I'm not taking these kids alone. You need to ride with me and take them down to football and you can tell them the car pool's off."

So we rode down to the high school (I hadn't said a word) and the car doors opened and everyone jumped out. I sat in the front seat. Nobody said a word. My friends just looked at me, closed the door, and walked off. The minute the door was closed and we started to drive away, I knew that it was the wrong decision, that I didn't want to quit. It was a real struggle and I was too proud to say, "Stop the car and turn around; I've done the wrong thing." So we drove home and I sat around the house. An hour later, the phone rang and it was the back-field coach. He said, "Are you sick?" I say, "No, coach, I've decided football's not my game. I don't think I'm gonna play." (I still wouldn't let go.) All he said was, "I think there might be a place for you on the team if you stick it out." And that was just the crack I needed.

I tore downstairs and asked my dad to take me back to practice. When I got there, the skull session had ended and everyone was already dressed. The coach looked at me strangely, but nobody said a word. I know he knew what had happened.

As I reflect on that today, I think about that coach. If he is still alive today, I'm sure he has no idea that it was one of the key moments of my life. If I had quit, stayed home for three more hours and really quit, it would have changed the way I thought about myself probably for the rest of my life. In my own mind, I would have been the kid who could have played but chose to quit. It was a coach being willing to put himself in play that kept me going. We just don't know the outcomes. That is why it is so important to constantly keep yourself in play.

Setting high expectations while letting go of outcomes is one of the toughest balancing acts we must attempt as parents. In order to begin on the right foot, we will likely need to examine our own experiences in our families of origin as we inevitably carry these experiences into our parenting. As one mother writes about the expectations in her family of origin:

When I was younger, I always wanted to be the best at something, and if I wasn't the best, I wasn't going to do it. The outcome was always the only thing that was important. And so, I would have these high expectations, but if they didn't get me to someplace that was great, then I was a failure. That wreaked havoc on my personal life because I didn't have anything to feel good about if I didn't have this great outcome in the end. I have learned that if you don't let go of outcomes for your kids, then you can really help them self-destruct.

Perhaps if we model letting go of the outcomes of our own expectations, our children will learn to do the same.

FAMILY EXERCISES AND ACTIVITIES

Effort Bank

Materials: Shoe box with lid taped down and slit in the top, white slips of paper, pencil

Time: 30 to 60 seconds to make deposit; box may stay out for weeks, months, etc.

Explanation: Refer to the explanation of the Effort Savings Bank on page 159. Write the family name on the shoe box and place it in a high-traffic family area (kitchen or family room). Ask family members to make out a deposit slip every time they extend an extra effort. Examples include:

Trying out for an athletic team
Learning a new skill (computer, left-hand dribble)
Reaching out to someone who is difficult
Speaking up in a group situation
Singing
Learning to dance
Working out

After the box has taken deposits for a period of time, open the box and sit as a family and talk about the efforts that were made. Some questions to think about:

- What has happened as a result of that effort?
- How did you feel at the time?
- How do you feel about it now?
- What does it take to try new things?

The One Thing

Materials: A sheet of paper, pen, tape
Time: 10 minutes to create sheet; weekly or monthly check-in
Explanation: Have each family member come up with a One Thing that they *will do* each day, not *try* to do. Write each goal on a sheet and put it up on the refrigerator. You may also put smaller index cards at the corner of bathroom mirrors. Then weekly or monthly, check in with the family. Have each person go around and talk about how their One Thing is going. If they are not doing it, what is getting in the way? You may celebrate the person/persons who are following their One Thing by giving them a special dinner or activity. Some examples of One Things:

- Walking/working out thirty minutes each day.
- Talking to a family member five minutes each day.
- Writing one e-mail or letter to friend a day.
- Spending five minutes reading about current events.
- Sitting still for ten minutes a day to reflect.
- Shooting fifty foul shots a day.

The One Thing goals will change and need to be updated. Keep it simple and doable, but commit to doing it daily!

Family Reach Project

Materials: Only what may be needed for each specific project, camera, and scrapbook

Time: Varies depending on project

Explanation: Sit down and talk as a family about doing something as a family that will demand everyone's best effort. Some examples might include:

- Spend a day in a soup kitchen
- Yard work for an elderly person in your neighborhood
- All learn how to dance (disco, ballroom, etc.)
- Learn about another culture as a family
- Climb a mountain

The point here is to set a goal that will have family members reaching beyond their grasp as well as test everyone. It may be more difficult for some than others, but no one should feel absolutely comfortable. Then figure out the specifics of how it will be carried out. (You may find it easier to do a one-day project at first to get your sea legs.) Assign someone in the family to take pictures and another to get quotes from family members throughout the project. Put the images and quotes together in a family album and place it on the coffee table to refer to later.

Important: Let go of the outcome of this project. It may be good or horrible, but if you aim high, you will all learn something to draw upon again and again.

JOURNALING QUESTIONS

1. What were the expectations I felt as a child growing up?
2. Who were the people in my life who demanded my best? How did I feel then and how do I feel today about them?

3. Describe an incident (or time) in my upbringing when I set high expectations and went after something. What happened?
4. Was there ever a time as a kid when I quit on something? Explain.
5. What are the expectations in my family today? How much do we hold each other to our best?
6. Is there any difference in the degree to which I hold outside people in my life (coworkers, friends, etc.) to their best and in the degree to which I demand the best from my family?
7. How difficult is it for me to let go of "outcomes" in myself? In my children?
8. Describe a time when I "raised the bar" on either myself or someone else. What happened? How did I feel?
9. What is my greatest fear about my own high expectations?
10. When have I been inspired by the commitment to high expectations?

Priority 5,
Value Success and Failure

"When the One Great Scorer comes to write against your name, He marks not that you won or lost, but how you played the game."

—Grantland Rice

This Priority is closely linked to the previous one. We cannot value failure if we are overly preoccupied with outcomes. Although life must be lived forward, it can only be understood in reverse. We comprehended many of the concepts in this book only after we had tried to teach or parent with approaches contrary to them. After all, most of us do not seek failure. Furthermore, our initial reaction to failure is sadness or discouragement. Often, time is necessary for us to understand the value of our failures. Malcolm notes how he learned to Value Success and Failure as a young coach:

In my early days as a coach, I was overly focused on my teams' win-loss records. I remember taking my 13–2 women's basketball team to the New England Tournament. In the first round, we drew a strong team from Phillips Andover Academy. The official tossed the ball up for the opening jump ball, and it seemed that before it came back down, we were losing by fifteen points. When they pressed us, it seemed as though they had six girls on the court. We soon began settling for "long bomb prayers" on offense. I'll never forget the look on the faces of my team during the series of desperation time-outs I called. It was a look that said: Who changed the script, Coach? We know what to do when we're winning. We have no idea what to when we're losing. We never really went over that.

Things never really improved in that contest. As we headed home from the tournament a bit earlier than I had hoped, I tried to put the season in perspective. It wasn't long before I realized that I had been a big part of the problem. I was overly focused on our win-loss record. I was proud of that 13–2 record. In fact, we had avenged both losses later in the season. Thus, when we entered the tournament, we may well have been the only team that could boast that it had beaten every team it had played. And yet, here we were, headed home after the first round. It soon dawned on me that the 13–2 record probably hurt us. We probably would have been better off had we played a few superior teams that would have exposed weaknesses that otherwise never really surfaced until we hit the tournament.

The focus on success was, and is, as deeply ingrained in Malcolm as it is in our culture. To add a touch of irony, this focus is also one of the great strengths of the American social fabric, so long as it is kept in proper perspective. (It's one thing to get back on the horse that threw you; it's another to begin manipulating your schedule so that you never ride one capable of throwing you!) In Malcolm's case, he required a few more years to gain that perspective. Eventually, he began to visualize the ideal athletic season schedule, which he calls "a season of thirds":

A third of our games we should be expected to win;
A third of our games we should be expected to lose;
A third of our games should be 50/50 propositions.

Eventually, Malcolm grew to value the anticipation of wondering how the players would execute in games they ought to win. He wanted to see how well they kept their poise when they were overmatched. He wanted to see how the team's focus and sportsmanship held up in the heat of truly balanced competition. The students Malcolm first coached are now in their forties. When they meet to talk of "old times," they rarely speak of win-loss records. They generally speak of the lessons they learned in adversity. These lessons stand the test of time long after the records are forgotten. They bear out the wisdom of Grantland Rice's words. He was right. It *is* how you play the game. We *do* learn more from our failures than our successes. If this is true, why, then, do we have such a hard time synchronizing our parenting and our teaching in accordance with this wisdom? Probably because we have one foot in the Achievement Culture and another in the Character Culture. Where is the weight of your foot?

In the previous chapter, we noted how our experiences in our families of origin can influence our difficulties with setting expectations and letting go of outcomes. Similarly, this dynamic can also have a significant impact on our perceptions of success and failure. A Hyde mother writes:

> My parents wanted to protect me from failure, among other things. Things were done the right way and you couldn't do it the wrong way. You couldn't find out for yourself. I remember an incident in my early teens. I got it in my head that I wanted to build a birdhouse. I told my dad about this and he was thrilled. He didn't have a boy, but he and I could do stuff together. So we rushed out to the hardware store and he got all the right stuff and we went down to his workroom and I had to watch him build the whole thing because he wanted it done just the right way. He wanted to build the perfect birdhouse. I think about that a lot with my own kids: I don't want to build their birdhouses for them.

Thus, to repeat a theme that helps form the core of this book, we must come to understand our own upbringing as a prerequisite to implementing a new vision for our families. Sometimes this understanding can help us move beyond some of the hang-ups we associate with our own childhoods. A Hyde mother writes:

How was success and failure handled in my family? My father would never look at what I got right in the stuff I brought home from school. He would usually look at what I got wrong. I think I have tended to pass that along to my children. It was done out of love, but it didn't help us grow.

On another note, our experiences in the workplace can have a profound influence on our perceptions of success and failure. This dynamic was discussed at the beginning of the book in the Who Am I? exercise when we looked at the Achievement Culture versus the Character Culture. A Hyde father writes:

It has been real important for me to be valued by my colleagues, and there have been a couple of times during my career when a grant proposal was not funded or something of that sort. It was very devastating for me, really threw me for a loop, and it took me a long time to recover. In some of those instances, I think that in the end, I responded well to the failure and learned from it. It took me off into directions I wouldn't otherwise have gone. Yet it was so hard at the time.

One of the most common tendencies we see is when parents lead double lives in regard to home and the workplace. They act in accordance with the expectations of the Achievement Culture at work (a friend calls it "the permanent game face") and then try to change personas in an attempt to reflect the Character Culture once they cross the thresholds of their front doors at home after work. Kids see clear through it all.

The Hyde Schools hire a fair number of teachers fresh out of the finest American colleges and universities. In one job interview, an honors graduate from one such school said something to the effect of:

I feel a bit cheated. I did everything they told me to do for sixteen years. Why don't I feel better about myself? I remember my adviser winking as he encouraged me to drop a challenging course that threatened to lower my grade point average. At the time, I followed his advice with enthusiasm. Today I find myself wondering if I wouldn't have been better off had I struggled with the course until the bitter end. I ended up with a great transcript balanced with an uncomfortable degree of self-doubt. Maybe I would have been better off with a shakier transcript balanced with the self-knowledge that I had persevered. Why did no one advise me to follow that course of action?

What this person and others like her have come to understand (usually after graduation) is that they experienced an education that had little use for failure. That's right . . . *failure*. While failure may not be an intended goal for anyone, it ought to be a fairly regular outcome for everyone, especially for students. While most of us give lip service to the notion that we learn more from our failures than we do from our successes, few of our homes and even fewer of our schools are actually structured to emulate this truth. Far too many students are encouraged to avoid any circumstances where failure might result. Again, the Aptitude Culture eventually squeezes out the value of failure.

We spoke with a friend who attended a high school graduation where the valedictorian stood before his entire high school community and explained the strategy he had employed to earn his position of distinction. He noted how he had carefully selected those courses where he knew he would succeed and avoided those courses that might cause his grade point average to suffer. In his speech he noted how he was not proud of the approach he took and he stated that he intended to exercise more intellectual courage and genuine curiosity in college than he had exhibited in high school. What was the motivation behind this student's actions? Did he experience an education intended to build his character and intellect, or did he experience an education intended to satisfy adult expectations?

A NEW VIEW FOR PARENTS
AND TEACHERS

We think it's time for a new view of parenting and school. Perhaps a new emphasis on attitude, effort, and character could result in a new family, a new school, a new community, and ultimately a new culture. In any case, schools and families would undoubtedly be healthier with such realigned priorities. The Aptitude Culture is ultimately debilitating for *all* students, however they're categorized.

Before we can truly value Attitude over Aptitude in our teaching or our parenting, we must be aware of and think about the old habits and pervasive culture that actually values these qualities in reverse. We believe American schools and families are trapped in valuing talent as a means to success. The 10 Priorities are designed to help jar us out of that paradigm, to help us move from being preoccupied with talent to focusing on character, from being preoccupied with success to focusing on fulfillment. Many families and schools are far more entrenched in the "talent/success" trap than they realize. Consider some of the oft-repeated phrases we parents utter, albeit with the best of intentions, in our efforts to inspire our children on to a better performance:

- "I don't care about your grades as long as you try your best."
- "I don't care what you do with your life as long as you are happy."
- "You're a very bright student; you simply need to apply yourself."
- "If you will work hard, you can be and do anything you want in life."

As discussed earlier in this book, we break with convention by stating that we believe this last phrase is false. Furthermore, we even believe that it can do more harm than good. While the statement might encourage children to momentarily try harder, it fails to divulge the inevitable unpleasant stops we will make along the way to our destiny. It does not encourage kids to seek a deeper purpose in life or a different destiny than we might have intended for ourselves. The following is Malcolm's story of a former student, one we taught in the early eighties.

STEVE

Steve came to us from Washington, D.C., as a participant in a scholarship program we have conducted for many years with the Boys and Girls Clubs. He was a very serious, polite, and dedicated young man from the very first day of his freshman year. I would evaluate him as one of the hardest-working students we had in the eighties, indeed one of the hardest-working students we have encountered. He was also an especially talented basketball player. During his years with us, our basketball team was one of the premier prep school teams in New England. A number of our students went on to play Division I basketball on full scholarships, a goal to which Steve committed himself from the very start. He worked hard in the classroom to satisfy the scholastic requirements for competitive college admissions, and there was no basketball player in our program who worked harder than he did.

To this day, I might rank him as the most adept and skilled ball handler Hyde has ever had. He had an uncanny court vision that was undoubtedly enhanced by the fact that he was also a first-rate quarterback on the football team and was accustomed to finding open teammates under pressure. He was also a very unselfish team player who looked to pass before looking to shoot. He was a coach's dream in that he had impeccable sportsmanship, never lost his cool, and could always be counted upon to maintain control of a game in the pressure-packed final minutes. He also had one significant drawback: He was five feet nine inches tall. If you know basketball, you know there aren't many five-foot-nine players in major college basketball. In any case, Steve congratulated his older teammates as they received college scholarship offers and anxiously waited his turn as a senior.

No scholarship offers came. One coach at a southern university offered him the chance to enroll at his school and attempt to make the team as a "walk on." (An invitation to take the risk of trying out for the team with the understanding that successfully making the team will result in financial assistance. However, if the individual fails to make the team, he or she is responsible for the full financial burden.) Having no other offers and without the money to pay for college on his own, Steve decided to play the hand he was dealt. He went to the college and tried out for the basketball team. Although he made the team, he ended up holding down a spot near the end of the bench and rarely saw playing time. He strove to transcend his disappointment, hanging with it throughout the year in accordance with his long-standing work ethic. Refusing to let go of his dream, he transferred to a university on the West Coast where yet another coach offered him the same "walk on" invitation. Once again, he accepted the challenge, tried out, and made the team. Once again he found himself glued firmly to the bench.

After staying with it throughout the year, he took an honest inventory of his standing as a basketball player and as a student. He came to a simple conclusion, one at odds with his dream: "Maybe it simply wasn't meant to be." Given Steve's substantial investments in his Effort Savings Bank, it's not hard to imagine how tough it was for him to come to this conclusion.

Steve decided to transfer his high effort from the basketball court and apply it to the classroom, making the commitment to become a top student. The result: After graduating in the upper reaches of his class, he went on to earn an MBA at Harvard Business School with additional graduate work at MIT's Sloan School of Management. Today he is a successful and respected Wall Street analyst.

So, *can* you be whatever you want to be as long as you're willing to pay the price? Well, Steve deeply wanted to be a college basketball player, and he unquestionably paid the price to do it. And yet he did not accomplish his goal. Now, let's take a deeper look. Although Steve may have fallen short of his dream, the overwhelming majority of those he played basketball with (or against) would be extremely tempted to exchange places with him today. Although he didn't achieve his goal, Steve seems well along the way on the path to his destiny.

Malcolm has told Steve's story to many students. Its message is simple: Even if you go after your dreams with your very best effort, there is no guarantee you will attain them. There *is* the guarantee that you will experience failure along the way. However, you can trust that these failures will lead you to destinations you will be very excited about. You will lead an exciting, fulfilling life. This is the wonder of the Effort Savings Bank discussed in the previous Priority. Steve went through some very difficult times and often thought about quitting. He ultimately transferred the work ethic from basketball to his studies. He began making "deposits" and reinvesting those he had already made in a separate "account." He aimed high. He paid the price, and he had to let go of the desired outcome in order to connect with his destiny.

Thus, perhaps we might amend the earlier statement as follows: *If you work hard, you will maximize your chances of connecting with your destiny and of discovering a deeper purpose in life.*

Before they can call upon their children to risk failure, parents must also be willing to model the idea for their children. One mother writes:

> For the past ten years I've been the one waiting in the warmth, hot chocolate in hand, for my family to come off the mountain from the day of skiing. I recently faced the fact that the only reason I didn't ski was fear. It had nothing to do with the cold, or my nonathletic ability, or my being too old or too fat. It was fear alone that held me back. Well, last winter I took a few lessons and this winter I took a few more. I have just returned from a week of skiing in Utah on the highest mountains I have ever seen.
>
> The work is difficult, as I'm a bit old, a little too fat, and a lot out of shape. The fact that I'm not naturally athletic means I have to work harder. There are times it feels more like torture than pleasure. And ever present is that fear. I keep telling myself that my "midlife crisis"

is to challenge myself in just such an area, one that is difficult and tor-turous and painful. Now after a run, there's a wonderful feeling of pride and accomplishment; it's been a long time since I've felt that way. The good feelings outweigh the fears.

MORE ON THE CULT OF SELF-ESTEEM

Aiming high and valuing success and failure are not merely offered as suggestions. We believe that failing to honor them can have a much higher cost than a mere missed opportunity. If we fail to aim high, we run the risk of falling victim to the Cult of Self-Esteem, as discussed earlier in this book. Malcolm elaborated on this concept in a high school commencement address in 1998:

> One question educators often ask: Are kids different (read: worse) than they were in the "good old days"? I don't know the answer to that one either, but I doubt it. I do, however, believe that the way they are taught is different. I believe that those who work with kids—schools, teachers, parents—have been locked in the debilitating grip of what I call the "Cult of Self-Esteem." I suspect it grew out of the Values Clarification emphasis of the early seventies. In any case, the approach seems to say: If we make kids feel good about themselves, they will do great things. Our approach here at Hyde looks at this through the other end of the telescope: If kids do great things, they will feel good about themselves. The former sees self-esteem as a gift in the form of a birthright that can be bestowed simply for the asking. The latter sees self-esteem as hard-earned. If the broken wheel serves as a metaphor for why we might have stalled as a culture, I believe that the Cult of Self-Esteem has contributed directly to many of the specific problems we have in our schools today—drug usage, absenteeism, cheating, guns and violence, for example. If self-esteem can be easily given, it can just as easily be taken away. On the other hand, when self-esteem is earned through one's actions, it may be harder to gain, but it can never be taken away.

Self-esteem is a laudable goal. Students should graduate from our schools with a healthy amount of it. Parents and teachers ought to direct their efforts toward developing it. Unfortunately, self-esteem has been cheapened by many of the very people who claim to nurture it. Rather than regard it as an inspirational force in the lives of our students and children, we have come to regard it as a rationale or justification for unmet expectations or negative behavior. For example, it has become common to respond to a child who is failing with "He cannot succeed until he has self-esteem." We might fail to reprimand another who is "acting out" because we "don't want to damage his self-esteem." Let us treat self-esteem as the valuable quality it is. Let us view it as a rare combination, consisting of attitude, character, conscience, and hard work. It most certainly is not free for the taking. It is, however, within reach of anyone willing to pay the price. That price includes "aiming high." That price is a bit easier to pay when we let go of the outcomes.

FAMILY EXERCISES AND ACTIVITIES

Essay Assignment on Success and Failure

Materials: Paper, pens
Time: 20 to 30 minutes to write, another 20 to 30 minutes to share and discuss
Explanation: Ask each family member to complete this assignment and bring it to the next family meeting:

- In the last year, what has been your greatest success? Explain.
- In the last year, what has been your greatest failure? Explain.

(Younger children may just write a few sentences; others need only write two to four paragraphs.)

Sit down as a family and share your papers. You may comment on each paper and talk about why success and failure are important teachers in life. Put the letters away for a period of time (six months to a year), and then bring them out to discuss again. Do family members feel differently about what they perceived as successes and failures?

Success/Failure Collages

Materials: Magazines, newspapers, scissors, glue
Time: 30 to 60 minutes
Explanation: Divide the family into two teams. Have the first team create a collage on how "success" is portrayed in the media and society (for example, cigarettes ads showing strong images of success with smoking: "You get the car and the girl when you smoke"). Have the second team create a collage on the media portrayal of "failure." Allow your children to interpret the two terms as they understand them. Then put them up and talk about the Achievement Culture that we live in where failure is not valued and success is often defined by the final outcome. Talk about the idea that the only real failure is the failure not to try something and often what we thought was failure at one point, ultimately opened another opportunity for us.

Time Line

Materials: Paper (long computer paper works great), family photos, markers, tape
Time: 30 to 45 minutes
Explanation: This is a great family exercise and may even become part of the family written history. Take the paper and draw a line across the middle, creating a top and a bottom half. On the top of the page, write down "moments of truth," "important moments," and "highs and lows." You may also include family photos that show either you

at the specific time period or the actual event (tape these right onto the time line). Examples of such moments include:

- Moving to new place
- Trying out for the team
- First date
- Accident of some kind
- Having a child
- Death in the family
- Summer camp

On the bottom half of the page, list the feelings that you were having at that time. They can be feelings about the specific event or general feelings that you had at that time in your life. Put the chart up and share with the family. (Younger children will have fewer experiences to draw upon, but still have important moments to share.) You may even want to create a "family time line" at some point.

JOURNALING QUESTIONS

1. How were "success" and "failure" handled in my upbringing?
2. What were some of the important "successes" in my childhood? Explain.
3. What were some of the important "failures" in my childhood? Explain.
4. How do I feel about those experiences today?
5. How do I feel about my child's successes?
6. How do I handle my child's struggles/failures?
7. Have I ever tried to manipulate the outcome of one of my children's potential "failures"?
8. How do I deal with "success" and "failure" in my family today?
9. Have my children ever seen me fail at anything? Explain.
10. How could I help my family understand the long-term view of both "success" and "failure"?

Priority 6,
Allow Obstacles
to Become Opportunities

In the face of hard times, we often tend to wish for a differ-ent set of circumstances. This Priority suggests that instead we should wish for a different set of attitudes.

All of us come up against hard times personally, professionally, and in our families. In the face of hard times, we often tend to wish for a different set of circumstances. This Priority suggests that instead we should wish for a different set of *attitudes*. As new parents, many of us start with an ideal vision of what family life should be like. We imagine a living, breathing Hallmark greeting card depicting a won-derfully connected team of people gliding through life with sunlit smiling faces accompanied by inspirational background music. Obstacles are something to be dispensed with quickly in order to allow the family to move down that virtual yellow-brick road.

Recently Laura was talking to an old friend whose children are grown and who now have children of their own. At onc point in the conversation they were talking about the struggles of someone else's child and Laura's friend said, "I was lucky. My children never gave me any trouble." Laura nodded in agreement almost unconsciously, as if to say, "How great." Later on she thought about it: Was that really true? If it was true, was she really so lucky? The urge to downplay difficult situations is common to all of us. Think about all those rail-thin models who casually claim, "I eat cheeseburgers, French fries, and just love banana splits!" *Riiiight!* The truth is probably much closer to the idea that they are working overtime to stay thin. We can all fall into the trap of nonchalance. For some strange reason, our society has decided that outcomes achieved with little effort are worthy of awe.

In the Biggest Job workshops, we ask parents to throw out whatever words and phrases that come to mind when they hear the word *obstacle*. Some responses come up again and again.

Obstacle
Problem
Something to fix
Barrier
Hurdle
Get around
Get over
Embarrassment
Struggle
Uncertainty
Wanting to hide it

Then we ask parents to do the same for the word *opportunity*.

Opportunity
Something good
Vision
Unknown
Belief
Positive
Growth
Taking advantage of situation

What a difference in these two categories! We have seen a powerful connection between the way in which we view obstacles and their ultimate role in our journey as people and parents. While our society will hail the individual who overcomes amazing odds (e.g., Helen Keller overcoming her deafness and blindness to become one of the most outstanding individuals of the twentieth century), we still perpetuate the image of the ideal parent as someone who always knows what to do, who can solve any problem. Our children are supposed to achieve and naturally become upstanding, morally grounded individuals. What's more, all of this achievement is supposed to look effortless. How many times have you found yourself visualizing such a scene with your family, only to find that not all the players have been clued in to their roles in that dream?

This Priority is about letting go of the myth that problems are a sign of weakness and realizing that the opposite may be closer to the truth. Obstacles come as a result of high expectations. The more you strive to accomplish, the more you will be asked to struggle. Problems are evidence of the struggle that necessarily comes from higher expectations and the courage to take risks. If we can start to value obstacles and struggles, we will not only liberate our families from the trap of having to look good all the time, we will ignite a powerful energy to foster growth within our families.

One mother shares the role obstacles have played in her life:

Obstacles have done more to form who I am today than successes. It started early on as an only child. My parents both worked and thus were not home a lot. I really learned independence. Then I had learning disabilities. I can remember sitting in the "bluebirds"—we had the bluebird class and the redbird class—and that's where you read out loud. Despite the fact that nobody ever described the difference between the bluebirds and the redbirds, we all knew that the bluebirds were the slower group.

I could not figure it out. I knew that I wasn't stupid, but I couldn't do some of the things that the other kids could do. What it did was force me to work through it and learn to read. It all helped me discover who I am today and what I am capable of. I have a daughter with a chronic disease, but learning how to deal with those real obstacles and moving through them to the next spot has been where the biggest growth has occurred.

Obstacles come in many forms. Some shake us to our core, while others may seem like nuisances in our lives. All have the potential to either enslave us or move us forward. Malcolm shares a childhood obstacle that turned out to be a blessing:

"Gauld, Coach could time your sprints with a sundial!"

I heard a lot of comments like that from teammates and coaches on the athletic teams of my youth. Although they didn't diminish my love of athletics, they didn't exactly pump up my self-esteem. Whether trying to beat out a single to first base or skating after a loose hockey puck, I continually found myself the slowest player on all my teams. I remember being called "Flash" in the schoolyard in much the same way the biggest kid in school might be called "Tiny." My preoccupation with my speed, or lack thereof, began to color my psyche. Although I continued to play sports through high school, I never had the success I imagined in my childhood dreams. I did have some success in lacrosse and began to daydream about playing it in college. However, these dreams were tempered by my ever-present speed problem. I talked to my coaches and I intently watched my fleet-footed teammates in hopes of picking up clues.

In my senior year (1971–72) it just so happened that the U.S. Olympic Track Team was scheduled to train at nearby Bowdoin College prior to heading to Munich. There was great excitement in the area as local citizens anticipated the arrival of the Olympic athletes. One of the reasons they were coming to Bowdoin was to work with the college's renowned doctor, Daniel Hanley, a longtime U.S. Olympic physician. One day an inexplicable motivation possessed me to give Dr. Hanley a call at his office: "Dr. Hanley, I'm a local high school student. I understand that you are familiar with running techniques. Well, I have a problem: I'm slow. I'd like to be faster and I was wondering if you might help me." I can only wonder what he must have thought. Perhaps he was angry with his secretary for allowing the call to sneak through. In any case, he said, "Come on over to the track next Tuesday. Wear your sneakers and we'll have a look."

I arrived at the Bowdoin track at the appointed hour and Dr. Hanley asked me to sprint down the track a few times. I remember hoping that he was conjuring up some scheme that would result in my becoming fleet of foot. Panting, I asked if he had any suggestions for me. He stunned me with his response: "No. I can see the problem, but you've been running that way for so long that changing your stride might do more harm than good." He then proceeded to offer a thoughtful and reasonable explanation of the mechanics of my stride. I nodded, thanked him for his time, and nearly dissolved into tears before reaching my parents' car. I was feeling pretty down for the next few days. Then I remembered my goal: to someday be a college lacrosse player. I had bought into the premise that there was no way to do this without being fast. I began to toy with the idea that maybe it was possible to be slow and still accomplish the goal. Then and there I made a simple commitment to be the best stick-handler on any team I played on. I hoped to offset lack of speed with great stick work.

I did play college lacrosse, even ultimately setting a college record for most goals scored in a single game. The point of the story is not the success I experienced. The point is that an obstacle–my lack of speed–actually contributed to my eventual success. The initiative to seek the truth, coupled with Dr. Hanley's frank, dead-on diagnosis, led me to accept the obstacle. Then I sought the hidden opportunity. I doubt I would have developed my stick work had I been faster. What I once perceived as a curse was now perceived as a benefit.

Malcolm continues to get grief for his lack of swiftness but is still heavily into athletics as he approaches his fifties. Ironically enough, running has become a big part of his life. In fact, he has competed in 10Ks and has completed several marathons.

COMING TO GRIPS
WITH OBSTACLES AT HOME

Some obstacles hit like a tidal wave, sweeping us in a storm of feelings, emotions, and physical demands. It is difficult to find our feet as we struggle to get through each day. Summoning the courage to look for opportunities may begin only after we decide to move forward, step by painful step. This was the case in our family. We were crushed when doctors in Boston told us that our youngest child had been diagnosed with developmental delays. The diagnosis of mysterious medical terms went over our heads until we heard the word *autism*. The doctor's use of the "A" word hit both of us like a gunshot. We wanted to "stop the clock" and have a five-minute audience with God: "Ah, excuse me, God, but there must be some mistake. This isn't the son we ordered."

After a few days of tears, Laura took the lead. We would commit to the goal of "recovery." Then we rolled up our sleeves and began an intense journey to pull our son out of his world and into ours. In her book *Let Me Hear Your Voice,* Catherine Maurice, a mother who led her two autistic children to recovery, writes: "You need to work like it all depends on you and pray like it all depends on God." This became our mantra in working with our son.

Laura shares her thoughts on our journey with Harrison:

We were over the top when Harrison was born, the youngest of three children, rounding out the family. His two sisters were equally excited. Through the blur of caring for three young children, my memories of that time were wonderful. Harrison was a good baby and achieved all the developmental milestones his sisters did. I continued along with my job at the school and, as I had with the girls, often walked around with Harrison on my hip at work.

When he was almost two, I began to notice that he said very few words and seemed to enjoy sitting quietly by himself. My first fear was that he might be deaf. I would come up behind him and clap my hands in his ear. I voiced my fears to Malcolm and we would try to talk each other out of really worrying. "His sisters talk all the time so he doesn't need to." "Boys develop later than girls." As my fears continued to grow, I started to think that maybe something else was wrong. I saw how readily Harrison would zone out in front of a video. I thought about autism, but felt he didn't have some of the obvious signs. (Or what I thought were obvious signs—i.e., lack of emotional attachment and affection.) The nagging doubts continued. At the time, I was teaching and found myself reluctant to reach out to others to publicly share my concerns and fears about Harrison. I justified this by saying, "I work incredibly hard here and give my all. I do not need to bare my soul here."

The truth was I didn't really trust a process that I had taught for seventeen years. I had worked with individuals, pushing them to open up and share with their families. Now I needed to do the same. One night we were in a faculty seminar. This is a regularly scheduled gathering where the faculty get together to share their struggles and hopes and give feedback to each other. As I was sitting there, I could feel the emotion rising. The thought went through my head, "I need to get out of here because I don't want to share with these people." Something kept me in the room and I found myself starting to talk. The emotions quickly came as I shared my fears about Harrison with the group. After a few seconds of silence, people began to share feelings about their own families. They talked about similar fears. They talked about Harrison. They also just offered their support. As I listened, I felt a weight lift off. As a veteran Hyde teacher, I also learned a powerful lesson: Asking for help is an important action step (see Priority 9). I left that room with a sense of relief that my "secret" was out. I also left with a resolve to find some answers.

We took Harrison to a world-renowned children's hospital and scheduled him for daylong evaluation. The next day, we returned to hear from the diagnostic team. As I sat in the office, I felt I was having an out-of-body experience as others discussed my son. They gave him a diagnosis of PDD, pervasive developmental delay. I learned later that this diagnosis has different meanings to different people, but basically it means that the child's communicative capabilities lie somewhere on the autism spectrum. As they discussed treatment options in their flat clinical tone, my thoughts were reduced to figuring how I could get out of the room without completely breaking down. I couldn't look at my husband because I knew he would be close to tears and his rare displays of emotion would send me over the edge. We nodded as they suggested who we needed to speak with and we thanked them.

As we got out in the hall and pushed the elevator button, I slumped into Malcolm. I felt as if someone had kneed me in the gut and there was no wind in my throat in which to transmit sound. The tears fell down my face as we silently held hands in the elevator. The door opened a floor below and a young boy was wheeled into the elevator in a chair that almost looked like a bed. The boy was slumped over and drooling with an expressionless face looking off to the side. My heart went out to this child and for a few seconds I forgot about my own heartache. Was God trying to tell me something? A flicker of gratitude entered my heart. We went to my folks' house. My mother met me at the door with a big hug and her usual optimistic chatter. I only wanted to hold Harrison. As we drove him home to Maine that night, I found myself pulling him out of his car seat and cradling him in my arms.

After two days of crying intermittently, I was sitting in a meeting with the local child development coordinator when our speech therapist handed me a book titled *Let Me Hear Your Voice*. It was written by a mother who had two children diagnosed with autism. The book discusses the idea of "recovery" using an intensive teaching approach, which broke down the learning process into small steps. I got into my bed and read the book from cover to cover. Despite the pain of her tremendous struggle, there was hope. Not only did this woman lead her children to recovery, her story impacted the whole field of autism and brought attention to an approach called ABA, Applied Behavioral Analysis. As I was reading, I kept thinking, "I need to find this woman. If she can do this, we can, too." A few days later, I was talking to a friend on the phone. As I was explaining the book in rapid-fire sentences, she said quietly, "I think I know her." A few days later, the phone rang at 9:00 P.M. It was the author of *Let Me Hear Your Voice*.

Years ago, when I was the dean of students at Hyde, I would have many late-night calls about students. As I would talk to parents, often I would hear, "Slow down, I'm taking notes." I used to think, "Have these people no minds of their own? What I'm saying is basic common sense." Yet here I was, taking down almost every word that came out of this woman's mouth. The tears were coming down my face, but the feeling was entirely different. Suddenly, there was hope.

At some point over the next three days, we made the decision to raise the bar on Harrison and "recovery" became the motto that symbolized that expectation. We threw out the labels. While hearing the word *autism* was important because it woke us up to the truth about the real obstacles facing our son, I knew that if we invested too much into that label, we would accept far less than his best. I took much of the following year off and we mobilized a force of ABA teachers, speech therapists, Hyde students, and family. In order to be on the "team," the only requirement was a belief in the highest expectations. As we discussed in Priority 4, letting go of the ultimate outcome is difficult but essential if you are to really aim high.

Harrison was not quite two and a half when he began his formal home program, one of intense interaction for thirty hours per week. As hard as that was, every other waking moment was filled with human contact. ABA starts with simple expectations accompanied by uncompromising standards: eye contact, imitation, standing and sitting on command, and so on. It involves three basic components: command, correction, and reinforcement. A command is given, "Harrison, look." This is known as the stimulus discriminate. Then, after a few seconds, either a correction–"That's looking, Harrison"–or a reinforcement for the correct response–"Great looking, Harrison." All the responses are charted daily so that progress can be objectively monitored. As opposed to sitting around and saying "I think he's doing much better," all one had to do was look at the data. Once he accomplished something in his room, then we moved out of his room to generalize the skill.

The first two months were some of the toughest times of my life. I watched my happy-go-lucky son with the incredible grin cry and scream as he was asked to perform basic tasks. In order to be truly effective, I needed to remain objective when his pleading eyes sought me out to rescue him. My training as a Hyde teacher allowed me to rise to the challenge, but the nights were a different story. The resolve would come crashing down. Between the tears, my questions kept coming: "Am I doing the right thing? Am I making him do something that he is not capable of? Will he hate me for this?" For the first time in my life, I began to pray on a regular basis. Malcolm provided a calm strength to my intensity. His attitude was, "I am with you on this. I also want you to know that I love him no matter what happens."

As I noted, the first two months were difficult. There were times when I closed my eyes and said silently, "Hold on. Time will eventually end this session." Yet there were moments of hope even in the beginning: a correct gesture, more sounds, some smiles. I hung on every moment of success and that got us through. After a couple of months in the program, the progress started to come exponentially. Soon sounds turned into words. Along the way I worried that progress might halt. "What if he never puts two words together?" Yet he kept improving in all areas. Words did begin to go together. Then came basic sentences. A list was put up on the refrigerator and there was great joy and celebration whenever we added another word or phrase. Malcolm spent one morning a week in the room with Harrison and the girls got involved. It became a family experience.

At some point in that year, a realization hit me. This "obstacle" had changed me for the better and seemed to be affecting the whole family in a positive way. Sure, there were still fears and breakdowns, but most of the time there was a bounce in my step as I headed upstairs to work with him. I started to really enjoy being in that room and the difference was that I started to focus on myself. I spent so much of the time judging the day on how he did. Evaluating the day's work started out with the question "How did Harrison do today?" Slowly a shift happened. The most important questions were now "How did I do today?" "Did I stay focused and neutral?" "Did I follow through?" It was a great feeling to recognize that his actions did not have to dictate mine.

Not that every day ended on such a high. Many days I dragged my body through the programs. One particular morning was like a scene right out of *The Miracle Worker* (the Helen Keller movie). Harrison didn't want to eat his cereal. Why? Who knows? I could have enlisted a team of experts to analyze why he was afraid to use his spoon, but the outcome would still be the same: me–his mom–figuring out a way to feed him. So on that morning a decision was made. ("Harrison, you will not leave the table until you have used the spoon by yourself to eat this cereal.") Then the "fun" began. We sat together, he on my lap, with the cereal in front of us. I would lift up the spoon. Harrison would open his mouth, ready to be fed. I would then put the spoon down and prompt him at the elbow to lift the spoon himself. He would let out a cry and push my hand down over the spoon. He was not ready to give up a good thing (i.e., mom taking care of this for him). This continued and as I became calmer, I realized that I was ready to raise the bar. The anger was replaced with a steely calm. At one point, the girls and Malcolm had finished their breakfast and were ready to head out the door. "How long are you going to sit here?" Malcolm asked me. My reply: "As long as I have to." I added, "I may need some backup later."

I think we sat there for two hours. The cries turned into screams and the cereal looked about as appetizing as a bowl of mush. Most of the time there was silence. Finally, he made an attempt to pick up the spoon. I gave a whisper, "Nice job, Harrison." Again, silence. He tried again, and this time he actually put some cereal on the spoon and put it in his mouth. I went crazy. "Great job. You did it!" I thought to myself, "*I* did it!" I let go of trying to figure it out for him and just demanded his best.

I will forever be grateful for that lesson in our kitchen. It showed me the strengths and obstacles of my parenting. It also showed me the power of closing one's mouth.

Harrison continues to climb his mountain of recovery. Thanks to his efforts and that of his committed teachers, he is making his way in a mainstream first grade. We thought long and hard about writing this section about him. We were fearful that sharing his struggles might constitute an unfair invasion of his privacy. Having done so, we hope the story will serve as a source of pride to our son and as one of inspiration to other families.

While the PDD/autism label that he was given at two years of age brought us out of denial, we instinctively knew that we would need to reject the limitations that are often placed on students bearing labels. Far too many people hear labels and lower the bar. A career of working with kids has shown us that labels are well-meaning but do not speak to the power of one's Unique Potential. That doesn't mean that we have not sought out experts to help us with our son's obstacles. We certainly read a great deal and learned much from the developmental experts that came into his life. It was just that we had to also adopt our own approach to this obstacle. For example, one expert said to us, "These kinds of kids don't handle transitions well, so you need to keep such times at a minimum." Our rebel mind-set responded, "*This kid* will handle as many transitions as we can set up." With each such statement of "These kinds of kids . . .," we have learned to say, "I don't know about 'these kinds of kids,' but *this kid* is going to have to deal with this." The tiger that came out in us at times surprised us. Raising the bar on our son, in turn, helped us raise the bar on our two girls and ultimately on ourselves.

Many opportunities have come out of this obstacle, for which we are grateful. We learned that wishing away the obstacle was wasted energy. It didn't help our son and it only served to bring our spirits down. While we won't even pretend that there aren't dark moments when we worry about his future, we know at the deepest level this obstacle has been placed on his doorstep as part of his ultimate destiny, part of his Unique Potential. He will be what he is meant to become as a result of this struggle and his triumphs over his obstacles. There are many tough days. As we write this, he is struggling with serious tantrums that seem to arrive with no advance notice and quickly take over this endearing boy. The difference now is that we talk as a family about the trials and triumphs. We share our feelings on the tough days and listen to the strength of each family member. Mostly, we marvel as his progress unfolds in the spirit of "The Tortoise and the Hare." Along the journey, there are joyous signs of his development. Recently, he met up with his kindergarten teacher at the playground. (Catherine Tait has taught all of our children over the years, and Malcolm refers to her as one of the best teachers he has ever witnessed.) As Harrison alternately flirted with Ms. Tait and played with Scout, his language was flowing freely and he was clearly "in the zone." It was as if he were showing off all of his new skills. Ms. Tait was excited, and he seemed to feed off this interaction. At one point, he said, "I'm doing good." When we left, he shouted "Good-bye," and as we turned the car to head out of the parking lot, Harrison undid his seatbelt, reached over to lower the window, and shouted again, "Good-bye, Mrs. Tait. . . . Thanks!" We are in this for the long haul. As Bruce Springsteen sings, "You've got to learn to live with what you can't rise above." We are still rising above. Perhaps we always will be.

Another opportunity that arose out of this experience was that Laura began to pray on a nightly basis. It started out with the Lord's Prayer (the only prayer she knew!) and that has remained constant. "Yet," Laura says, "after I say the prayer, my thoughts are different each night. It has become a source of strength for me. Most days, I would not change the last three years."

On a personal level, Malcolm learned that obstacles were opportunities in dealing with his use of alcohol. He tells his story:

> I gave up drinking alcohol fifteen years ago—1985. Although drinking never put me in the gutter, I always sensed that I did not have a healthy relationship with it. I don't know if it would have eventually led me there, but I am certain that it would have prohibited me from being all I'm capable of being as a father, a husband, professionally, or personally. I began to make efforts to curtail my drinking two or

three years before I finally quit. Those were miserable years. I resented friends who seemed to be at peace with social drinking. I resented the fact that normal drinking habits seemed to evade me.

Eventually, I went to some AA meetings, a measure I had studiously avoided, perceiving attendance at such things as a sign of weakness. Once there, I remember hearing speakers refer to themselves as "grateful and recovering alcoholics." Cynically, I thought they were paid plants, like those in tent show revivals where a man gets up out of the wheelchair or a blind woman can suddenly see. Yet I could not deny the conviction they seemed to feel. Years later, I understand. My life—my marriage, my relationships, and my work—took a dramatic upward swing once I accepted and addressed the obstacle of alcohol. Once again, avoiding or wishing away the obstacle brought misery. Addressing it head-on enabled me to stride forward. Rather than wishing for different circumstances, I chose to wish for a new attitude. Ironically enough, I ended up with different, and much better, circumstances as a bonus!

This Priority encourages parents to view obstacles in a new light. As parents, we share a natural compulsion to want to remove obstacles from our children's paths, to make life easier for them. This is not how we learned, and it does them no favors. Sometimes the only way we accept this is to see firsthand what happens when we step back. A mother talks about an obstacle that turned out to be an opportunity she had never anticipated:

We were the type of parents who made it to everything our kids were involved in. We prided ourselves on that. We were always there, at every game, every event, in the bleachers cheering.

Our younger son, Mark, was going to play in a final soccer match for Hyde that would decide the number one ranking of two rival teams. At the same time, our older son, Peter, had been placed on academic probation at college because of poor grades. His attitude was indolent and he was in a real slump. Mark was right in the middle of the Hyde process and doing well. He had a great attitude about learning and was a little uppity toward his brother when he came home. It caused a lot of tension and bickering.

Meanwhile, not considering the possibility that Mark's team would make the finals, my husband had made hotel reservations and purchased tickets for the Monet exhibit in Boston. This created a huge conflict in our minds. We agonized and finally decided to choose art over soccer.

Later, we were in our hotel room and the phone rang. It was Mark. He tearfully told us about his heartbreaking loss in the soccer game. Then he said, "I am not emotional because I lost my game." As it turned out, when the game was over, he was walking off the field hanging his head and crying. He heard someone calling his name amid the chaos. He looked up and saw his brother coming toward him. With arms outstretched, Peter extended his arms and gave him a big hug and hung on to him. He told him the outcome didn't matter, he had played his heart out and he loved him. So they walked off the field and jumped into the car and got something to eat together. They connected in a huge way and they talked about the fact that their relationship had soured. Mark realized that he had been wrong in judging his brother. He had allowed himself to forget who Peter really was. He had set up unrealistic expectations for his brother, and because his life was going well, he had become intolerant of Peter.

That was a turning point in their relationship. It allowed both of them to see their weaknesses. Had we been there, it would have been Michael and I hovering over Mark, making sure that he was OK. Meanwhile, Peter would have been relegated to the background. I learned the importance of stepping back because I never knew how to do it. Stepping back and allowing my children to feel their pain and letting them come to me. I got the call and heard an inspiring story about my children connecting. I can't think of a greater gift. The obstacle of not being able to be in both places at the same time turned out to be an incredible opportunity for all of us.

OBSTACLES AS OPPORTUNITIES

HOW TO MOVE TO A POINT
WHERE OBSTACLES
BECOME OPPORTUNITIES

First, let go of the Hallmark-card fantasy. Many of us start out with a vision of what family life is supposed to be like. As Malcolm's mother once said, "You can visit your fantasy world, but you cannot live there." Let go of that fantasy vision and allow obstacles to help bring you toward a true connection.

Break the fantasy vision down into two parts: our highest expectations (hopes) and our dreaded reality (fears). It can be helpful to write down or tell someone your hopes and fears for your children. While this may be helpful to you, hopefully it will also allow you to see that hanging on to hopes and fears can derail you by leading you into the trap of harmony over truth. Give as much responsibility as you can to your children to face their own dilemmas and work out their solutions. Ask yourself, "Is this my issue?" If not, then refrain from speaking. (You may need to count to ten!) Use this classic line: "It sounds like you're struggling, what are you going to do about it?" We have found that the more we talk as parents, the more we automatically rob our kids of the opportunity of owning and overcoming their obstacles.

You may even need to physically move away from your children so that you will not be tempted to step in and give advice. That doesn't mean that help and advice cannot be given, but the simple challenge of having to ask for help can reinforce in them the importance of gaining ownership of their own obstacles. This is a critical first step for them. To be specific, you could say before you walk out of the room, "Let me know if you need any help." (Just make sure that you get out of the room!) By walking out of the room, we create a circumstance where they, not us, must make the next move. They must ask us for help. They must seek us out to use us as a resource. This is much easier said than done, as we learned with our middle child, Scout. Laura writes:

Last year Scout asked if she could walk home from school by going through the Hyde School campus. She explained that she wanted to use the computer to check her e-mail. I nodded, thinking, "Love those technology instincts!" and forgot about it.

A few weeks later I learned that she was redirecting her route in order to avoid facing a bully. When I pressed her on this, she broke down and said that she had a confrontation with the bully and was afraid. As I tried to talk with her about this, it became apparent that she had a deep-seated fear about this young girl. I shared some of my school memories of the "bully." I encouraged her to face her fear. Nothing seemed to work. I then said quietly, "Scout, you will always have this fear unless you face this girl. You are going to have to work through this." "No!" she screamed, and ran out of the room.

Part of me wanted to call the school and have them handle this. I had questioned her and her sister enough to know that this was not a potentially dangerous physical situation. (I even hid in the bushes one day to check out the scene!) But I decided to step back and put the onus on Scout to address her fear. There was a night of tears and in the morning, Scout came to me and said, "Mom, can I face the bully every other day instead of every day?" I thought for a moment and decided to go with her plan, since it was *her* plan. I said something like, "That is a step in the right direction." She left for school the next day with a wrenched face. (She wears her emotions on her sleeve.) My heart ached for her, but I knew she had to face this.

There were many tearful days, actually tearful alternating days. In the end, the obstacle gave Scout and me some great opportunities to share with each other. While I so wanted to take away her pain, I decided instead to share more of my own fears with her. Slowly, the big bad bully began to fade from the forefront of Scout's day. One day, her sister said, "Scout, you seem to be over the bully." Scout gave one of her prize-winning toothy grins. "Not really," she said, "but it's getting better."

It is hard for parents to see their children struggle with obstacles. We want to get in there and make it easier or bring the whole process to a conclusion quickly. Why? Look at your own life. What were the moments when you learned the most about yourself? Chances are, they were times when you struggled with something and, in so doing, earned an understanding. Our children need to have their own opportunities to learn from their dilemmas and earn their own understanding. In order to step back and let them work out their struggles, you must start with a premise that speaks to the title of this Priority. Can you accept the notion that obstacles can actually represent opportunities? In order to embrace this, you must accept the idea that we are in this life for the long run and that we need to be able to work through tough issues in order to fulfill our own potential.

Kahlil Gibran's classic poem, "Your Children Are Not Your Children," has always helped us to remember our mission as parents.

Your Children Are Not Your Children

Your children are not your children.
They are the sons and daughters of life's longing for itself.
They come through you, but not from you.
And though they are with you, they belong not to you.

You may give them your love but not your thoughts,
For they have their own thoughts.
You may house their bodies, but not their souls,
For their souls dwell in the house of tomorrow,
Which you cannot visit, not even in your dreams.
You may strive to be like them
But seek not to make them like you,
For life goes not backward, nor tarries with yesterday.

You are the bows from which your children
As living arrows are sent forth.

The archer sees the mark upon the path of the universe
And he bends you with his might
That his arrows may go swift and far.
Let your bending in the archer's hand be for gladness,
For even as he loves the arrow that flies,
So he loves also the bow that is stable.

Read this poem a few times. What are the words and phrases that jump out at you? Many parents comment on the phrase "house of tomorrow." Others react to the idea that we do not have ownership of our kids. They are not ours. Every time we read this, something different usually resonates. The phrase "[The archer] bends you with his might" hits home. We often try and bend our kids in the direction we think would be best for them, forgetting that we are the bow and not the archer.

When it comes to viewing obstacles as opportunities, it is helpful to remember that our children are on a path to the "house of tomorrow," which we cannot comprehend. Therefore, when obstacles arise, how are we to know their ultimate significance? If we step in and try to solve the obstacles, we may be taking away an important opportunity that is connected to their destiny. Our instincts as parents are first to protect our children against danger. That is a primal instinct. Yet in most daily situations, our intervention is not only unnecessary, it can be destructive. It also may interfere with a "moment of truth" on the way to the house of tomorrow.

As we start viewing obstacles with a different set of glasses, we may even get excited about the struggles of our children. I remember a Hyde School parent once lamenting about her son's battle with substance abuse. Someone asked her, "If you could wave a magic wand, would you take this problem away?" She replied, "Of course. What a silly question." Suddenly, another parent in the room quietly but firmly spoke: "I am the CEO of a major organization. I struggled with alcohol and got sober in my thirties. I know that I wouldn't be running this operation had I not had to deal with that issue. I also would not be the person I am today."

ALLOWING THIS NEW VIEW TO HAPPEN

Whether you are dealing with a four-year-old arguing with her sibling or a teenager battling an issue with a teacher, allow them to turn their obstacle into a learning opportunity. We chose to begin this Priority with the word *allow* because it more precisely describes the process of letting go of control. Whether you have a child with a learning disability or one with a physical limitation, try to embrace these obstacles as important opportunities for growth. This is not easy. It can be tough to see your child struggle. At times, you may have to keep yourself busy so you won't step in to solve the situation. Once you have accepted the idea that opportunities can evolve from obstacles, you will be in a better position to assist your child when they really need your help. As with any one of these Priorities, you need to place the weight of your foot in stepping back. After stepping back, you may well decide that you need to jump in with both feet and take control. But there is a better chance that you'll be doing so in order to satisfy a genuine need your child has as opposed to an emotional one you have. (We will talk more about when to take hold and when to let go in Priority 7, Take Hold and Let Go.)

ALLOW AND ENCOURAGE OTHERS TO PUSH YOUR CHILDREN

The example of Helen Keller is one that speaks to the human spirit and its potential to create opportunities through obstacles. *The Miracle Worker*, the story of Keller and Annie Sullivan, never fails to inspire us whenever we watch it on TV. As parents, we often wonder: Would we have the strength to demand the best from a child who had such obvious difficulties? It was easy to see how Helen's parents had made the decision to love her and try to keep her at home. What they couldn't see was that she needed someone in her life who was more interested in uncovering her potential. Annie Sullivan came into her life and saw through the obstacles. She was committed to helping her achieve her best, not keeping her from her worst. But she needed to actually move Helen down to a cottage on the property in order to establish the learning bond between student and teacher. We need other people to come into our lives. Whenever you see someone who is creating obstacles for your child by demanding their best, step back first and think: "Is this going to help my child?" If your instincts say yes, then you need to allow it to happen.

Laura writes:

During a summer swim lesson, I took along my new baby-sitter to see the routine. Harrison was in the water with a young man who had not worked with him before. At one point the teacher said, "Harrison, push away from the wall." I watched as Harrison continued to tread water. I knew that he did not really understand the instructor's request, but I sat there holding my breath. The teacher said, "Harrison, I am going to count to three and if you don't push away from the wall, you are going to get out of the pool." One . . . two . . . three. "OK, get out and sit on the bench." Harrison got out and sat down, still not fully comprehending why he was being reprimanded. My baby-sitter turned to me and said, "Aren't you going to do something?" I thought about it (step back and assess) and decided to allow it to unfold.

Then the teacher said, "Harrison, I am going to give you another chance. Now jump in and push away from the wall." Oh boy, I thought, here we go again. Next the teacher said, "Harrison, if you don't push away by the count of three, you are out of the pool for the rest of the lesson!" One . . . two . . . three. "OK, get out, Harrison. You are done for the day." Again, the baby-sitter looked at me incredulously. I waited a few more minutes until the lesson was over and then went down to speak with the two young teachers.

I said, "I'm Harrison's mom. I do not want you all to change the way you are working with him because it is great that your expectations are high. He has struggled with delays in his development and there may be times when you need to physically show him what you

205

expect out of him. But please, continue to push." The young girl said, "Thanks for telling us that. I will work with him on this." The young man said, "I have seen him do this before, so I know that he can do it." I responded, "That's great, then keep pushing him." As I drove away, I felt good about stepping back and waiting those ten minutes. As I watched him, I knew that he was not in physical danger and even though my heart ached for him, he would survive this "unfair" moment because the larger lesson was more valuable. He needs people in his life who will act as if he can do it. I cannot get in the way of that.

We also continue to see that despite allowing others to raise the bar on our children, we need to raise it on ourselves and on each other. We need to embrace obstacles as important milestones in the journey and not try to fix or minimize them. As we advance as parents, we might even learn to welcome them in the newfound knowledge that they offer a promise of future blessings. When we hit an obstacle, instead of launching into "fix mode," we may even get excited about the possibilities. Allow yourself to wonder, What opportunity lies around the corner of this obstacle?

FAMILY EXERCISES AND ACTIVITIES

"Two Words"

Materials: Paper, pen
Time: 20 to 30 minutes
Explanation: Think about your children. (If children are present, have them think about their parents.) Write down two words for each of them: one that is the biggest strength they have, and one that is the biggest obstacle. Then apply the same examination to yourself. Write one word that is your biggest strength and another word for your biggest obstacle. Now look at your words and think about the following questions:

- Are there any connections between your words and the words you wrote for your kids?
- Thinking about the words for your children, which came to you first, the strength or the obstacle? How about for yourself?
- Look at the word that you wrote for your obstacle. Does an opportunity lie in this area of your life? How about for your children?
- Are you addressing your obstacles and believing in your strengths in equal measure?
- Have you shared your obstacles with your children?

"Flip a Coin"

Materials: Coin
Time: 20 to 30 minutes
Explanation: This exercise can be done anywhere. It can be done with the whole family or just two members. Take the coin and start with one family member. Have them or others state an issue in their life—for example, slow speed, academics, music class, working out, singing. Then have the person toss the coin. If it lands heads, rattle off a quick assessment of the obstacle involved in that issue. After that, turn it over and give the opportunity side. If the coin lands tails, start with the opportunity side. Then toss the coin to another family member and give them a turn. The key here is to be quick so as to allow spontaneity to emerge.

Problem versus Higher Purpose Orientation

Materials: None
Time: 20 to 30 minutes
Explanation: Ask yourself, "In striving for personal growth, am I focused primarily on my problems or on a higher purpose?" We sometimes use our problems—or perceived problems—as foils to prevent us from truly examining a higher purpose in life. Our prob-

lems can actually provide a sense of security. We might never have heard of remarkable people like Ray Charles and Stevie Wonder had they been educated by some current approaches to schooling. Chances are a greater emphasis would have been placed on their blindness than on their desire to be musicians. Lucky for us, their commitment to music came first and guided their efforts to address their obstacles (blindness). Commitment to a higher purpose inspires us to address our problems. The reverse may not lead to a higher purpose. Discuss the following questions:

- What is the purpose of my life?
- Which personal problems do I need to address in order to seek this purpose?
- Which personal problems do I need to let go of in order to reach this purpose?

JOURNALING QUESTIONS

1. How were "obstacles" viewed in my upbringing?
2. How do I view my own "obstacles" and struggles?
3. List three strengths that I have. How do I feel about these?
4. List three obstacles that I have. How do I feel about these?
5. Describe the opportunity within one of these obstacles.
6. What gets in the way of my seeing my children's obstacles as potential learning experiences?
7. What steps could I take to allow my children's obstacles to become opportunities?
8. What steps could I take to allow my own obstacles to become learning opportunities?
9. Do I ever connect my children's obstacles to myself in some way? Explain.
10. What specific step will I take to view obstacles in a more positive light?

Priority 7,
Take Hold and Let Go

When the going gets tough, the kids need to learn how to
"hang on" and the parents need to learn how to "let go."

As parents, we face an ongoing dilemma: When do we step in to take action and when do we step away from it? We often want to step in and take charge when we most need to listen and step back. Likewise, we can be afraid to take action when "our gut is churning" and we are unsure about the outcome. How do we deal with this inevitable confusion as we parents attempt to balance the seemingly opposite concepts of taking hold and letting go? In this chapter, we explore this tension. While it can be maddening, the pull between "taking hold" and "letting go" can also guide us to our best child-rearing instincts.

Laura has vivid memories of what she considers to be her first major "screw-up" as a parent: trying to help our daughter in the rituals of toilet training. Although humorous today, it wasn't all that funny at the time!

POTTY TRAINING OUR FIRSTBORN

Since we had tried for six years to conceive a child, and Malcolm was the headmaster of a close-knit community whose members had supported us through our tough times, Mahalia's birth was something akin to the Second Coming. She was showered with gifts, and the excitement we felt over having a beautiful baby girl often led me to break into impromptu tears of joy as I walked around town. This baby cooed, slept soundly, and generally was a delight to everyone who commented on her almond brown eyes and milky complexion. When I would recount to my mother my newborn's sleeping habits, she would reply, "You have no idea how lucky you are!"

I even remember calling my mother when Mahalia was eighteen months old and boasting, "I don't know why people make such a fuss about this parenting stuff. It's easy!" My mother chuckled, saying nothing. I felt on top of the world with my wonderful, cooperative prize. Not long after that call, I was sitting at the kitchen table with Mahalia as she was attempting to navigate the transition from bottle to "sippy cup." She was clearly in need of some help and I said something like, "Mahalia, if you hold it like this, you will be able to get the juice. See?" She took the cup, looked me straight in the eye, and intentionally turned the cup upside down, dumping the juice onto the table. I was shocked as much by her defiant look as by the force of her actions. Where did this come from? It marked the beginning of her emerging spirit as well as a stage of declining confidence in myself as a parent.

The potty training began innocently enough. I started putting out the potty and reading the how-to books at the right age. Mahalia showed very little interest. Friends and our pediatrician all said to give her space to work this out. Of course, that made sense for a girl just shy of three years old, but it made less sense once Mahalia passed the three-and-a-half-year mark. I was starting to panic. My achievement side was determined to accomplish the potty training while still appearing to look as though it didn't bother me that my daughter was still in diapers.

I remember talking to her doctor one day in his office. He suggested I talk to Mahalia. *Talk to her? Of course!* That sounded like a great idea! As we were driving home, I started to talk about the potty training. How did she feel about it? As she nodded and made some comments, the thought ran through my mind, "We're really communicating on this. Why didn't I think of this before?" When we got home, I asked Mahalia if she wanted to sit on the potty. She said, "Not now." Later, when she had another accident, all my frustrations came up again. This went on for about five months.

There were shameful moments, like the time I offered a Barbie as a reward for using the potty. Again, my friends gave me maddening advice. One of my sisters said, "You know, you need to let go of this." I nodded, "Of course, I know that." I would walk around repeating a mantra in my head: "Let go. Let go." Then one day my sister said, "When are you going to *do* something?" I retorted, "What are you talking about?!? I am doing something! I'm letting go!" She laughed and said, "You'll know when you are ready to do something." I shouted back, "Don't give me that pop psychology stuff! I *am* letting go!"

Soon after that conversation, my lack of serenity hit me squarely in the eyes. We were upstairs doing something and Mahalia was again refusing to use the potty. As I told her to go down to the bathroom, frustration got the best of me and I pushed her from behind. Feeling both ashamed and helpless, I went to my room and sat on the bed with tears in my eyes. I had crossed a line with Mahalia and I needed to take a hard look at myself. I went out for a walk and let the silence work its magic. Why was I so upset over this? Why was Mahalia so determined to fight me? My thoughts were jumbled and there was a mixture of shame that I had not been able to help her with this as well as the fact that I had lost my temper and had physically pushed her.

Slowly, the jumbled thoughts started loosening up like a tangled necklace and my breathing became slower. I thought about my sister's comments: "You need to let go," and "When are you going to *do* something?" I asked myself, "What are you really feeling here?" Two words came to mind: *expectations* and *fears.*

- *Expectations:* My vision for her was high. I had originally assumed that she might be the first in her age group to be potty trained, surely not the last in Bath, Maine!

- *Fears:* Mahalia was almost four and going into preschool in a month. I was afraid the other children would ridicule her and that this would wound her. (She puts up a tough front, but she's sensitive.)

As I sorted out these thoughts, I began to go back to the questions that focused on what I needed to do. I had no answers, but eventually I turned and headed back home. I walked in the back door and saw Mahalia sitting at the kitchen table having a snack. The words that came next surprised me, as they seemed to come not from a plan but from some deeper place: "Mahalia, I was wrong to push you and I am very sorry. I know that I can no longer change your diapers. We have two other children who wear diapers and it is just too much. I will give you a diaper at night if you want, but no diapers during the day." My voice was calm and as I walked out of the room, I felt a weight lifted. My husband said later, "What are you doing? She's going to leak and dump all over the house!" My answer, "It's OK. I feel good about this. She will figure it out."

The next morning, Mahalia came down to the kitchen with a counterplan: "Mom, how about no diapers at night and diapers in the day?" I looked at her and realized the example that I had set with all my manipulating. I laughed and shook my head as if to say "no."

It took two days. (Luckily, it was summer so she could use the yard to work through this!) We had one incident on the attic stairs that our middle child gleefully pointed out to me, "Mom, there's something I need to show you!" As Mahalia and I cleaned that up, I realized that the anger was replaced with something else: a determination to let go of what she needed to address and to take hold of what I needed to do.

We all get a good laugh about that family story now, but it was a powerful lesson for me. It was my first big realization that I can be part of the problem. I now know that my actions were part of the reason she took so long to accomplish this rite of passage. I also began to understand that taking hold and letting go were not separate actions; rather, they worked in concert with each other as a guide to bring out the best instincts in us. My better instincts finally came out, allowing me to set my course of action and, in turn, allowing my daughter to set hers.

Our experiences in working with families have caused us to perceive an irony that tends to evolve during trying times: *Kids need to learn how to "hang on" and the parents need to learn how to "let go."* Another mother, Jane, a family education director at Hyde, tells a story about learning a lesson in letting go after a visit to the emergency room:

At Hyde we were told to "let go." In my controlling way I could sit back and say, "Sure, I will let go of this because there are strengths there. I will let go of that because there are strengths, but I won't let go of this because I see weakness there." I sat back in my judgmental way and made evaluations of everything that I could let go of and could not let go of.

We were in a seminar and I somehow managed to slip in my chair and dislocate my shoulder. Although I was in pain and my arm was dangling down, I was trying to pretend that nothing had happened because I don't like to ask for help or be the center of attention. Eventually I decided that I had better leave the room or I would faint, so I quietly got up to go. My son James followed me out and ended up driving me to the emergency room where he stayed with me while they reset my shoulder. My husband came later.

I arrived back in time to actually go back to the seminar with James. Later, when asked what they had gotten out of the morning, James raised his hand and said, "I have been waiting seventeen years for my mother to need me."

This was a real moment for me, as I realized what it took for me to let him help me. I also understood how I had pushed my children and even my husband away because I hated to be dependent on anyone for any reason. In fact, I remember doing a Hyde worksheet titled "Who Can I Depend On?" I felt a sense of pride because I could depend on myself. Honestly, that day, I would have driven myself to the hospital and never would have realized what a jerk I was being. It felt good to have people helping me, to allow my son and husband to be there for me.

This past year I found myself in a funk about something, but there was a difference this time. I talked with my family. Now I reach out to my family more to help me. I don't feel I have to be all things to them. That has taken a huge pressure off me in my relationship with James and my husband. It is interesting that I had to have my control taken away in order to understand what it meant to "let go."

Sometimes when we hang on to the "ideal," we are prevented from appreciating some valuable moments. A mother shares her story about the holidays:

I had a dream for my family. But it was my dream, not my family's dream. It consisted of the ideal perfect family and manifested itself in many different ways. One way was the holidays. At Christmastime I would spend countless hours planning meals, getting the perfect little decorations, buying the presents, making presents, doing projects, having parties, making presents to take to parties, and, of course, the ultimate moment: Christmas morning.

The boys were always allowed to open one gift on Christmas Eve. Now that may sound special, but the gift was always the same: a pair of pajamas . . . identical pajamas. The boys were to wear the pajamas that night so they would look their best on Christmas morning. They were to wake up early in their perfect pajamas and I would be wearing my little robe. (My husband, Michael, would refuse to participate. His hair was always a mess.) The boys would sit at the top of the stairs, but they would not be allowed to come down until the fire was crackling, the lights were on the tree, and the pastries were laid out on the table. Inevitably, that dream would evolve into a nightmare as the day unfolded. The dog would get sick from too many treats. The linen tablecloth would get stained. The house would get very messy. The kids would be bouncing off the walls. Michael would be sleeping on the couch.

I had to take a look at why it was so important for me to get everything perfect. I eventually realized that my motivation was sincere but my quest for the perfect image was getting in the way. I had to let go of my vision simply because other individuals in the family were not into it. I spent so much time exhausting myself trying to make things perfect that I lost sight of what was really valuable. In exhausting myself, I didn't have any time or energy to put into the important things. My kids didn't enjoy me. It certainly wasn't inspiring to them.

Perfection is a word, a state of mind, an image of family life that seems to get in our way so often that some of us need to constantly let go of its seductive veneer. As one mother said so well, "Perfection is just another form of dishonesty." Another mother shared her own perfection story:

> I made it easy for everyone. I helped solve my husband's problems and my kid's problems with love and understanding. What I learned about myself was that I was not really sharing myself with my child. One night we sat in the garage for about an hour after I picked him up and I said, "I'm really interested in knowing what you think of me." He said, "Mom, I see you as a real perfect person. I'm the one with the problem." I said, "No, there are some issues with me and I can share with you what I'm learning about myself."

That mother let go of her image and took hold of "being real" to her son.

What prevents us from trusting the best in our children, from letting go? As teachers and administrators for the past twenty-five years, we often use the word *fragility*. As discussed in Priority 4, fragility has to do with just how fragile parents believe their children to be. Although there is obviously no way to measure how fragile a teenager is, we cannot remember too many times where a parent understated the fragility of his or her own child. In other words, kids are far more resilient than their parents think they are. Therefore, most parents could stand to improve on letting go. If we return to Johnny's interview at the beginning of this book, it is easy to see that

Johnny has not accepted much responsibility for his life because his parents have done his worrying for him. One mother writes:

> I have learned that letting go doesn't mean not caring. It means car-
> ing enough to give my child the freedom to fail or fly. His triumphs
> are sweeter when he knows he alone is responsible for them and his
> problems are also his own to deal with and not to blame on anyone
> else.

This Priority suggests the paradox that taking hold is actually the key to learning how to let go. The motion of moving forward provides an energy that, in turn, allows us to loosen the grip we have on something. On the Hyde campus in Bath, Maine, there is a high ropes course. It has been used by students, teachers, and families and has taught many people about courage and trust. The sections between the trees are called "elements." Each element has its own peculiar demands: sheer height, balance, coordination of feet and hands, and so on.

One particularly challenging element is called the "monkey vine." On this part of the course you are challenged to stand on a wire thirty-five feet up in the air while secured with a belay, or safety, line. Someone on the ground is at the other end of the belay line monitoring your progress. Should you fall off the wire, the weight of the person on the ground will counterbalance yours, preventing you from crashing to the ground. The monkey vine is so named because it has a series of ropes that hang about six feet apart along the wire. You start out hanging on to one rope and then inch yourself away from the safety of the tree platform that you are resting on. The next rope out is hanging a few feet from your grasp but just far enough away so that you must let go of the rope you're holding in order to grab the next rope.

The ropes course teaches us to trust in others. More important, it shows us the dynamic nature between taking hold and letting go. One depends on the other. Together, both can give us the strength to attempt what seems almost impossible. In order to let go, we need to reach out and take hold of something else. Taking hold of this new challenge forces us to release our grasp on whatever we once felt required our control.

In the Biggest Job workshops, we ask parents to think about a trying issue that has been occupying their thoughts. They then turn to someone they haven't met and talk about the issue using, as their guide, two questions: When you think about this issue, (1) what do you need to take hold of, and (2) what do you need to let go of?

These two questions can be very helpful in working through a tough situation. The following is another classic Gauld family story that tested Laura's ability to take hold and let go:

When Scout was five, she was taking swimming lessons at the local YMCA. Swimming was something I wanted my kids to learn, as I had grown up on the water and knew how important it was to be confident in that setting. The kids had all taken lessons and Scout had already learned the basics of the dog paddle. For some reason, she decided that she was afraid of the teacher, the water, or who knows what else. After we had signed up for the six-week course, she announced that she would not be partaking in the festivities. Not taking her seriously and underestimating her own determination on this, I brushed it off as we prepared to get ready for the trip to the Y. She was whining all the way in the car.

Once there, the whining escalated to full-out crying. I kept crouching down and encouraging her, wondering why she was so afraid of something that a few months ago she loved to do. For the first couple of lessons I encouraged, cajoled, even got into the water with her to allay her fears. (I was fully dressed in shorts and polo shirt!) Nothing was working.

Finally I decided I needed to take hold and demand that she follow through and get into the water. I said to her, "Scout, until you get into the water, you will be grounded." As Scout was the type of child who didn't like conflict, I figured that this was what she needed to break through her fear. On the second night of the grounding, she threw me for a loop, when I was putting her to bed. "Mom," she said,

"I love being grounded." What do I do now? I wondered. Clearly, the grounding was not working. I thought again about what I needed to take hold and let go of.

Let go: I had to let go of what all this looked like to others. We had to face and accept the fact that we had become a floor show for the Y that summer. I also had to let go of the outcome.

Take hold: I knew that she had to face the water, and since grounding her wasn't working, I needed to take hold of something that would be effective.

I talked to her the next day about her fears. I told her that at the next swimming lesson, she would either go in under her own steam or I would drop her into the pool. She nodded and assured me that she would go in the water. The morning of the lesson, she repeated her claim that she was ready to swim, yet as the lesson approached, her resolve faded into more whining. This time there was out-and-out crying as we got to the pool area. I crouched down and whispered in a low voice, "Scout, you can go in on your own or I can help you." She was screaming now as I peeled her fingers off the aluminum bleachers. I looked at the instructor and asked, "Is it okay if I drop her in?" His response, "Go for it."

I tried to walk with as much dignity as I could muster as I half carried her to the edge of the water. I made one last attempt to let her go in on her own and then dropped her into the water. Then I turned and walked by the row of parents, thinking surely they would not approve of my actions, and went out to the outer hall. One mother came out and said, "Great job! I wish I could do that!" The parents were supportive of Scout as she cried her way through the lesson—in the water! The next lesson wasn't much different, except this time she went into the pool on her own. On the third lesson, she jumped in and started swimming with a huge grin on her wide face. The parent section broke out in applause and one grandmother exclaimed, "She knows how to swim!"

Scout doesn't remember all that much about that moment, but we laugh about it and what it taught both of us. Laura learned that taking hold and letting go leads one through a meaningful process, despite the fact that it may not promise a pat answer. Scout learned that her mother was committed to helping her achieve her best, and that while she might not have the "answer," she was there for the duration. Overall, Laura relearned that demanding Scout's best demanded her own best in return.

A mother tells how she struggled with taking hold and letting go of her grown sons' girlfriends:

> One of the areas where this Priority has helped me the most has been when my boys have been in serious relationships that I didn't think were going to work. Growing up, my parents' usual response to any guy I brought home was something like, "I hope you're not going to get serious about *him*." There was always something wrong. There was never any explanation, just a subtle form of control.
>
> Now the shoe was on the other foot and I had some concerns about my son Ryan's girlfriend. I kept saying to myself, "You have to let go—remember how your parents did it. It's his choice." Yet I knew I needed to take hold of something in order to let it go. So my husband and I sat down with Ryan and said, "You know, we have some concerns and we just want to say them so that we can let go." And the surprising thing is that it worked. He listened and in a few instances said, "I see those things, but that is one of the things I find refreshing." What was bothering us about the relationship was pulling him in. I think we really took hold of what we needed to say and then were able to really let go.

Having children is such an intense experience that we will spend the rest of our lives learning to let go. As Malcolm's father, Hyde School founder Joseph Gauld, likes to say: "Typically, children and parents need to learn opposite lessons in facing the challenges of growing up. The kids need to learn how to hang on. The parents need to learn how to let go." If we are to fully take hold of our best parenting instincts, we need to also use the taking hold/letting go process as it relates to our own parents. As we mentioned in the introduction, many of the parents we work with are obsessed with the objective of parenting differently from the way they were parented. We often hear comments like, "I intend to take the good and discard the bad." As hopeful as that may sound, the process exacts deeper demands than those afforded by such oversimplification. It also demands that we deal with our own upbringing. Although it may be painful, it can ultimately be liberating. We need to accept the things that our parents attempted to give us and learn to forgive them for the things they were unable to do. Again, our society tends to push us to declare that we had a "good" childhood or a "bad" one. The former designation can lead us to deny anything that wasn't "great" and the latter is similar in that the negative seems to permeate everything. For most of us, we have to process the positive and the negative, even if we have an overall feeling of "good" or "bad."

One Hyde father talks about the relationship between two of his children and how it helped him take a step with his own father:

> I have four boys and one of the biggest disappointments that I had as a parent was the fact that my two oldest boys seemed to hate each other. The way they dealt with each other was just so disappointing. I envisioned something so different when we started a family. I knew there would be some difficulties, but they seemed to really hate each other. I didn't know what to do about it. One time, Aaron came home from school and got into a fight with his older brother. It turned into a physical and really ugly situation. So we stopped them and made everyone come into the den to talk. They were both giving us negative body language, leaning back in the chair and staring up at the ceiling. After talking for a while, it was clear that we were not getting anywhere.
>
> Then Aaron sat up in his chair and said to his brother, "All of my life I have looked up to you. I've wanted to be with you. I've wanted to be like you. And all of my life you have treated me poorly. Maybe you'll always be that way and there's nothing I can do to change that. But I want you to know that I love you and I forgive you." It was a moment that changed many things in our family. His brother, Dexter,

leaned forward in his chair and said, "Now I owe you." I asked him what he meant by that. He said, "Now I have to rise to your level."

Aaron took hold of becoming a man. That was one of the most mature statements that had been spoken in our household. He was able to let go of the hurt he felt from his brother and it allowed all of us to let go. As soon as he said those words, I knew that I needed to say the same thing to my own father.

It took me about a year. I went on a trip with my father and we were in a hotel and I said something like, "You know, growing up with this incredible unpredictable temper was a problem and had an influence on me. It was one of the things that I had to sort out as an adult." I had to tell him, "Look, if you want to be in my life, you can't do that. Maybe you're always going to be that way, but you can't direct it to me or to my family. That said, I want you to know that I love you and I forgive you." I said basically the same thing Aaron had said to Dexter. I didn't know what was going to happen. He cried. Then he said, "You know, I always knew I was losing my temper, but I always felt better afterward. I didn't realize it affected you and everyone else."

Aaron introduced the concept of forgiveness into our family and it was probably one of the most powerful sentences that's been said in the family. As I look back on it now, I had to let go of the boys' relationship and take hold of saying what I needed to say to my own father.

Another Hyde father, a physician, talks about taking hold and letting go when he was faced with a crisis of conscience with his daughter-in-law:

When Lisa was well into her pregnancy, it was clear that she wanted to have a completely natural childbirth that included delivering this baby underwater. I took a deep breath and thought, well, maybe I can help her work through this. I had really worked myself into a frenzy, as I had talked to some OB-GYNs who felt it was really dangerous. Lisa and I had some brief conversations about it over the phone and when she and William came down for a visit, she brought a book that she thought would help me understand the whole thing. I read the book and got more disturbed. I mean, I really worked her hard. I'm not letting up and she's not letting up, and finally Brian, my other son, said, "Dad, we need to ride to town."

When we got in the car, he turned to me and said, "Dad, you've got two choices. It's pretty clear that Lisa is going to have this baby underwater. You're not going to change that. Keep on doing what you're doing and you probably won't have a relationship with Lisa, Will, or this grandchild. Or, go back in there and apologize and maybe you will." I said, "You're dead right." When we got back from town, I pulled Lisa aside and apologized. I said, "This is your child. You've got to do what you believe is best. I want to tell you I love you and whatever you decide is fine with me." She wanted my blessing. That was important to her.

That was a real moment of truth for me where Brian and I had the kind of relationship where he could say to me, "Dad, your offtrack." Had I stayed on it, it would have probably severed any relationship with Lisa because I was not being very polite. He was right and Lisa was very gracious. I had to take hold and let go at the same time. I went and prayed to God and said, "This is yours now. Please protect them." It was an enormous lesson for me.

(Postscript: Lisa and Will are the proud parents of a healthy baby girl.)

We suggest using the taking hold/letting go Priority as a way to work through issues, both large and deep as well as minor and routine. Rather than seeing them as separate actions, view them as fluid and connected. The energy that it takes to reach out and take hold of something will help you loosen your grip on the very thing you believe cannot work without you. And as we work more on taking hold and letting go of our own issues, then we will find our children coming toward us more and taking hold of our wisdom as a resource.

FAMILY EXERCISES AND ACTIVITIES

Take Hold/Let Go Exercise

Materials: Paper, pen
Time: 10 to 15 minutes
Explanation: You can do this with either the whole family or just one family member. Consider an issue you are working on in your family: How might you "let go" of this? How might you "take hold" of this?

Take two slips of paper. On one slip, write your "take hold" statement. On the other, write your "let go" statement. Example: "I will take hold of my belief in myself and use the resources I have to deal with this." "I will let go of the fear and embarrassment." As you read your answers, drop the "let go" statements into a container and hang on to the "take hold" statements. (You may ask someone to bury the "let go" slips of paper.)

Take two to three minutes for each person. Try to listen without jumping in to comment. It is especially important for parents to share with their children. Don't worry if they don't understand everything you are saying. They will "get" that you are working on yourself.

Coming to Terms with Childhood Exercise

Materials: Paper, pen (family photos may be useful)
Time: 15 to 30 minutes
Explanation: This is an exercise for parents, but it involves the children when it comes time to share your thoughts and feelings. Spend a few minutes writing on the following subjects:

- Describe your childhood. What were the positive moments and times?
- What were the shortcomings?
- What do you need to take hold of and let go of in your parents?
- What attitudes from your childhood do you see in yourself today?

Share your answers with your family. You may also want to share the ways you see some of your attitudes in your children. This may also be a good time to dig up old photos and share them with the family.

Family Show

Materials: Whatever props you need to pull off a show
Time: Preparation, 20 to 40 minutes; show, 10 to 20 minutes
Explanation: Declare that you are having a family show. Pick a time for the show and either work on a theme together or ask everyone to prepare a number (song, poem, dance) to put into the show. Everyone is involved. After you have performed your show, sit around and discuss what came out of the experience. Some questions to ask:

- What did we learn about each other?
- What did we have to take hold of and let go of?

Take a risk and have fun!

JOURNALING QUESTIONS

1. When I think about the term *taking hold,* what comes to mind?
2. Does anything prevent me from "taking hold" of what is important and what may need to be done in my life?

3. Where in my life do I need to "let go"? Explain.
4. Describe a time where I have "taken hold" and made something happen?
5. Is there any connection between my ability to "let go" and the actions of other members of my family?
6. What is an issue in my life that I am dealing with right now?
7. When I think about this issue, what do I need to "take hold" of?
8. What do I need to "let go" of?
9. What steps could I take to work on the tension between "taking hold" and "letting go" in my life?
10. Where in my life do I most need to step back and really listen?

Priority 8,
Create a Character Culture

"Sow an Act and you reap a Habit;
Sow a Habit and you Reap a Character;
Sow a Character and you Reap a Destiny."
–Charles Reade

Many forces threaten to thwart our children's character growth. A major one is the ever-increasing power of the youth culture, which barrages kids with seductive images of drugs, sex, and an array of troubling peer pressures. There are also constant pressures on their self-image; those that come from the media instruct kids on how to look, what to wear, what size waist they need to have in order to present that "perfect body" to the world. How do parents compete with these foes? We certainly can't put our heads in the sand and hope for the best. We must create a strong positive culture in the home and in the family, one that arms both children and parents with the strength to discover who we truly are and to stand up for what we believe. We must resist the urge to search for "quick fix" answers.

The approaches offered in this chapter are simple, but they require follow-through. They help create a pattern, a routine, a tone, and a spirit that might not promise an immediate return but can give birth to a new dynamic culture in your home or wherever you gather with your family.

ACTION/REFLECTION CYCLE:
A CHAIN REACTION OF PERSONAL GROWTH

Professional golfers often speak of "visualizing" the shot before they swing the club. They stand on the fairway and imagine the path and trajectory of the ball. Then they swing. Similarly, we have found that kids and parents can also visualize their personal growth. We imagine a productive pattern or a dynamic family culture before we set ourselves to the task of creating it. At the Hyde Schools, we do this with a concept we call the "Action/Reflection Cycle." This term comes from a statement we sometimes use to define our school: "A socially embodied moral argument that works on an action-reflection cycle."

To explain, our *moral argument* asserts that every individual has a Unique Potential that defines his or her dynamic personal destiny. As parents and teachers, it is our job to help our kids ultimately connect with this destiny. We offer this help by challenging them with values-forming experiences, challenges that can only be completed through the testing and demonstration of personal character. Students then reflect upon these experiences privately and also discuss them among their peers. This is the Action/Reflection Cycle.

ACTION/REFLECTION CYCLE

Engage in a challenging action.

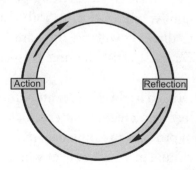

Act in a manner consistent with a new understanding of self.

This diagram provides a visual picture of how learning and character development can take place. First the student must act: complete a homework assignment, complete a chore, run a mile, sing a song, whatever. Then the student learns: "With each action, I begin to regard myself in a new light. As I accept this new view of myself, I act in accordance with it." Thus, the actions help form a new identity. Most students like the feeling of this new identity. They grow to like it enough to continue to engage in the actions that gave birth to it. The student begins to realize that this identity can only be maintained through continued constructive actions. Thus, the activity and identity reinforce each other in a perpetual chain reaction of personal growth.

We have talked a lot in this book about ways to increase the reflection moments in your family. Now we will focus on the actions using what we call the "Three-Point Plan." A wonderful quote from Charles Reade, which appears at the beginning of this Priority, captures the essence of this plan. Please take a moment to reread it. A new Character Culture in your home must begin with actions. Commit to the following program for one month without allowing yourself to take a break. Do not evaluate your progress while you are in the program. Just sow the act.

The three points in this plan are:

- Get a job!
- Family meeting
- Mandatory fun

GET A JOB!

Learning how to work is an extremely important lesson to teach our children. Laura writes about her experience with her stepfather:

> When my stepfather came into my life at age eight, I didn't have the slightest idea about doing a job well. He gave me a quick introduction

when he gave me one of my first jobs. I had to trim the hedges in our backyard. After showing me how to use the hedging shears and instructing me on how to flatten the top of the hedges, he left with a now infamous line in our family, "Let me know when you are ready for inspection." Little did I know how often I would hear that line from him. (I say it now to my children!)

After my stepfather left me alone, I proceeded to dillydally, doing a little here and a little there, assuming that all would be forgotten when it was time for dinner. At one point my mother came out and called me in for dinner. As I started to come in I heard my stepfather's voice: "Are you ready for inspection?" I said something like "Sure." He walked around and didn't need to look very hard to see the sloppy job I had done: branches scattered on the ground, hedging shears left open on top of one of the hedges. He told me that I wasn't done and then went back inside the house. Through the window, I saw the family sit down and eat. I sat down on the ground, stunned by the realization that my stepfather was serious and that I had to do the job right. I do not remember how long I was out there, but I now know that I was sowing an "action" that eventually evolved into a habit of learning how to work.

I remember all the everyday jobs—washing the dishes, pots, and pans; setting the table; serving as the "waiter" for meals. Mealtime was sacred in our household. We had dinner at six every night. The table was set and candles were lighted. It didn't matter if we were having hot dogs and beans, the table was always set. Phone calls were not allowed during meals, and everyone came to the table in proper clothes—shoes, no robes, and so on. Job assignments were posted on the back door of the kitchen. Saturday mornings were devoted to specific chores that generally involved learning a new skill: changing a tire, learning to plaster a shower crack, fixing a drain in the driveway. There were many skills to learn, among them: negotiating the subway system in Boston, swimming tests out to the farthest buoy, large mailings for my stepfather's business (he compensated us for those: three cents per stuffed envelope!), how to sail, how to ski. Overall, they were lessons in how to work—doing a job and doing it well.

In raising our own children, we know we need to take more of the same approach that we hated as children. Whenever we work with them and show them how to work, our home operates better for all. Also, when we follow through and expect the work to be done properly, everyone benefits and our children emerge with a sense of pride.

A mother and a teacher attended one of our workshops and shared this story about jobs in her home:

> I was trying to get my son to take more responsibility for cleaning his room. At the time, I had just taken a new job and had very little time to clean my own room. At one point when I was yelling at him, he said, "Mom, I don't see you picking up your things. Why should I?" I started to explain that I had no time with the new job and then it hit me that he also had lots of things to do with school and sports practices. I closed my mouth and made an effort to change my habits. He followed my lead.

Children of all ages can have jobs. Young children can put toys in a basket and books in a bookcase. Elementary school–aged children can clean rooms, set the table, wash the inside of windows, and load dishwashers. High school–aged kids can be responsible for maintaining areas of the house, special projects, yard work, trash, and laundry. It is important that everyone takes some ownership for the home.

Older kids can also get paying jobs. As teachers, we have seen the pride and responsibility kids feel when they are making their own money and holding down a job. Jobs also take care of other issues with older kids, such as vampire hours. If your teenage daughter goes to bed at 2:00 A.M. and wakes up at 11:00 A.M., then chances are pretty good you are picking up a fair amount of slack. A job will get your kids out of bed in the morning in a way you may not be able to. Teaching your kids to work and then expecting that they will have ongoing jobs is a gift they will appreciate later in life.

You might consider the idea of broadening your thinking on the whole concept of what a job is to include the category of "things we would like our children to know." Examples in this category include how to:

- Take a phone message
- Look someone in the eye and introduce yourself
- Give a firm handshake
- Write a proper thank-you note
- Behave in a nice restaurant
- Change a tire
- Mop a floor
- Iron a shirt
- Make a bed
- Navigate around an area
- Read a road map
- Speak in public
- Develop a skill in sports or a hobby
- Study up on an area and then visit it
- Cook breakfast
- Wash clothes (separate darks and lights!)
- Read a newspaper
- Visit an elderly neighbor and read to them or just chat
- Write a business letter or an e-mail
- Relate to all types of people

FAMILY MEETING

When we were growing up, family meetings took place in the living room. If a meeting was called, everyone in the family was certain that someone was in trouble. Stern faces confronted hanging heads and subsequent punishments were doled out. It certainly wasn't anything we looked forward to.

Weekly meetings keep us away from the trap of pulling together only in times of crisis. What we pay attention to is what we will reinforce. If our children get our full attention only when there is a problem, guess what we are teaching. There should be three parts to the family meeting:

1. Clear the Decks

This is a nautical term that calls for sailors to keep the ship's deck clear to avoid injury. We need to deal with festering issues within the family in order to prevent anger and resentment from building up. At the start of the meeting, ask if there are any decks to clear. This calls upon each family member to share the issues that have been churning within during the previous week. For example:

- To daughter: "I need to clear the decks about myself. Last week, I was really angry about your attitude, and I took it out on the whole family in a way that I didn't feel good about."
- To all the kids: "I need to clear the decks. I have talked to you all about the importance of honesty. This week I was dishonest about something really silly at work and my conscience has been bothering me. I admitted it to my coworker. I didn't really want to share it with you, but I know that I needed to."
- To son: "I need to clear the decks about you. I got sucked into your terrorist attitude and let you off the hook. I'm sorry."
- To everyone: "I need to clear the decks on the whole family. Lately, I've been picking up after everyone. I really need your help."

After someone clears the decks, there should be no response. This can always be talked about later, but for now it is important to listen and think about what the person is saying. Remember, you can't listen with your mouth open!

2. Review Week

During this part of the meeting we go around the room and talk about the week just completed. How did it go for us? What were the highs and the lows? What did we learn about ourselves? What did we get excited about? The following are some samples from our family meetings.

- Mom: "This week was good for me. I was so nervous about the workshop that we had in New York that I didn't think I had anything to say at the beginning. I couldn't remember anything. Once I started talking, though, it all came back and I felt great at the end. I also enjoyed working with Harrison in his room on Thursday. I also feel good about the early-morning workouts that I committed to. I really feel good about that. At work, I learned that I need to share more of what I'm thinking with my coworkers because sometimes I get going full-speed and they have no idea where my thoughts are heading. I am looking forward to our family trip next month."
- Dad: "I really enjoyed going to your soccer games this week. It's exciting to see the progress you're making out on the field. I think I'm still having difficulty balancing work with home life. (I know I say that every week!) I pledge to keep working on that."
- Daughter (age seven): "I had a good week. I worked harder on my schoolwork. I also made a new friend."

Again, when we are talking about our weeks, there does not need to be any response from family members unless someone wants to comment.

3. Set Goals

Here we look ahead to the coming weeks and think about what we would like to improve upon. By setting one specific action step, we give ourselves something to take forth from the meeting. This also sets up next week's "Review week." Here are some examples of weekly commitments:

- "I will commit to a one-on-one activity with each of my children."
- "I will speak up more at work."
- "I will make my bed every day next week."
- "I will cook one dinner next week with my dad."

Finally, you may want to add some of your own traditions to the family meeting. You may take one of the family principles and talk about that each week. For example, "integrity" may be the principle. Choose someone each week to begin the meeting with a story about that week's principle and what it means to him or her. One family we worked with wanted to work on taking more risks. Family members incorporated this into their weekly meetings and highlighted moments of courage.

As you begin the tradition, weekly meetings may feel flat, fake, and dry. They may only last five or ten minutes. Nevertheless, commit to doing it: Sow the action, and before long you will begin to reap positive habits. Pass around the responsibility of running the meeting so that it's not always the same person dragging everyone together. Even when the meetings seem uneventful, we find that we have more meaningful conversations during the week: in the car, while cooking dinner, at night before bed. We are convinced that the reflection muscles we develop every time we meet make impromptu sharing easier. In any case, think of deep family discussion as a habit. The weekly family meeting is the action that can begin to provide the fuel to develop and maintain this habit.

MANDATORY FUN

The premise behind this concept is simple: "We are going to engage in this activity as a family. Everyone is going to do it. Whether or not one perceives the activity as fun is irrelevant!"

We used the term *mandatory fun* when we were running a boarding school. Students would look at the weekly schedule and find the following:

Saturday Evening: Dance in Student Union *(Mandatory Fun!!!)*

Kids would moan and groan about having to go to the dance. Then at 7:30 they would be in their dorm rooms, both girls and guys, "primping for the prom," borrowing clothes, blow-drying hair, ironing shirts. Everyone had fun and all they needed was someone to say "You are required to attend."

Families are typically made up of people going in a hundred different directions. As our kids grow, they have more of their own obligations and interests to fulfill. Yet we all still have a vision in our heads of what family life is supposed to be, often a fantasy of family time. As one stepmother said, "I had seen *The Sound of Music* and so I knew what it was supposed to look like!" Our vision might cause us to imagine time together accompanied by background music, happy faces holding hands as we run along a sunlit beach together. Sound real? Let's take another look. Most family scenarios are more like: Mom is on the treadmill watching CNN, Dad is checking his e-mail hourly, one son is holed up in his room with his computer games, while another is playing with a GameBoy in front of the TV. Shared experiences? Hardly.

We ask parents in our workshops to describe the activities they are passionate about and what they like to do in their free time. Some of the typical answers are:

Exercise
Reading
Fishing
Going to museums
Bowling
Hiking
Road trips to view old houses
Sketching and painting
Swimming

Then we ask parents if they have ever tried to say to their family something like, "How about we all go hiking tomorrow?" Reaction may run from noncommittal grunts to outright sarcasm. ("Hiking is for losers, Mom!") Then our vision of family togetherness and shared vision gets in our way. We get hung up on wanting everyone to *want* to be together as a family. We want that relationship so much, we end up lowering the bar and demanding little from the family when it comes to being together. We end up doing nothing together.

When we look back on our own family vacations, they were often hellish. We would tromp around museums and historic monuments and there would always be several good fights that would erupt in public. Today we laugh about those times when we're together, but at the time we certainly did not see them as fun. Laura learned a valuable lesson concerning her own fantasy vision when our children were small:

We were wrapping up our annual trip to visit my parents on Cape Cod. They rented a beach house every summer for a week. On our last day, I decided that we would have a picnic on the way back to Maine. I made sandwiches and packed lemonade and snacks. As we were loading all the kids and gear into the car, I shared my plan with Mal. "It will be great," I said with overflowing enthusiasm. "We'll have a great time and save money. We won't have to drag the kids into a restaurant and pay a lot of money for food they don't eat anyway!" I didn't notice that Mal didn't respond. As we loaded the car and pulled out, I was hanging on to my vision.

Driving north, we would pass a park and I would say, "How about stopping here?" Then we came upon another park, this time with some water and a playground. "Oh look, a playground where the kids could play." Malcolm would say, "Let's get some more road behind us." As we approached Boston, the parks became fewer and farther between. There were still a few "green areas" visible from the highway. "There's a place!" No reaction. Finally, the first obvious clue came from Mal, "Maybe we should hoof it on home and eat when we get there." I bounced back with, "But the kids have to eat and I have everything already prepared." Still hanging on to my fantasy, I was growing angrier as I realized that Mal was not supporting me. He seemed intent on putting on his blinders and pushing for home in the shortest time possible. ("How about a late picnic in our own backyard?") By this time we had reached Route 1, where green gives way to an endless string of stores, malls, restaurants, and gas stations. My anger had evolved into deep resentment.

Suffice it to say that this story ends at a triangle of crab grass in front of a TJ Maxx store with our "picnic scene" looking something quite different from my vision. The kids were running around the parking lot, the food was lying on the ground, and Mal and I were not talking. The whole way home I did the "freeze out" routine.

As I think about that now, it is clear to me that I had only needed to follow the guidelines of mandatory fun. If it had been my turn to decide mandatory fun, I could have calmly announced, "We are going to have a picnic." Then everyone would have had to participate. If Malcolm didn't have fun, that would have been his problem.

We suggest that you try mandatory fun a few times each month. Give everyone a chance to lead the activity with his or her idea of fun. Obviously, some guidelines are necessary, but try to be a trooper. Let your children pull you into their passions. Our eight-year-old loves to swim. In the dead of winter, the last thing Laura wants to do is shave her legs, put on a bathing suit, and head out to a local pool, but when she does, she has fun. The whole family has fun. That's the beauty of mandatory fun. We usually have a great time. And if we are in agony, we will have fun later when we are recounting the story and the shared experience. Some ideas for mandatory fun are:

Bowling
Sledding
Reading aloud as a family
Hiking
Road trip
Drawing
Swimming
Biking
Taking a walk
Going to a museum
Cooking a meal together
Camping
Family movie
Beach walk
Dining out
Visiting grandparents
Going to playground
Library

Along with jobs, family meetings, and mandatory fun, you may also want to give back to your community as a family. Help a senior citizen in your neighborhood by raking her leaves or shoveling his driveway. Volunteer a day in a soup kitchen as a family. You may even create a family vacation around a community service project rather than an exotic locale.

If we want our kids to be interested in developing their character, we need to model the notion that character development is a lifelong pursuit. Sowing these actions will work our action/reflection muscles and strengthen a culture in the home that will support our best. We recently read an article about a family who had a simple sign on their back door: Return with Honor. We perceived the message to be: "You come from a family that has principles. When you leave this house, you are representing yourself and your family. Do so with dignity and integrity."

At one of our workshops, one father noted that his passions were not expressed in the family because no one wanted to spend a day the way he wanted to. He said something like, "I slowly disconnected my spirit from the family and let my wife take care of everything." His wife added, "I wholeheartedly took on all matters, even if it meant buying the football equipment. That was something I had no experience with, but that didn't stop me!" Sharing our interests shows our children a side of us they need to see. They may act as if they are not interested in seeing it, but they are interested and it will leave an impression. All of these efforts will create shared family experiences that will become a vital part of family folklore to be passed down through the years.

VISION, RIGOR, AND SYNERGY

This whole chapter has been about three qualities: vision, rigor, and synergy. *Vision* comes when we teach our children that there is a larger purpose in life and they need to stretch in order to discover their own Unique Potential. The family meetings help feed the vision of the family and keep the "top line" in sight.

Rigor comes when we commit to the daily actions that demand our best. The expectations of jobs and family meetings teach our children that life exacts a price that involves a commitment to excellence. Often, we protest against rigor because we want an easier way. Eventually, we tend to feel genuine gratitude toward anyone or any circumstance that requires rigor from us.

Finally, without *synergy*, our efforts will never fulfill their potential. We simply need the help of others in order to find the greatness within. As Hyde founder Joe Gauld says, "Others can see our

Unique Potential in ways we ourselves cannot." In our families, sharing our growth with each other will break unproductive patterns and create shared experiences. These experiences will lead to trusting relationships. Mandatory fun is an avenue that can combine all three: vision, rigor, and synergy. The rigor of compulsory involvement can connect our vision to the synergy that comes when all family members connect together.

We began this chapter talking about the need to sow actions. All these ideas will only work if we engage in them with a commitment to try in earnest for a period of time without evaluating the outcomes. You may be amazed at what catches on, but avoid the temptation to declare success. The point here is to focus on the sowing, not the fruits of the labor. They will come with time.

FAMILY EXERCISES AND ACTIVITIES

Job Survey

Materials: None
Time: 15 to 30 minutes
Explanation: This exercise can be done with young children, but use your judgment as to their readiness. Give each family member the following assignment:

> Find someone in your community who is in the workforce and ask to speak with them for a few minutes about what qualities they value in their own work ethic and in those who work with them.

Ask each family member to be ready to report to the family about what he or she learned. Then have a discussion about how family members can act upon lessons learned. For example: Mom: needs to take on less and focus on fewer things; Dad: daily pickup of bathroom; son: seeing a job through to the end.

Family Meeting Night

Materials: Dinner, music, candles
Time: Approximately 2 hours
Explanation: Decide on a night to have your family meeting. Make an event of it by cooking a meal and enjoying it by candlelight. Dinner assignments may be given out like setting the table, making the salad, and so on. Clean-up is done by everyone. After the meal, move to a family space to have the meeting. (Resist the temptation to do the meal and the meeting at the same time!)

Mandatory Fun Scrapbook

Materials: Camera, scrapbook
Time: 15 minutes per mandatory fun activity
Explanation: Keep a log on mandatory fun activities. Have someone draw a cover sheet (e.g., *Smith Mandatory Fun*) to glue to the cover. Then chronicle each activity with pictures (disposable cameras are easy and kids can use them), drawings, and quotes (nothing too long or people won't write them). Have the person leading the mandatory fun activity be responsible for putting them in the scrapbook. Keep the book on the coffee table or in a prominent place.

JOURNALING QUESTIONS

1. How much work was I expected to do as a child growing up?
2. Who were the people who taught me to work? What other lessons did I learn from them?
3. How did I take care of my personal belongings (room, bicycle, etc.) as a kid?
4. What were some of the important jobs I had growing up?

5. What was my first real job? Have I ever shared this with my family?

6. How do I feel about the work ethic of my children? Of my parents?

7. What steps could I take to bring a better work ethic into the family?

8. How often do we sit down to talk about ourselves as a family?

9. Who takes on the role of pulling together for a meeting in our family? How could we spread this responsibility around?

10. What were some of the "fun" times that I had as a kid that maybe I didn't think were so much fun at the time?

11. What is my idea of fun? How would other family members react to my ideas?

Priority 9,
Humility to Ask
for and Accept Help

"I don't know what the center of the universe is; I only know that it's not me."
—Popular slogan at the Hyde Schools

As a parent, Laura believes humility is the deepest lesson she has learned. When we were young faculty members, we would often join in when colleagues complained about parents. It seemed so obvious to us that many of the parents of our students were weak, that they caved in much too quickly to the attitudes of their children. Now, as we listen to the young teachers talk about how "out of it" a certain parent is, we find ourselves correcting them: "You, too, will be 'out of it' when you become a parent." It is the nature of the journey. We love our children so much that we fall in love with their potential, often blinding us to their issues. We also have such an unrealistic view of our kids and our parenting that we often set ourselves up to get knocked to the ground by reality.

We have learned the most as parents when we have been offtrack. The potty-training story was Laura's first lesson in humility as a parent. Her need to control and manage got in the way of letting her child figure out the potty-training issue herself. Laura now knows that this was Mahalia's issue. She also knows that it can be very hard to arrive at such clarity when you're focused on trying to be a good parent.

Adding to our difficulty is the fact that we generally feel the pull of a fairly steady pressure to downplay our offtrack parenting moments. We are supposed to know what we are doing. Our children are supposed to behave and reflect well on their parents. It is seen as a sign of weakness for us to need others. Often our culture encourages us to deny the existence of anything resembling a problem that can't be fixed. Therefore, for many of us, things have to get pretty tough before we ask for help. As one mother writes:

> This whole idea of asking for help has been a big one for me. I think I've defined my sense of self-worth through my ability to be self-sufficient and responsible. I mean, it goes way back as I look over my life, just really taking charge of what I needed to do myself. My first thought is not to ask for help.

One day we will see the backwardness of this notion. Asking for help ought to be seen as a sign of strength. We should welcome the help of others as a way to move us and our children forward. We should regard obstacles as catalysts for our own personal growth. Our society doesn't recognize that our capacity for getting help is connected to our potential. We cannot do great things if we do not develop the capacity to ask for and give help. This change needs to begin with us. If we can become better at asking for help, our children will trust us at a deeper level and will even begin to seek us out as a resource. A few thoughts on how to do that follow.

HOW OFTEN DO WE *REALLY* ASK FOR HELP?

Laura writes:

> While I have gotten a lot better about asking for help, it is still something that doesn't come easy for me. I view myself as a strong

woman and therefore I should be able to figure things out for myself. Of course, I can see in my children how they need to ask for help. One of the first sentences Mahalia put together was, "I do myself!" I was trying to help her do something and she made an emphatic declaration. I looked at her and thought, "Wow, she's tough." Yet where did she get that? Much of it came from her mother.

Now this does not mean that I do not value self-reliance. Self-reliance is an essential quality I want my children to have. From my own parents I learned the importance of making something happen for myself. Yet life has taught me that in order to demand high expectations of myself or my children, I need to involve others in the journey.

Years later, Mahalia and Laura had another moment of truth with asking for help. Mahalia was struggling with completing her homework. Although she was a leader in class, she would rush through to be the first one finished and the result would often be sloppy work, certainly not her best. While dealing with her on this we had some intense, heated discussions about her level of effort.

At one point she broke down and cried, "You know, I don't really know my multiplication tables! I know some of them, but there are many answers I don't know." She went on to say, "I'll ask Scout [her younger sister] a multiplication question and she'll yell out the correct answer while I have my fingers behind my back trying to figure it out." I thought it was a great moment for her to be able to admit this. The harder realization was that I had modeled this for her. There have been many things in my life where I have portrayed a sense of knowing what I was doing while my fingers were behind my back trying to figure it out. I fight the idea that if you ask for help, people aren't going to respect you.

HOW OFTEN DO OUR CHILDREN
SEE US REALLY NEEDING HELP?

Our kids face situations every day that challenge them in new ways. As adults, we often tend to live our lives in a comfort zone of our abilities. We appear confident, capable, and usually do not stray into areas that frighten us. Our attitudes may "pop" at home, but they rarely do so at work. Laura notes that the high ropes course was a challenge that really brought out her worst and best as a person. All of this came out in the workplace for all to see.

Laura writes:

As I looked up at the trees, I started to remember that heights were never something I felt comfortable with. There was a rope ladder that hung loosely. In order to climb the ladder, you needed some arm strength to pull yourself up to each rung. As I started to climb up the ladder, my heart started pounding, but I made it to the top and hooked myself onto the tree.

The next element was the "monkey vine." This required me to grab hold of a single rope hanging down as I simultaneously inched forward on a thin wire thirty feet above the ground. Just ahead another "vine" hung down just out of reach. In order to grab it, I needed to let go of the rope I was holding and lunge forward. Thus, for a split second I would be "between vines" and vulnerable. I was told that if I fell off the wire, the belay line would keep me from falling to the ground, and that my partner below would increase the tension on the line, allowing me to hang suspended in the air until I either came down or could get back on the wire.

Of course, I saw falling off the wire as some kind of failure. I was afraid to let go of the rope and lunge forward. I started to panic. The small crowd below was annoyingly cheerful. "You can do it!" they shouted. I thought, "Great, Laura! You had to show off to the faculty and volunteer yourself!" I blurted out, "Shut up! You don't know what this is like!" "Yes we do. We've done it. You can dooo it!" came back the chorus. I don't know how long I stood on that wire, but I finally lunged forward and grabbed the rope.

I felt a sense of pride that I had gotten through with the help of my husband and coworkers. The thought also hit me that for most of my life I stayed within my comfort zone and that allowed me to present a consistently positive disposition. On the ropes course I found I was unsure of myself and I allowed my attitude to come out in front of others. While it was painful at the time, it was also liberating. I came away from that experience ready to spend more time in areas of challenge and uncertainty.

The ropes course has been a key experience for many Hyde families. For many, it is one of the few times that the kids see their parents vulnerable and needing their help.

Most parents feel a desire to present a picture of confident strength to their children. Yet we have found that our children are often inspired when we are willing to let them see us in need. That may come from dangling off a ropes course. It can also happen when we are sitting on their beds at night and sharing our fears about something. When our kids see us in that light, they trust their struggles more. They see their own struggles as a normal part of life rather than something to hide. They can also help us in some very powerful ways. The night Laura shared with Mahalia her fears for Harrison, she patted Laura's back and said, "Mom, it's going to be OK." Her young, optimistic vision really helped Laura.

LEARN TO ADMIT MISTAKES
WITH ENTHUSIASM

It is easy to get caught up in the belief that our strengths and achievements will inspire our children. When we show our children our ability to admit mistakes and move forward, they will truly respect us. Although not easy, working this muscle will strengthen it and will make admitting mistakes easier. Humor and laughing at yourself will go a long way to help with this. Malcolm's sister and her husband learned the importance of this when their son, Zachary, was just a toddler:

> We were driving to Washington, D.C., and the car got a flat tire in very heavy traffic. I got out to take a look at the tire. I went into the back of the car to try and figure out what to do next. Instead of having the humility to pull out the directions, I started to fumble around and figure it out for myself. I knew that my wife and three-year-old son wanted to get home. My assembly process was not working and as I tried to figure it out, I heard our son say, "Mommy, we're in trouble. Dad doesn't know what he's doing!" We all laugh about that now, yet it obviously would have been better had I looked at the directions and not tried to appear as if I had it all together.

ALLOW OTHERS TO ENTER THE LIVES OF OUR CHILDREN AND TEACH THEM

Some of the most important things we want our children to learn, *we ourselves cannot teach them.* We can, however, get out of the way and allow others to affect them. This takes humility. When our children see that we are not overly possessive, they will feel freer to ask others for help. We remember a dad from Maine who related a story from his youth about running around the neighborhood and swearing at one of his friends. A mother heard the comment and said, "Johnny, you go home right now!" He walked home, only to find his own mother on the back steps with a bar of soap in her hand. The neighborhood network had spoken and there was nothing to explain or defend. He accepted his accountability, eventually realizing that the commitment of the neighborhood was to help him reach his best. While that particular method of accountability may seem dated and harsh now—Malcolm remembers what his mother used to say to his friends' parents when he would sleep over: "You know where his fanny is!"—we need to establish the equivalent of that network today.

We also need to give others permission to tell us when we are off-track. As simple as it may sound, it takes humility to say to our friends: "You have carte blanche to tell me when you think I'm off-track as a parent. I may not like it, but I really want to hear it." Sometimes we may cry about it and sometimes we will laugh about it, but we need to hear it.

Laura admits that she recently pulled the basic bribe maneuver and didn't even realize it. Harrison had spent a tough day in school and his teacher had called with a request that we pick him up for early dismissal. When Laura arrived, Harrison didn't want to leave school. She stayed calm as she walked this crying boy home. She avoided getting sucked into his tantrum, but calmly read the newspaper until he calmed down and then gave him some attention. She did, however, give the line, "Harrison, if you are a good boy tomorrow, Daddy will take you for an ice cream." Later, as we shared this with our friends, we all had a good laugh. It was no better than the shameless bribing we have witnessed over the years with new Hyde parents:

- "If you go to summer school, you can get that dirt bike!"
- "If you make the honor roll, we'll buy you a new snowboard!"
- "If you do well, you can take a trip this summer!"

We need to invite other people to see what we are really doing. In our case with the ice cream, what was really going on was that Laura was afraid Harrison would have another bad day, then another, and then all his progress would collapse. What would have been better would have been to share her fears with someone and get some help for herself and not focus on trying to "help" her son have a good day. That decision needs to be his.

There are times where we can make an unspoken pact within the family. Our children do not want to tell us the truth, and we parents do not want to hear the truth. When it comes to getting the help we need, allowing honesty to flow within the family is the first step. When truth is established as more important than anything else, we give our children permission to help us. Families whose members ask

251

for and receive help will invariably find that they are enriched with individual and collective personal growth. A father writes:

> The most rewarding experience for me as a parent has been the change in my personal philosophy of life. I used to believe in the concept of rugged individualism, of providing for my own needs, distrusting others and keeping them at arm's length. At Hyde, I learned how rewarding it can be to expose my true self to others and how showing my vulnerable side adds to my life rather than diminishes it.

One veteran Hyde parent writes about a defining moment where her son helped her with his honest evaluation:

> I came to realize that I had succumbed to the temptation to live out scripts for me that were written by someone else. I had to look at that and I had to realize that I had identified myself through other people and through the roles of being mother and wife. I had to be the perfect mother, the perfect wife, the best hostess; the picture had to be just right. At some point I realized that wasn't me, but I didn't know where to start the process of redefining myself.
>
> A major moment of truth for me came when my son and I had been in a Hyde family seminar. David said to me, "Mom, I am afraid that you'll just play tennis for the rest of your life." It's funny that he doesn't remember saying that, but it just blew my mind. At first it shocked me, and then it scared me, because that picture was pretty empty. It did start me on my journey of discovery.
>
> Today, our relationship is totally open. I share my struggles with him and he with me. We talk about our concerns about how to get where we need to go. Ours has become a deep and caring adult relationship. David has been one of my greatest teachers.

Many inspiring stories about kids helping their parents begin with the parents getting to a level of deep humility. Laura remembers a particularly moving one involving a young man she once taught:

He was new to Hyde and his parents were nice people, the kind of people most of us would want for parents. They were happy that their son was at Hyde but were unsure about sharing their private thoughts and feelings in the family seminars. At one point in the year this young man was clearly struggling with something, but when we asked him to share, he said, "I really can't talk about it." I pushed the parents a bit, but they clearly did not want to talk about it. I was caught. I did not want to push them to reveal something they did not feel comfortable about, and yet I could see that their son was caught between his desire to be honest and his loyalty to his family.

The defining moment came during a family weekend. The mysterious issue came up again. This time the son turned to his dad and said, "This is getting in our way." The father looked agonized and there was an awkward silence. I held my breath and waited. The room was still. Finally, I took a risk and said to the dad, "I can't tell you what to do, but there is an opportunity here." After a few seconds, the dad shared his struggle. His kids had found some pot in the house and it had been his. He talked about being with some of his old high school friends and smoking pot. He didn't feel good about it, but also didn't know if he wanted to openly deal with it. At that point, another dad spoke up. "Is that it? I thought it was something really bad!" Everyone in the room laughed and a weight was lifted from this family.

The following year, this same student was a senior and the parents became leaders in the community. We were having a discussion about parenting that was being filmed for a national television show. The dad was one of the parents who came to the meeting and easily shared his story with the interviewers. Later, I ran into the parents in the gym. We were joking around, and at one point the wife turned to her husband and said, "You realize that story might end up on national television." Without missing a beat, the father said, "I have my son's respect. I don't care who knows."

Another dad talks about reaching out to his son for help and the impact it had on him:

With your kids, it's hard to ask for help. A couple of summers ago I had this uneasy feeling that went on for a while and I knew that it was connected to my son. I didn't know what was going on or why I was feeling the way I did. I was scared and one night I stayed up late waiting for him. I said, "I need your help. I need to talk with you. I feel like I'm going backward with you and expecting the worst, thinking the worst." We ended up having a really good conversation. He didn't hide anything from me and I didn't hide anything from him. I felt it was an important moment in our relationship in asking him for help with the two of us. It moved us to another place.

SET AN EXAMPLE OF HUMILITY IN YOUR FAMILY

Do you sometimes feel that your children do not appreciate the things they have been given? Not only do we feel this at times, but we have watched countless students over the years harbor a sense of entitlement about their possessions, vacation trips, and educational opportunities. Most of all, we have seen many students view their biggest assets—caring, committed parents—as liabilities. How do we help our children understand the true gifts they have been given? We can start by understanding our gifts. Have we set up a life that has us at the center? Do our possessions mean more to us than our purpose in life? If we run our lives with our egos ahead of our conscience, then we should not be surprised if our children believe that they are entitled to everything. Understanding our role in the larger community helps to establish humility in our families. One father talks about his own humility:

> For me, humility has been a big issue. I've been arrogant and self-righteous as a person and have brought that into our family a lot. Within the family, I had the attitude that I knew what was right. This was brought home to me when my wife and I went on a vacation. It was probably the first time that we had been alone as a couple since

the children were born. There was a lot of tension that came out once we were out of our normal daily roles.

At some point in the Hyde process, I began to realize the extent to which I was rigid and hard-nosed in a way that was not productive for anyone. It was a period of humility for me and started a significant step of asking for help. I've always put up walls around me and built an image based on my fears of failure. I am developing the humility to let those walls come down and expose myself.

Another mother shares a time where she found the humility to honestly show herself to her daughter. This is an example of the many seemingly small and insignificant everyday opportunities that surface where we might do well to ask our kids for help.

I have always hated sewing and have never been any good at it. I get frustrated when I have to rip out stitches. For many years I've avoided it. But this one time my daughter needed quite a bit of sewing done on her dance costumes. Instead of sending it out I thought I could handle it. The day before it was needed I realized that I had messed it up and it was too late to send it out to a professional. I started to cry and thought, "I really lost it now. I'm crying over sewing!"

My daughter walked in and saw me wiping my eyes. My natural inclination was to cover it up with a story about something wrong with my eyes. I decided to lay myself bare, so I told her how much I hated sewing and how I couldn't do it. "I need some help!" Immediately my daughter started helping me. Everyone pitched in and now it's one of those things we refer to. It turned out wonderfully, but it was a hard role for me.

As part of our commitment to raise our children to be the best people they can be, we need to establish ourselves as spiritual parents to our children. This can be a difficult subject to explore because people are often uncomfortable with subjects of spirituality and religion. We certainly do not pretend to understand all aspects of the spiritual side of parenting, but we have come to believe that there are three components to the family growth process: (1) We as parents have a role; (2) our child has a role; and (3) a higher power has a role.

Joe Gauld, Malcolm's father and the founder of Hyde School, defined a spiritual parent as someone who "humbly accepts that his or her child has a purpose and a destiny dictated by a higher power." When asked what is meant by a higher power, he says, "Although you don't necessarily have to believe in God, you do have to accept the fact that you are not the center of the universe." If we behave as if we are at the center of the universe, then we teach our children to emulate that model. If we play too large a role in our children's development, then we may inadvertently teach them to be accountable to us as opposed to the deeper truths of life. If we control too much, then we deny them the learning opportunity they need to experience before they can enter the "house of tomorrow" that Gibran spoke about. If we take a passive role, they may never develop a sense of self-discipline. We need to remember that we are always teaching, whether we intend to or not. Whatever we choose to pay attention to (or not pay attention to) will speak loudly to our children.

There are some questions all parents can ask of themselves as a way to maintain focus:

- To what extent do we control our children's growth?
- To what extent do we trust something beyond ourselves?
- Do we raise our children by principles or by personality?
- Who takes ultimate responsibility when our children fail?

Accepting the limitations of our role in the spiritual growth process does not mean that we abdicate an active role in parenting. It does mean that we must accept that there are forces that are out of our control. Sometimes, when we let our kids deal with the consequences of their actions, they can find their own higher potentials. If they know in the heat of the moment that we will step in, they will act accordingly with less responsibility. As a general rule, the larger role we play in a child's life, the smaller one he or she will play.

We recently attended the funeral of a coworker. There were many stories told about this woman, but her son spoke the line that stuck with us: "Our mother would stand by us if we were right, but we also knew that she would never lie for us." This mother understood her role and did not interfere with the other components in the child-rearing process: the child's role and the role of a higher power. Both of us look to that line to remind ourselves to allow our children to understand the deeper lessons of life. Life will not treat them the way we treat them. If we do our part as parents, then the foundation they are given in our home will serve them, not enslave them.

In the mid-eighties, Malcolm took a weekend mini-course with a group of headmasters at the Hurricane Island Outward Bound School ropes course in the Maine woods. A reading by Eda J. LeShan left an impression on him and we have used it ever since.

I met an oceanographer who asked if I knew how a lobster was able to grow bigger when its shell was so hard. I had to admit that learning how lobsters grow had never been high on my list of priorities. But now that he had mentioned it, how in the world could a lobster grow?

The only way, he explained, is for the lobster to shed its shell at regular intervals. When its body begins to feel cramped inside the shell, the lobster instinctively looks for a reasonably safe spot to rest while the hard shell comes off and the pink membrane just inside forms the basis of the next shell. But no matter where a lobster goes for this shedding process, it is very vulnerable. It can get tossed against a reef or eaten by a fish. In other words, a lobster has to risk its life in order to grow. . . .

We all know when our shells have gotten too tight. We feel angry or depressed or frightened because life is no longer exciting or challenging. We are doing the same old things and beginning to feel bored. Or we are doing things we hate to do and are feeling stifled in our shells. Some of us continue to smother in old shells that are no longer useful or productive. That way we can at least feel safe—

nothing can happen to us. Others are luckier; even though we know we will be vulnerable–that there are dangers ahead–we realize that we must take risks or suffocate.

We will only connect with our greatness if we develop our capacity to ask for help. The more we embrace our humility, the more our children will see us as a resource. They will also learn to ask for and accept the help they need to fulfill their greatest potential.

FAMILY EXERCISES AND ACTIVITIES

Honest Evaluation

Materials: None
Time: 15 minutes per evaluation
Explanation: Think about three people in your life from whom you would like to get an honest evaluation. (Try not to think about whether you want this. Think about how much you will benefit from it!) Ask them the following questions, or make up your own.

- How do you perceive me?
- What do you see as my strengths?
- What do I need to work on?
- What do you think is getting in the way of my doing my best?

Try to just listen–don't argue–and thank them. You may also want to ask family members as well as friends.

Job Swap

Materials: Whatever is needed for the particular job
Time: Varies according to job

Explanation: Have each family member identify a job that he or she currently does that consistently brings about some feeling of resentment, stress, being overwhelmed, and such. For example: paying bills, putting dishes in the dishwasher, cleaning the toilet, picking up wet towels, and cleaning out the car.

Ask another member of the family to assume this job for a day, a week, or a month. (Note to parents: You may have to let go of the idea that you do not think this person could do the job as well as you.) After the swap period is over, have a family meeting about what has been learned.

"Process"

Materials: None

Time: 20 to 30 minutes or more

Explanation: This is something that we do in our extended family. The code word is *process* and it means you need to get help with something. (Sometimes saying the code word gets you started.) Think about something that is occupying your thoughts. It could be about work, a friend, or family. Ask someone to "process" and share with them what you are having difficulty with. Then the key part comes: *Listen.* It is important to really listen and think about their response. Then if you can, commit to an initial action step that can begin to address the person or situation you are thinking about. Good luck.

JOURNALING QUESTIONS

1. What does the word *humility* mean to me?
2. When in my life have I needed help and asked for it? What happened?
3. Where in my life has it been difficult to ask for help?

4. How do I feel when someone asks me for help?
5. How often do I ask my children for help?
6. What are my deepest dreams and visions for myself?
7. What is the role that conscience plays in my life?
8. How have the members of my family inspired me?
9. What does my family mean to me? Does anything get in the way of sharing this with them?
10. What specific step could I take to honor the highest vision in our family?

Priority 10,
Inspiration: Job 1

What do your kids most want from you?

At the beginning of this book we asked you to name your best hopes for your kids twenty years down the road. We listed terms like:

Happiness
Honesty
Fulfillment
Self-reliance
Concerned citizenship
Financial security
Good health
Moral foundation

In this chapter we ask you to peer through the other end of the telescope. In other words, what do your kids most want from *you?*

Before you answer, our experience forces us to conclude that parents generally misunderstand this essential question. Recall your own adolescence and think about how you might have answered this question about your own parents as you moved through your own teenage years. As Malcolm has said at the Biggest Job workshops, "I think I probably would have wished for my parents to be a bit 'cooler' when we were together in restaurants or other public places."

Chances are your kids are at that phase where they don't want to be seen with you in public places at all. Some of this feeling on their part is simply teenage angst, and as parents we have to accept some temporary rejection. Knowing what Malcolm knows now, he is certain that there was something he wanted from his parents. We would bet that it was the same thing your kids want from you: They want you to inspire them.

They may not even know they want this from you, not consciously anyway. However, their desire to be inspired may well be the strongest yearning and the biggest hope they have.

One father came to this realization after a heated exchange with his son. He writes:

> We were in our first group session at our first three-day Family Learning Center weekend. My wife, our son, and I were all seated in a circle with the other ten or so families. It was our turn to talk about each of our perceptions of family issues and I jumped in to go first, as usual. I began pontificating about progress when our son interrupted. "That's B.S., Dad. You always talk and sound good and look good and my friends think you're OK, but I couldn't tell what you stand for. I can tell you what you have accomplished, but what are your values, and what are your principles? You've never said them and I do not see them in your actions. Leadership? You never show leadership . . . you always duck the issues and hide in your rowing or reading. Courage? Sure you flew jets off carriers, but you're afraid to confront me, like when my brother and I fight. Dad! Listen! Sometimes I just wanted you to say 'no' to me!"

This father came to realize that the heights he had achieved in the Achievement Culture had failed to inspire his son. In fact, they had served to establish a barrier between them. Not only did the son have doubts about his own ability to attain those heights, he also didn't feel as though he could share those doubts with his father. Like many parents, he believed that he might inspire his children with his successes and accomplishments. Thanks to what we call "the willingness of recognition," he learned that we can only inspire them with our earnest efforts to live in accordance with our convictions. This father went on to forge a new and meaningful relationship with his son and the rest of his family.

If the reader takes little else from this book, we hope it will be the message that our children are most inspired when they see us try to improve ourselves as people, when they see us strive to develop our own character, when they see us strive to practice what we preach, when they see us:

- Put *truth* over harmony in our own relations with spouse and peers.
- Honor the spirit of the law *(principles)* as much as its letter *(rules)*.
- Put *attitude* over aptitude in our daily lives.
- *Aim high* in our personal and professional lives.
- *Risk failure* in our efforts to be successful.
- Accept life's obstacles as *opportunities.*
- *Take hold and let go* in our professional and personal lives.
- Strive to uphold a *Character Culture* in our families.
- Demonstrate the *humility* to ask for help.
- Seek to live *inspired lives.*

ROAD MAP TO INSPIRATION

We have talked about how achievements alone will not inspire our children. In fact, achievements can actually alienate our children from their own potential, as they may perceive us in unrealistic terms. ("My dad is so strong and just seems to always do everything right.") As one student said to his father, after a Biggest Job workshop, "Dad, I used to look up to you for being good in sports. Now that I have seen you get emotional and share yourself, I have a new respect for you."

We have observed three basic ways in which we inspire our children:

1. *When we share our struggles and our feelings.* This is hard for most parents. We often try to convince ourselves that our children may not be able to handle us in what seems like a vulnerable role. Our struggles can be deep and tough or they may be of the everyday variety. Regardless, our kids deserve to see this side of us. Since it is likely that they are struggling at some level with something about which we are not aware, they will be comforted by our honesty about the things *we* have not figured out!

A Hyde father talks about taking the risk to share his feelings with his own father:

> The gift that Hyde gave me was not only in my own family but with my father. He had never been able to tell me he loved me and I had never told him how important he was to me. I sat down to write him because I was worried that he might have a sudden illness and my chance would be gone. Once I told him, it was amazing how it opened up our relationship. He's been able to, since that time, tell me he loves me.

A Hyde father of three talks about a tough decision he had to make and sharing it with his family:

> I felt a lot of things when I made the decision to resign from my job. Mostly, I thought about how my kids would be impacted and how I thought they would feel about it. To my astonishment, I think my kids felt the best they've felt about any decision I have made, because they think that I did something that was important and right for me and I was up front about it. It has changed my whole approach to them.

2. *When our reach exceeds our grasp.* As adults, we can often live our lives within a range of comfort. In this mode, our risks are calculated and we might justify this in the interests of being a responsible parent. In reaching beyond your grasp, we do not suggest that you take up skydiving or rock climbing. However, reaching beyond our grasp demands that we face our fears. It can involve exhibiting the courage to take a class, run a race, share your feelings with your mom, learn to sing, climb a mountain, paint, and so on. It is also about the courage to live our lives based on deep principles. The reality is that when we takes risks, our attitudes "pop" in a way that shows our children who we really are. Bill talks about his father and the inspiration that he feels now, but perhaps didn't comprehend when he was younger:

> As a kid, I resented my father a lot for his temper and the way he dealt with me. If I look back on it now, he's the one who has inspired me. His father died when he was young, and he basically had to be a grown-up at an early age. The most inspiring thing that he did was change his job. He was a successful executive and started to realize some things in his job that didn't agree with his principles. He left his job and went from Park Avenue to the basement of our house. There were some tough times financially. I thought he was crazy and stupid and it made me angry. Looking back now, I was inspired that he would go with what he thought was right.

A mother writes:

> My father could be very earnest, but he certainly didn't take himself seriously. Unlike people of his generation, I did see my father cry and we had a close relationship, but the real inspiration was the way he lived his life. He grew up very poor, and he had to leave school at sixteen to go to work because his father died. We didn't hear about how hard his life was. He never had any formal education except an occasional business course, but he ended up president of a small bank. One of the proudest moments was when he worked with a nearby college on fund-raising and they gave him an honorary Ph.D. He didn't take that too seriously. When he died, we went through his things and found the certificate. We had to unearth it. It never sat out in public.

A father whose son graduated from Hyde talks about a defining moment when his son was confused with his new growth:

> My son Tom and I were in a family seminar and when it came to us, my son was crying and said, "I am lost." I didn't have any idea what he was talking about and I asked him what he meant. He said, "I've always wanted to grow up and be like you, the life of the party. I spent sixteen years watching you and thinking that is what I wanted to be. Then you stopped drinking and you changed the rules." It was a turning point in our relationship and it started a new level of sharing. From then on, it has been amazing to see our relationship grow.

3. *When we model daily character.* Getting up every day and trying to do the right thing is a challenge. Our kids notice everything, even those little acts of character. Throughout our day, we have many opportunities to sow such acts: picking up litter, being honest, taking the high ground, showing concern, supporting the right thing to do, helping a friend, listening. We do not need to look far to find these opportunities. A father talks about his daughter facing her fears and inspiring him:

> My daughter had finished high school and one summer we went up to visit a relative in North Carolina. She asked me about the roller coaster up in Myrtle Beach. I said, "Yeah, there's a big roller coaster there." She said, "I'm afraid of roller coasters and I think I've got to ride that roller coaster to get rid of the fear." So I said I would ride with her. She was afraid. When we got there, I was afraid, too, so I said, "Elizabeth, I don't have this fear of roller coasters that you do." She surprised me, "That's OK, Dad." And she got on that roller coaster by herself and rode it. After she got off, she said, "OK, I've done that, let's go home." It was quite an inspiration to me that my daughter could face her fears like that and I couldn't.

A father talks about the character of his own father:

My father worked as a buyer. He had never gone to college and there were always rumblings that my mother could have "done better." My dad got transferred to a new plant and received a promotion. I remember one afternoon I went down to his office to help him clean up and the janitor of the building came over and said to my dad, "I wanted to tell you how much it meant for me to have you stand up for me." He and my dad exchanged some more pleasantries and that was that.

It turned out that one of the secretaries was getting obscene phone calls and the blame fell on John Henry, a black man. (Remember, this was back in the days of Jim Crow.) They were getting ready to fire him. My dad stuck up for him and said, "John Henry is not the guy who did that." That delayed things long enough so they found the guy who did it. It wasn't John Henry, of course. I remember thinking at that age, here's this interesting juxtaposition: My dad got the promotion my mom always wanted him to get and yet this is what really counts. He had the courage to stand up and say something.

A dad shares one of those daily moments in which he realized he was modeling the wrong thing:

When Dennis was ten, I was buying a pair of shoes. I bought two pairs of shoes and when the cash register was ringing it up, I thought, "I think they undercharged me thirty bucks." What I thought was a big department store, little old me. I just got a nice gift and no one is going to get hurt. My son noticed it, too, and he started to say something. I said, "Shush." For all the talk about honesty, here I was modeling the exact opposite.

To personalize this idea of inspiration, Malcolm offers two stories of growing up with his own parents:

I was nine years old when my father decided he wanted to head his own school. Thus, he offered his fifteen years of teaching, coaching, and administrative experience to the marketplace. A number of schools were interested in him and he had been named a finalist for the position of headmaster at one well-regarded school.

One night when my parents were talking I overheard my mother say something to the effect of, "Joe, that school is segregated. We can't do that." My father responded, "Well, yeah, I've given them an ultimatum: Either make a commitment to integrate in two years' time or remove me from consideration." (This was 1963.) As I listened to this conversation, I wasn't really sure what words like *segregated* even meant, but I did perceive something that left an indelible impression on me: My parents were prepared to deny themselves something they deeply desired all in the name of principle.

My parents were showing me how to live. Nearly four decades later, I now know that my parents were doing for me what I most wanted from them, and they were probably not even aware that I was watching and listening. But as educators themselves, perhaps they knew that kids are watching their parents and teachers all the time.

The second story occurred later in Malcolm's life, well after he was married. It involves alcohol, an obstacle in the lives of many families.

My mother was a wonderful woman, thoughtful, wise, caring, and trustworthy . . . when she was sober. Another side came out when she drank, a side characterized by biting sarcasm. There was the morning my sisters and I came downstairs to find a poster-sized professionally designed portrait of my mother greeting us on an easel. It depicted her with a disapproving frown on her face, pointing a finger at us in admonishment. She had left our home on the previous evening vowing never to return and wanted to leave a parting shot. There was the time that she suddenly appeared, inebriated, in my college dormitory my freshman year. I remember wanting to melt into the floor as I felt my friends collectively grasp the notion that this very intoxicated woman who had invaded the dorm was "Malcolm's mother."

I can remember coming home with friends after school and praying that the "good" mom would be in the house when we got there. The "other" mom was impossible to deal with and a real embarrassment. I remember believing that no other teenager in the world faced circumstances like this at home. (Of course, I later learned that some of my closest friends experienced the very same trauma in their homes.) Once I crossed the threshold of our front door, it never took me more than a few seconds to determine which mom was home. There was a look in her eye, a certain degree of clutter to the house. This determination was always followed by either incredible relief or high anxiety.

Throughout my teens and my twenties I obsessed about my mother's drinking. As I entered my thirties, I came to understand a simple truth: Although I may not be able to control what my mother's drinking is doing to her, I *can* control what it is doing to me. I told my mother that I loved her but that I could no longer hang my emotions on the false hope that her earnest decision to quit drinking alcohol was "around the next bend." If she wanted to drink, that was ultimately her decision. I would no longer hide bottles or walk on eggshells. I would spend time with her if she was sober. I would not spend time with her if she wasn't.

This was very hard. My parents had divorced and my sisters were no longer living near our mother. As the child living closest to her, I felt a responsibility to help keep my mother as part of our "family." To make matters worse, I was struggling with my own use of alcohol—a problem drinker trying to help a problem drinker!

At any rate, I "let go" of my mother's drinking. I walked away. I would no longer make sure that her heating bill got paid. I would no longer make it a point to be on the lookout to try and intercept her as she walked out her front door on her way to her car to shop for groceries. In short, I would no longer enable her drinking. I resigned myself to an acceptance that she would never quit drinking. This acceptance led the way to a deeper acceptance of my mother, a sense of forgiveness. I decided to value her for the wonderful things she did for me and my sisters. I developed a genuine appreciation for what she tried to do for all of us. I would not judge her for what she was unable to do in her life. I was at peace. But I was not prepared for what happened next.

Shortly after I announced this to my mother, she both shocked and inspired me. She quit, truly quit, drinking. Although she had been in and out of Alcoholics Anonymous for twenty-five years, at age sixty she made a true commitment to it. Her decision evolved into a fairy tale when my parents reunited and decided to remarry after ten years apart. (They said, "After ten years, we declare our divorce a failure.") It was a very proud and happy day when my sisters and I attended the marriage of our parents. To this day, I get a kick out of people's reactions when I say, "When my parents got married, I gave the bride away." My mother had shown me that she had a major role to play well after I left the nest. As parents, we are never too old to inspire our children. As children, we are never too old to be inspired by them. I discovered that I still had that yearning to be inspired, despite the fact that I had buried all hope of its possibility.

Although this story is about how my mother inspired me, it also taught me volumes about the lessons of Priority 7, Take Hold and Let Go. I learned that many of my well-intentioned efforts over the years had actually served the problem more than the solution by enabling my mother to continue drinking. Today, I do not believe that my decision to "let go" was the cause of my mother's decision to quit drinking. I do believe, however, that my prior inability to "let go" had been a direct contributor to her failure to do so over a number of years. My mother died at sixty-two, less than two years after she had remarried my father. The years of alcohol had exacted their toll. But her last two years were perhaps the happiest of her life. They were sober ones characterized by serenity, for her and for her family. She saw all three of her children have children of their own, the last one becoming a parent only a few months before her death.

Both of us feel a great sense of gratitude to our parents for the commitment they made to our growth. In the past year, both of our children's grandfathers (each named "Papa") have celebrated significant birthdays. The family members at each party wrote letters to the birthday "boys," thanking them for what they have meant to us in our lives (see Thank-You Letter exercise at the end of this chapter). The following were letters each of us wrote to our fathers.

Malcolm writes to his dad:

July 2000

Dear Dad,

Although you have provided me with too many blessings to count in a single letter, I will limit my expression of appreciation to two areas: one pragmatic, the other more spiritual.

First, the pragmatic realm: Thanks for creating an organization that has afforded me such an enriching professional career. Whether mowing lawns for Ev Quimby, washing pots and pans for Glenda, teaching history and coaching a variety of sports, or serving as headmaster, I have always been proud to be employed by Hyde. However, it would be both shortsighted and naive for me to stop there. After all, I have not only enjoyed a rich career, I have enjoyed one characterized by an incredibly fast ascension through the ranks. I began teaching English and history in the fall of 1977. By the fall of 1987, I was the Hyde headmaster. Although I may be fairly arrogant, I am not so full of myself as to believe that this quick rise was due solely to my own talents. If I were not your son, perhaps I would have become a headmaster anyway—FWIW, I doubt it—but I know it would not have happened as quickly as it happened for me. I owe a huge debt of gratitude for these great opportunities I have had.

The second area of thanks has to do with a spiritual legacy you have left for all of us, one that will be passed down to your grandchildren. Over the years I have known people who felt trapped in the shadows of successful family members who preceded them. It isn't long before someone says something to the effect of, "He seems to be holding his own. After all, he's had a tough act to follow." Others present will nod in agreement. Certainly there have been times when I have felt the burden of a tough act to follow. Sometimes I have resented it. Yet perhaps it has been my association with Hyde that has allowed me to see deeper into this whole dynamic. In any case, I have come to believe that

271

there is one fate far worse than having a tough act to follow. That would be the fate of having an easy act to follow. Your act has not been an easy one to follow. However, I do not curse you for it. On this, your birthday, I sincerely thank you for it.

Love, Malcolm

Laura writes to her stepfather:

March 2001

Dear Dad,

Happy Birthday. We are here to celebrate your 70th and to share with you all that you have meant to us. It's hard to know where to begin. I will start with what you have taught me.

- *"No such word as* can't.*"*
- *How to change a tire.*
- *How to plaster a shower.*
- *How to clean out a septic tank.*
- *How to do lawn work.*
- *How to polish silverware.*
- *How to stuff envelopes.*
- *How to answer phones.*
- *How to drive a camper at 6:00 A.M. on a superhighway.*
- *How to travel.*
- *How to arrive ten minutes early (don't know how much I learned this one).*

The list could go on and on. You also taught me deeper things. You taught me to be a person of integrity, with the large and small things in life. You taught me to work hard for my dreams, and you taught me the value of standing against the crowd when you have to. You taught me that change must be embraced constantly.

Dad, you made a commitment to raise all of us as your own and my life would not be the same without that. Mom gave you permission to be our parent and it took a while to understand that. You also embraced Hyde and grew along with me.

We did not always have harmony, but we did strive for truth, and the love I feel for you today is a result of the commitment you made to our growth. Enjoy this birthday and many more to come. I love seeing you with the grandchildren. Your legacy will be passed through us.

Love, Laura

WORDS FROM INSPIRED TEENAGERS

At the Hyde School, we consciously seek to offer character-forming experiences so that our students and their parents can work together for personal and family growth. Each academic year concludes with a poignant graduation ceremony where each graduate speaks for two minutes as their parents stand in the audience. A few years ago we sensed that we lacked an opportunity for formal closure for the work our parents had done in our Family Learning Center program. So we began to offer a breakfast ceremony on graduation morning where the parents receive their own diplomas. Rather than having the parents speak, we read a brief citation that their children, the graduating seniors, have written in their honor. The following examples were read at a recent graduation:

BRIAN

To his mother: "Mom, I remember how inspired I was by your courage on the ropes course. You did not let your fears stop you from finishing. I had such an overwhelming feeling of pride. You set a great example for me to follow."

To his father: "Dad, your courage to face your issues, and your devotion to God, have been an example to follow. Your commitment to community, the parish, and Oakland speak to your compassion for others."

RON

To his mother: "I have never seen you give up on anything. You are my greatest inspiration. Your returning to school to get your degree in the midst of raising us kids on your own speaks to your strength. We have struggled through many bumpy times together and you have been my spiritual guide."

SAM

To his mother: "Mom, you have inspired me to become a person of character by your willingness to change. You have had tremendous challenges to face in the last few years with dad's death and becoming a single mom of three boys. We gave you many challenges and attitudes to deal with. An ordinary person would have given up long ago. I hope I have half the commitment to my family that you have shown us."

JOHN

To his mother: "I am sure most people who have done the ropes course feel that it was a great experience for them, but it was especially significant for you. I belayed you, and you put all of your trust in me, which proved to be truly inspiring."

To his father: "Dad, you swore to never go camping after you got out of the marines. You broke that promise when you accepted the challenge from me to do a Wilderness FLC. You not only rose to the challenge, but you were a leader throughout the four-day trip. You made me very proud."

ISAAC

To his mother: "I have been inspired by both your involvement with the Family and Children Crisis Program and getting your teacher recertification, which has allowed you to teach again."

To his father: "You have inspired me by addressing and seeking to change the lack of emotional fulfillment in your life and your overemphasis on work."

TYLER

To his mother: "Mom, you inspired me when you started your own business and began painting. I hadn't known you to be an independent person. When you began your work and painting, I saw it as an inspiring act of unexpected strength."

To his father: "Dad, you inspire me by your running, your charity, and your work ethic. You take every opportunity you get to keep yourself in shape and push yourself to new levels with your running. The selflessness you demonstrate when you give to others is something I deeply admire. Your work ethic is something you show in every other area of your life."

As these statements indicate, our kids are inspired when they observe us striving to improve our own character. They are inspired less by our accomplishments and more by our own efforts to face the unknown in ourselves. They are moved when we tackle a personal challenge with an uncertain outcome, when we strive to better ourselves as people, when we work on those factors we listed under the heading of Character Culture.

When you think about it, children and parents actually want the same things. They want to be inspired, and we would very much like to inspire them. We can do this through our own character development. Our own growth can create a ripple effect throughout the family. It begins now. It begins with us.

FAMILY EXERCISES AND ACTIVITIES

Share a Hero

Materials: Newspapers, books, magazines
Time: 20 to 30 minutes of research
Explanation: Ask each person in the family to identify a hero. It could be someone still living or not, someone who is greatly admired for their character and example. Make a collage, write some notes, or bring in a book to share.

Each week, have a family member share their "hero" at the weekly meeting. You may want to put up the picture or some key quotes to inspire everyone to remember that hero's legacy as they go through their day.

"Our Greatest Fear"

Materials: The following poem by Marianne Williamson, quoted by Nelson Mandela in his 1994 Inaugural Speech:

> *Our greatest fear is not that we are inadequate,*
> *Our deepest fear is that we are powerful beyond measure.*
>
> *It is our light not our darkness that frightens us.*
> *We ask ourselves, Who am I to be brilliant,*
> *Gorgeous, handsome, talented, and fabulous?*
>
> *Actually, who are you not to be?*
> *You are a child of God.*

Your playing small does not serve the world.
There is nothing enlightened about shrinking
So that other people won't feel insecure around you.

We were born to manifest the glory of God within us.
It is not just in some, it is in everyone.

As, as we let our light shine, we consciously give
Other people permission to do the same.
As we are liberated from our fear,
Our presence automatically liberates others.

Read the poem as a family, perhaps as part of a weekly meeting, and talk about the meaning. Some of the following questions may help:

- What hits you most when you read this?
- What is your light?
- Why does it frighten you?
- How might you shine your light in order to "give other people permission to do the same"?
- How might you liberate yourself from fear in order to liberate others?

Thank-You Letter

Materials: Paper, pen
Time: 20 to 30 minutes to write
Explanation: Start with the oldest family member. It may be a grandparent or an extended family member. Ask members of the family to write that person a letter, starting with the line: Thank you for what you have meant to me in my life. . . .

Ask people to write the letter from their soul. The kids will understand this! Then have a family meeting or family dinner. Sit around and read the letters to the person. You may want to collect the letters afterward and put them in a book for the family history. This could become an annual event where, each year, someone new is honored.

JOURNALING QUESTIONS

1. When I was growing up, who did I admire? Explain.
2. When was I inspired by my parents?
3. When was I disappointed in them?
4. When have I inspired myself with my courage and risk-taking?
5. What are my dreams for my child/children?
6. What are my deepest dreams and vision for myself?
7. What role does conscience play in my life?
8. When have the members of my family inspired me?
9. What does my family mean to me? Does anything prevent me from sharing this with them?
10. What specific action step could I take to honor the highest vision of our family?

Conclusion

LIBERATION FROM NORMAL

Four years ago, our life changed dramatically when our son was diagnosed with delays in his development. Laura took most of the year off to work intensively with him. With a great deal of help from his teachers, extended family, many Hyde students, and friends, we set the bar at "full recovery" and then proceeded to work like warriors to carry off this vision. It has been one of the most intense and difficult times in our lives, but it has taught and continues to teach us many valuable lessons.

Perhaps the most important lesson came with the discovery that a publicly visible issue within our family can serve to liberate us from the notion of the perfect family without problems. We relearned what we had learned at Hyde about unique potential: We are all unique, and our character can lead us to connect with our destiny. We learned that our problems could actually take us farther than our so-called successes. We learned that obstacles can serve as real opportunities. We also learned that we never really solve our problems, but we can move beyond them.

In fact, in the 10 Priorities, two speak directly to the character-building value of so-called problems—Priority 5, Value Success and Failure, and Priority 6, Allow Obstacles to Become Opportunities. Learning to let our children own their own obstacles is an ongoing challenge no matter what their age.

A Hyde mother talks about her early approach to her son's obstacles and what she learned:

My youngest son and I would often work on his homework. He would dictate to me because I type faster than he does. We were working on a report. He would tell me something and as I was typing, I would suggest certain changes. He would express frustration over this and I knew I shouldn't be doing it, but that didn't stop me.

At one point, I said, "Now you know, I can't keep doing this forever! You are going to have to start doing this by yourself." His comment shocked me: "You can't stop helping me because I will just fail. Every time I tell you what to say, you think it's not good enough and change it." He got a strong message from me that he couldn't do it, that his way wasn't as good as mine. And I thought I was helping him by making constructive suggestions.

I learned that we give our kids messages all the time about our confidence in them, and while we may think we are being subtle, they pick it up loud and clear. I didn't want him to be embarrassed by the quality of his work, so I helped him. I felt that by doing this, I would be demonstrating how one should approach these kinds of problems. I guess I have come a long way from that afternoon. My children own their highs and lows today.

A Hyde father of two talks about how his daughter's "problems" led him to address some of his issues and ended up liberating the whole family:

I also wanted to be the good father. I just didn't realize that being a good father was such a personal thing. About ten years ago, when my daughter was fourteen, she was dressed exclusively in black—up, down, and sideways. I resented her. Why was she doing these things to me when I was such a great dad? Why was she pushing me away? Today we laugh about the fact that she could scale down her bedroom window to sneak out but couldn't pass seventh-grade gym.

After a few months at Hyde, a teacher suggested, "Maybe you should take a look at yourself." At first, I couldn't deal with that. Then I started to share some things that I did at her age. I realized that my honest sharing could help her with her honesty. I started to change as

I shared my deepest feelings and fears: Maybe I have a gambling problem. Maybe I shouldn't smoke pot on the weekends. I began to see that being a good father was more than taking your kid to Little League and coaching baseball and being there at the school play. I was not a good example to my kids until I was conscious of the fact that I better start setting an example. Today, my daughter is a social worker who is terrific and my son is doing some exciting things with his life. So the beat goes on. . . .

Sometimes, relentlessly addressing the issues of our children keeps the focus off our own journeys. At one point, as our son was progressing, Laura sensed that she needed to take a hard look at her life. She writes:

I was in a box. While I knew that my son needed me at this point in his life, I also knew that I couldn't be his advocate forever. I asked myself the three essential questions that we have asked students, parents, and faculty over the years: (1) Who are you? (2) Where are you going? (3) What do you need to do to get there?

As I opened up the possibilities of doing anything I wanted to, my answer led me to taking the wisdom we had collected about parenting and family to a wider audience. I knew that the Hyde approach to education and family was powerful, but it needed to be put into a language that could be understood by the outside community–rich or poor, black or white, rural or urban. We started giving workshops almost three years ago with just some ideas on a simple outline. We found that parents and professionals connected to the Priorities. I brought Malcolm along because I wanted there to be a male up in front of the room so that this wouldn't just be a mother talking to other mothers. I knew that mothers would find the time to do this, but fathers need to understand just how critical they are in the parenting process.

We have met with parents from around the country to listen to their stories. Some of these parents have been to one of the Hyde

Schools. Many of them have watched their children graduate. Some of their children did not stay, but most felt that the experience was life-changing. We also talked to some families who came to a Biggest Job workshop and some who did the follow-up monthly program. Powerful sharing has come out of these meetings.

One mother writes:

I get teary-eyed just thinking about what I have gotten out of the Hyde process for myself and my son. I have found that I have a life. I have feelings. I don't have to be numb. I can express myself.

A dad writes:

We were first attracted to the Biggest Job program because of our son. He's always been brilliant, but he had character issues. If you asked him the color of the sky, he would say green just so he could be different. So we wanted him to work on his character. God knows there was nothing wrong with me!

Somewhere in the first year, the realization set in that everything's not OK. There's stuff that we need to deal with. I view this program as another link in the chain that helps me to be the best person I can be. If I had had this growing up, I can't imagine where I would be. If I could have dropped the garbage back in high school, it would have been such a burden off of me. My relationship with my son has gotten a lot better. I never realized how much we are alike.

A mother talks about her journey to help her grandson:

If I think about what I have gotten out of this process, it would be love and support. I was almost convinced that Jay was incapable of being educated—we were in private schools, Afro-centric schools. We tried everything. We have been doing this for two years. He is growing and so am I. I have seen wonderful changes in both of us. When Jay was home, he used to spend 99 percent of his time with the door closed. Hyde is helping us to communicate.

One young high school senior from the rural Midwest brought a chuckle at a workshop when he talked about the year his family spent in the monthly meetings. He said:

> I guess we got involved in this program simply because we're one of those kinds of families that does this kind of thing. I knew that my mother would be front and center in terms of not only having our family involved but in bringing other families along.

He then went on to say to his father, "Dad, I always respected you as someone who was good at sports and successful, but this program has shown me another side of you. You have shared your emotions and I have a new respect for you." His father listened silently as his eyes welled up with tears.

A mother from an urban center talks about her relationship with her son:

> I got my son back. When he was sixteen, he was in high school and frankly there were moments when he would be sitting across from me and I didn't know who he was. He was foreign to me. We had superficial communication between us. I didn't know how to approach him. I'm not even sure I was angry. I think I was sad. As a result, I turned against my husband because I needed a scapegoat.
>
> As we were working on some of the programs, one of the instructors said to my son, "You've got to look at your mother when you talk to her." I think it was one of the first times in a long time that we really looked into each other's eyes. It was extraordinary. I know we will have ups and downs, but we now have a way to communicate. I have a technique to be honest and in touch with my feelings.

NOT EASY, NOT IMPOSSIBLE

In our workshops, we regularly say to parents, "This program is not a quick fix. You will leave here excited, but the work takes a daily commitment." As one Hyde mother said:

> You can't just walk in and read the stuff and say, "Yeah, I know how to do this." It's a process. And it is a process that often reverses the whole way you're accustomed to running your life. Like when something goes wrong. Well, you normally wouldn't even think about letting your neighbors know. You just don't talk about it. Well, I've learned that stuff happens and it isn't anyone's fault. It is what it is and you deal with it.

Although this book has focused on parenting and families, it has hopefully offered a map and compass to help us navigate a journey that we are all experiencing. We all have dignity and worth. Taking the responsibility to work on our character can connect us to our destiny.

We have talked a lot in this book about letting go of the relationship with our children. Sometimes a vision of the ideal close-knit family unit must be put on the back burner. A wonderful irony can unfold when we try to live our lives in accordance with character and principles. On the one hand, our children may resent or even claim to hate us at times. However, we are building a permanent foundation for a deep relationship, one that will last a lifetime. If you're unsure of this, we would simply say we have observed a consistent quality present in the families who have completed programs outlined in this book: *Family members tend to have very close, trusting, and loving relationships.*

A father gives his view of how his family grew:

> I think what I got in this whole process was finding myself. For many years I did not know who I really was. I had principles but did not

practice them. I lied to my wife about stupid things . . . definitely harmony over truth. I learned I was human, that I, too, can be concerned about people and have integrity.

Remember the mother who wanted everything to be perfect at the holidays? She writes about the growth her family has experienced:

Even though I intellectually knew that my "perfect" vision was not my family's vision, that didn't keep me from trying to bring it to reality. What motivated me to continue on that path? I had to look at my own upbringing with my family of origin. There were many times we avoided the difficult words or issues and instead put up this beautiful picture, with everything in its place and everyone saying the right things.

Now it may still get off course, but there is talking and laughing about the issues. My son might say, "Here we go again with Mom!" I don't jump through hoops like I used to. We talk about things. I might say, "This is what I really want to do for the holidays. What do you think about it?" I ask for help now. If we decide to have a candlelit dinner, we delegate and make it all a part of the family's collective vision. The table represents one member's efforts, a side dish belongs to another, and so forth.

COMMON LANGUAGE

There are so many parenting moments in a day. Think about the way we usually address them. How can I get this child back to center as quickly as possible? It also usually involves some kind of bribe that we assure ourselves will be the last time we use such methods. It is not unlike the dieter who indulges in the candy bar with the promise to eat well starting tomorrow. We have all been there as parents. We are so tied to the moment that we would sell our souls for a little harmony.

Just like eating well, the 10 Priorities provide an approach that will sustain us for the long term and give us a common language in which to process our parenting. One mother and daughter from New York went on a Biggest Job wilderness trip, a three-day canoeing and camping experience on a lake in western Maine. When asked a year later what had been most valuable on the trip, the mom said, "We learned some phrases that have helped us work things out as a family of two. For instance, Truth over Harmony has meaning to us. It means no bullshit."

Our efforts can be enhanced with a common language among family members. Examples of common language might include:

- "What is it that you need to let go of, Mom?"
- "I am totally into harmony here."
- "Let go of the outcome, honey."
- "There is an opportunity somewhere in this obstacle."
- "Keep the expectations high."
- "Sow an action, keep sowing those actions."
- "What is the important thing here?"
- "Is this my obstacle?"
- "What do I need to take hold of?"
- "I need to raise the bar."

As we work these Priorities, humor will creep in and help solidify the Character Culture that is forming in the family. (Remember the story about the parents who disconnected the family phone during the dinner hour in Priority 2, Principles over Rules?) We also need a common language with the people around us who are helping to raise our children. We can use the Priorities to create a culture of honesty where we both want the truth and know that it will be given to us. We can think of many times when the input from our family and friends stung but helped us move forward. And remember, every time we move forward as parents, our children benefit.

Work hard on creating this common language and you will use the Priorities more in your life. Without this, you may well lose whatever wisdom was gained by reading this book.

LET GO OF BEING RIGHT

Effective parenting does not mean always being right. Our job is to try and do our best as consistently as we can. In fact, much of our real learning as parents occurs when we get offtrack and have to confront that. It means getting back on track when we are way off. It means apologizing to our kids when we get sucked into their terrorist attitudes. It means having the courage to change and go after our highest visions. It means giving other people carte blanche to be honest with us. It also means learning to laugh at ourselves in order to restore humility to our parenting base.

Why as parents do we feel that we need to be right? A mother shares her struggle with this:

> When we found Hyde, my daughter recognized right away that this was going to be a place where she could become the person she wanted to be. Then I began to look at myself and a big revelation I had was that after the divorce, I had adopted the role of the righteous victim. I was the one who was right. I was doing everything right and I expected respect for the success that I had made of my life. I wasn't sharing with my children or anyone else the struggles I was going through.
>
> I was finally able to step away and say, "I am not always right and why do I have to be?" I have learned to get in touch with a deeper sense of humility, something that I wouldn't allow myself before. . . . I think I was afraid I would lose my capacity to rationalize and thus overcome things.

In our society, a myth has been perpetrated that parents are supposed to know what to do with their children in all situations. Our kids are supposed to follow our authority and achieve. Unless there is really a problem, we are not supposed to ask for help or expose the true issues within the family. Thus, we spend a lot of time covering up issues and denying problems. Through thirty-five years of character education, we have found that when a family has high expectations, there are going to be obstacles—no way around it!

CALL TO ARMS

We do not pretend to have the expertise to solve all the family and school dilemmas that currently exist. We do believe that neither conventional wisdom nor standard current practices will lead to the fundamental changes that need to happen. This change will come from countless parents who embrace their own commitment to change and grow as the foundation to guide their children to their fullest potential. This change starts with the belief that there is no job more important than raising our children. If you are a parent, your performance will be the most significant contribution that you make to the planet in your time here. The bottom-line message is this simple: *If you want your children to be people of character, you need to be working on your own character on a regular basis.*

The call to arms is simple. Be real to your children. Let go of the notion of being the perfect mom or dad. Put harmony on hold and call the truth as you see it. If the family is out of control, face it and stop trying to arrange the deck chairs on the *Titanic* with a smile on your face. Stop yearning for happiness, but believe that it will find you in moments and times when you least expect it. Enjoy those moments and take the time to appreciate each step forward. Have the courage to set a vision for yourself and your family. Place the weight of your foot in the principles that are sacred to you. Create a unified vision in the family and make a commitment to stay as close to the truth as you can. Learn to "eat crow" and enjoy it. Know that a more appetizing course is headed your way.

Let's go back to the dad who was working overtime to project the successful lawyer image to the outside world while taking his kid's bar mitzvah money to pay bills. As he said:

I learned perhaps the biggest lesson of my life. None of the outside stuff compared to having the respect of my kid. I think I have become more in sync with who I was inside. I had a hundred different reasons why I had to act in ways that were inconsistent with my values, being untruthful because I couldn't deal with the disharmony that I thought honesty would bring.

The mother, divorced when her son came to Hyde, adds:

I think we were living the fantasy of harmony over truth, but the harmony was for other people to see. And the disharmony and turmoil was turned inward in perpetuating harmony for the rest of the world. I came from a family where appearances were everything. I don't think we were shallow people. We cared about the right things, we were good people. We weren't cheats and liars to others, just to ourselves. What I got out of Hyde was the lesson that if I am true to myself, I can be true to everyone I love and care about.

I have a different kind of relationship with my children than many of my peers. I don't pat myself on the back for that. I am proud that together we could get there. Another big thing that came out of Hyde was my relationship with my ex-husband. We can now really support each other and parent the children together.

Near the end of our Biggest Job workshops, we offer two quotes for discussion. The first is by the nineteenth-century French painter Eugene Delacroix: "When we do the right thing, we raise ourselves in our own eyes." The second is by Ralph Waldo Emerson:

Our chief want in life is someone who will make us do what we can.

Considered together, these two sentences can help keep us on track. The Delacroix quote reminds us that there exists a pressure in our culture that can cause us to spend a great deal of time trying to raise ourselves in the eyes of others. Parents may try to impress bosses.

Teenagers may try to impress teachers or peers. Our best hopes of inspiring our children may require us first to impress ourselves by being the best people we can be. Emerson reminds us that we cannot do this without the help of others. In the future, our children will someday realize that they need to voluntarily enter into relationships with people who will "make them do what they can." Until that discovery dawns on them, we will probably have to serve as unwanted volunteers for the job. As our children come to value our service in this role, the bond of our relationships with them will strengthen. If that is not reward enough, consider the fact that you are modeling the very behavior that your children will pass on to your *grand*children!

At the beginning of this book, we made three points about exceptional parenting:

1. It is *hard.*
2. It is *doable.*
3. It is *never too late.*

As each family adapts the message of this book to its own dynamic, we would stress again that there is no substitute for hard work. If any big job requires great effort, it certainly follows that the Biggest Job will test the deepest reserves of our attitudes, our efforts, and our character. However, it never hurts to have a little luck.

In the interests of luck and superstition, we end every Biggest Job workshop with a story about the great cellist Pablo Casals, a musician noted for his beautiful sound and relentless practice. Casals was once approached by a reporter who asked, "Mr. Casals, you have long been considered the greatest cellist in the world. At age ninety-six, why do you still practice six hours a day?" Casals reportedly replied, "Because I think I'm making progress."

We believe that the best parents, indeed, the best people, are those who approach their own character development the way Casals approached the cello. Although neither of us plays the cello, we would suspect it's a lot like parenting: it's hard, it's doable, and it's never too late.

Acknowledgments

From the moment we envisioned this book in the mid-1990s, we have been blessed by many people who believed in and contributed to it. At the risk of leaving several out, we wanted to single out a few contributors to this team effort.

Providence was working on our behalf when our friends Felicia and Marek Milewicz introduced us, thankfully, to Sarah Lazin, our superlative agent. Sarah expressed a belief in the project at a time when we doubted its possibilities. She and her staff then guided us through the arduous process of the book proposal. Without Sarah this book would not have happened.

Sarah's work with us on the proposal led us to Jake Morrissey at Scribner. Jake got excited about the proposal, and we dove into the effort of writing the manuscript. Jake along with Brant Rumble and the folks at Scribner expertly guided us through the writing and editing process.

We owe an incalculable debt to the scores of students, teachers, parents, and alumni at the Hyde Schools who contributed stories to this book, presented here under pseudonyms to preserve anonymity. Although representative of different eras in our teaching careers, the writers of these stories reflect the unanimity of pride and character that has long characterized the Hyde community.

A number of friends and colleagues in the Hyde community played critical roles throughout the project. Pam Hardy continues to be instrumental in helping us develop the Biggest Job workshops from a local program specifically designed for parents at the Hyde Schools to one with a national focus. Rose Mulligan contributed her expert review and editing of the manuscript. Julie Greenlaw assisted us with research and typing. Others helped us with the typing, copying, and collating of hundreds of pages of manuscripts, especially Frances Murray and Tessa Heath.

We would also like to express deep appreciation to Mark Jaffe, an old pro in the book world. We began having discussions with Mark about a book on family and character in the 1980s. (One early effort was titled "40 Ways to Teach Character.") Without Mark's encouragement, it is doubtful we would have sought an agent in the first place. (After all, we had never heard of either agents or book proposals!)

Special thanks to Marc Brown, author of the *Arthur* children's series, for contributing the foreword to this book and for expressing his consistent belief in its value.

Index

Index

MALCOLM GAULD, president and chief executive officer of the Hyde Schools, oversees Hyde's two boarding campuses in Bath, Maine, and Woodstock, Connecticut, and public school initiatives in New Haven, Connecticut, and Washington, D.C. LAURA GAULD directs the Family Education Programs for the Hyde Schools. They live in Bath, Maine, with their three children.